THE JUST
ECONOMY

by J.E. Meade

A Principles of Political Economy

1 The Stationary Economy
2 The Growing Economy
3 The Controlled Economy
4 The Just Economy

A Geometry of International Trade
A Neo-classical Theory of Economy Growth
Efficiency, Equality and the Ownership of Property
Introduction to Economic Analysis and Policy
Planning and the Price Mechanism
Problems of Economic Union
The Control of Inflation
The Intelligent Radical's Guide to Economic Policy
The Theory of Customs Unions
The Theory of Indicative Planning
Theory of International Economic Policy
Wages and Prices in a Mixed Economy

also
The Structure and Reform of Direct Taxation
Report of a Committee chaired by Professor J.E. Meade
(The 'Meade' Report for the Institute for Fiscal Studies)

THE JUST ECONOMY

BY

J. E. MEADE

C.B., F.B.A.

Being Volume Four of A

PRINCIPLES OF POLITICAL ECONOMY

London
GEORGE ALLEN & UNWIN
Boston   Sydney

First published in 1976
Second impression 1978

© George Allen & Unwin (Publishers) Ltd 1976

ISBN 0 04 330279 3

Printed in Great Britain
by Billing & Sons Limited,
Guildford, London and Worcester.

CONTENTS

PREFACE

This is the fourth volume in a series of which *The Stationary Economy, The Growing Economy,* and *The Controlled Economy* have already been published. This still leaves three topics uncovered.

First, there remain all the marginal and structural problems of economic efficiency, which cannot be handled by a *laissez-faire* competitive market mechanism; such problems include, for example, the whole range of economic externalities including public goods and the problems of monopolistic conditions which may be the inevitable outcome of economies of large-scale production. I would cover these topics in a volume with the title *The Efficient Economy*.

Second, no reference has been made in the first four volumes in this series to any questions of international economic and financial relations. These volumes have all been based upon the assumption of a closed economy. An obvious title for a volume which tried to repair this gap would be *The International Economy*. But so far as economic policy is concerned, international problems constitute only one example of a wider set of issues, namely the relationships between different and separate governmental institutions and decision-making bodies. Such bodies may be quite independent of each other (e.g. national sovereign governments); they may exist on the basis of co-operative agreements or treaties (e.g. many international economic institutions); they may be subordinate to each other (e.g. local government authorities operating within constraints determined by a central government); or they may divide the range of activities between them under a single over-riding constitution (e.g. state and central governments in a true federation). It would be attractive to treat international economic policies as one part of this wider set of problems of the relationships between separate governmental decision-making bodies; and in this case an appropriate title for the volume might be *The Decentralised Economy*.

Finally, there would remain a need for a volume which brought together the various threads of economic policy discussed in connection with the separate issues covered in each of the previous volumes. This wicked, second-best world being what it is, such a volume would inevitably be concerned with the choice between various workable mixes of different types of institution and policy; and for that reason I would call it *The Mixed Economy*.

I have written the present volume as if *The Efficient Economy* and *The Mixed Economy* were about to be published. The reader of the present volume will find a number of unqualified references to these as yet non-existing publications. But in fact it is not at all certain that they will ever be produced. In a small volume entitled *The Theory of Economic Externalities* (published by A. W. Sijthoff of Leiden for the Institut Universitaire de Hautes Etudes Internationales in Geneva) and in an article entitled 'The Optimal Balance between Economies of Scale and Variety of Products' (published in *Economica* in November 1974) I have made some recent notes for *The Efficient Economy*. In a short book entitled *The Intelligent Radical's Guide to Economic Policy* (published by George Allen & Unwin) I have treated in the tone of a political pamphlet much of the ground which would be covered more tediously in *The Mixed Economy*. Indeed I have gone so far as to endow *The Intelligent Radical's Guide* with the subtitle of *The Mixed Economy*.

But while it is possible that *The Efficient Economy* and *The Mixed Economy* will be written, it is virtually certain that *The International Economy* or *The Decentralised Economy* will never appear. The reader will have to make do with the 1,334 pages of my *Theory of International Policy,* consisting of *The Balance of Payments* and *Trade and Welfare* with their mathematical supplements. That work covers one part of the ground; but I would write it differently if I were to try again. Indeed, I would write *The Stationary Economy, The Growing Economy,* and *The Controlled Economy* differently if I were to try again and I would very much like to do so. But to go back to the beginning would eliminate any remaining chance of reaching the end.

The present volume deals with the distribution of income and property and I hope that it will speak for itself. I have not tried to deal with the ethical problems involved, though the title and much else is inspired by Professor Rawl's great book *A Theory of Justice.* I make no claim to originality for any of the ideas in this book; they have been culled from innumerable sources. In particular I owe much to the works in this field of Professors A. B. Atkinson, E. H. Phelps Brown, D. G. Champernowne, A. Sen, J. R. N. Stone and J. Tinbergen. Professors A. B. Atkinson, E. H. Phelps Brown,

Yew-Kwang Ng and J. Tinbergen have commented on parts of my typescript and I owe them a special debt of gratitude. Table VIII and the commentary on this Table (pages 176–81 below) is directly based on the analysis on page 63 of Professor Atkinson's *Unequal Shares*, and the thought in the footnote on page 178 is due to Professor P. Hart. In Chapter IV I have incorporated some paragraphs from the Sidney Ball Lecture which I gave in Oxford in May 1972 entitled 'Poverty in the Welfare State' (published in *Oxford Economic Papers*, November 1972); and in Chapters IX, X and XI I have included a large part of the Keynes Lecture which I gave at the British Academy in December 1973, entitled 'The Inheritance of Inequalities' (published in the *Proceedings of the British Academy*, 1973). To all these sources I should like to make grateful acknowledgement.

Christ's College   J. E. MEADE
Cambridge
December 1974

CHAPTER I

THE OBJECTIVES OF ECONOMIC POLICY

In a *laissez-faire*, market, competitive economy there are important forces at work promoting economic efficiency. If a factor of production is employed in one activity in which the value of its marginal product is relatively low, it will be offered a higher reward in an alternative activity in which the value of its marginal product is relatively high. The movement of factors from activities in which the values of their marginal products are low to activities in which the values of their marginal products are high will increase the value which purchasers place, at current prices, on the total output of the community.[1]

These beneficent competitive market forces should be exploited wherever possible in the design of economic policies and institutions; but there are at least seven fundamental economic reasons why they cannot in all cases be left to operate unchecked and uncontrolled without loss of economic welfare.

(1) It may be impossible to leave planning for an uncertain future solely to the competitive market mechanism of forward markets. The cost of running the astronomically large number of potential forward markets needed to cover all goods and services for all future times and for all future states of the environment would be quite prohibitive. Measures for centralised indicative planning may be desirable.

(2) It may be necessary to introduce controls over the total economic system in order to stabilise it at a level giving full employment to available resources without explosive inflationary tendencies.

---

[1] This statement is a very crude way of expressing a subtle truth. More sophisticated discussions of the ways in which competitive forces will lead to an efficient situation in static conditions and of the way in which they will cause a dynamic economy to move on an efficient time-path are contained in Chapter XII of *The Stationary Economy* and in Chapter XXIII of *The Growing Economy*.

(3) It may be desirable to take measures to redistribute as between the rich and the poor of any one generation the total real income and wealth which a competitive system will produce.

(4) It may be desirable to take measures to influence the distribution of income between present and future generations by influencing the amounts of real resources which the present generation will save up for the benefit of future generations.

(5) It may be desirable to take steps to influence the size and composition of future generations by influencing the levels of fertility of the present generation.

(6) There may be important blemishes in the competitive price mechanism which give rise to external economies and diseconomies, in the sense that costs and prices in the private market do not take account of some of the marginal social costs and benefits to which the activities in question give rise.

(7) Full competition among a full range of all available products may be impossible because of indivisibilities and economies of scale. For this reason it may be a matter of social concern to influence the structure of economic activities, e.g. to influence the choice of which products to produce and which not to produce.

In *The Controlled Economy* we have already considered at length the sort of policies that might be desirable to stabilise the economy and to aid in the problems of planning for an uncertain future. In this volume we shall not, therefore, deal with problems (1) and (2) in the above list. We shall think in terms of a full-employment stabilised economy which is making the best feasible plans to meet future market conditions.

The remaining five problems in the above list can be divided into two very broad groups.

Items (3), (4) and (5) are concerned primarily with questions of a fair and just distribution of income and wealth. This is obviously true of item (3) which concerns distribution between the rich and the poor of any one generation and of item (4) which concerns sacrifices by one generation for the benefit of another generation. The inclusion of item (5) in a list of problems which concern justice and distribution is not quite so obvious; but nevertheless the connection is in fact a very real one. Suppose that an increase in the population would cause some fall in the average standard of living of an existing population. Would it necessarily be desirable on those grounds to limit the population? Is it just for the born, in defence of their own standard of living, to restrict the unborns' entry into a pleasant life? The determination of what one means by an optimum population clearly raises basic moral issues.

Items (6) and (7) on the above list are, on the other hand, concerned primarily with questions about policies to promote economic efficiency and to increase the size of the cake which is to be made available for distribution. These items deal with the possibility of improving the allocation of economic resources either by a more accurate determination of the real social costs and benefits of the various economic activities which are already being conducted (item 6) or else by the selection of a better structure of activities (item 7).

In this volume, *The Just Economy*, we shall be dealing with the set of problems (3), (4) and (5) and we shall leave to a subsequent volume on *The Efficient Economy* the set of problems (6) and (7). This distinction is a convenient and useful one made only because one cannot discuss everything at once. But, alas, in fact the choice of economic policies makes up a single coherent problem; and in Chapter III we shall consider at some length the difficulties encountered in separating the problem of prosperity or efficiency from that of justice or distribution – that is to say, the problem of what affects the size of the cake from the problem of what affects its distribution. In fact all that we can do is to discuss in this volume the effects of certain factors on the distribution of income and wealth with some side references to their effects on efficiency and in the next volume to discuss the effects of certain factors on economic efficiency with certain side references to their effects on distribution.

But the matter is more complicated than that. Prosperity and justice are not the only two basic social goods which may be affected by various economic policies. Equality of opportunity, personal freedom, security and participation in the making of decisions which affect one's life: these are all things which citizens may value and which may be much affected by the choice of economic policies and institutions.

Many clashes between these various social objectives can occur. Three examples must suffice to make the point.

(1) Suppose that complete equality of incomes were considered to be the most desirable arrangement on purely distributional grounds. It would be quite possible to devise a set of economic policies (with 100 per cent rates of tax on incomes in excess of the fixed level and

100 per cent rates of subsidy to incomes below that level) which resulted in complete equality. But that would remove all incentive for people in search of high rewards to move themselves, their capital, their land, or any other factor which they owned, from occupations in which the value of their marginal product was low to occupations in which it was high. As a result either there would be a serious loss of economic efficiency and prosperity or else people would have to be directed to shift any factors which they owned (including their own labour) to the more useful occupations with a consequential serious loss of personal freedom.

(2) Economic policies may be adopted which encourage research and development in the invention of new products and new processes of production. As a result the economy may through rapid technical progress produce a rapidly increasing level of economic prosperity. But this may be at some considerable cost in personal security. Frequent replacement of one technique of production by another or of an old product by a new product may mean frequent losses of jobs by persons working in the discarded economic activities. The general standard of living may be higher, but individual insecurity may at the same time be greater.[2]

(3) Participation may be easier to organise and have more meaning in small-scale than in large-scale organisations, whereas large-scale production may for technical reasons be more efficient. The replacement of large-scale capitalistic enterprises by small-scale labour-managed co-operatives may, therefore, purchase participation at the expense of prosperity.

The choice between some of these basic social goods can in some cases be left to *laissez-faire* market decisions. Here again three examples must suffice to illustrate the point.

(1) It is perfectly possible to allow both large-scale capitalistic enterprises and small-scale labour-managed co-operatives to exist and to compete side by side. If the large-scale organisations were more efficient, the wages which they would pay would be higher than the partnership profits earned by the small-scale co-operative workers. In the absence of any trade union or similar restrictive practice citizens could freely choose between high prosperity with

---

[2] This, of course, does not imply that no measures can be taken to reduce the loss through insecurity. But such measures may themselves reduce incentives (e.g. social guarantees of income) or may impinge on personal freedoms (e.g. limitations on the freedom to use new products in order to protect declining activities).

low participation in the large-scale enterprises and low prosperity with high participation in the small-scale co-operatives. Some might prefer the former and others the latter style of life.

(2) If it were legally permissible, a man might sell himself into slavery at a high price, thereby purchasing a high standard of living at the cost of his personal freedom. His master might accept the bargain, since it might pay him to have an able and useful, though expensive, servant who had to do exactly as he was told. Less extreme and fanciful cases of this general principle are more realistic. A man may enter into a long-term contract which limits his future freedom of action for a sufficiently high price which the purchaser is prepared to offer for the security of an assured supply. The seller gets prosperity for freedom and the buyer gets security for prosperity.

(3) An even more obvious case of the market pay-off between security and prosperity is the choice before an investor of lending his money at a low but certain rate of interest or investing it for a high but uncertain dividend.

The above are all illustrations of cases in which an individual citizen can in the market exchange one basic social good for another – prosperity for freedom, security for prosperity, and so on. But there are other cases where these basic social goods cannot be treated as private goods to be exchanged in the market place between one citizen and another (like food and clothing) but must be treated as public goods of which each citizen must enjoy the same amount (like clean air or the absence of noise). In this latter case there must be a public, political decision as to the amount of the particular basic social good which is to be sought and at what cost in other goods.

The outstanding example of this is the distribution of income and wealth, which is the subject matter of the present volume. It is not possible for the rich to choose to live in an inegalitarian society (in which they can continue to enjoy their riches unhampered) and for the poor to choose to live in an egalitarian society (in which some of the riches of the rich are transferred to the poor for their enjoyment). All citizens must live either in an egalitarian or in an inegalitarian society. There must be some political public choice as to the degree of progressive tax rates on the incomes of the rich and the degree of subsidies of one kind or another to the incomes of the poor

Some political process for social choice is necessary not only for this basic problem of deciding upon a just distribution of income and wealth but also for a host of other public decisions relating, for example, to the scale of expenditure on national defence, to many environmental goods (such as the purity of the air, the absence of noise or the purity of the water supply), and to many structural problems such as the country's network of road and rail transport. We shall be discussing these problems in the next volume in this series on *The Efficient Economy*; and we will postpone any discussion of the political machinery of public choice for that occasion.

In this volume we shall consider some of the factors which determine the distribution of income and wealth, some of the governmental measures which may be used to influence that distribution, and some of the various ideologies about what should be the objective of political action in regard to the redistribution of income and wealth. But there may be very serious differences between such ideologies and very serious differences of opinion about the amount of other basic social goods (of prosperity or freedom, for example) which one should be prepared to give up in order to achieve a given improvement in distribution. We shall not in this volume be concerned with the mechanism of political decision to make a social choice between such conflicting ideologies.

The size of the cake and its division among the participants at the feast constitute what one most naturally regards as the basically *economic* aspects of the good society. This volume is about the division of the cake with frequent reference to the relationship between the division and the size of the cake. The effects of the slicing of the cake upon other basic social goods (upon equality of opportunity, freedom, security, participation, for example) are less a matter of technical economic analysis, though they may be of extreme importance. Reference will be made to them in this volume rather incidentally.

In the choice of policies for the redistribution of income and wealth it is, of course, desirable to select that form of policy which has the smallest adverse effects not only on the size of the cake but also on the other basic social goods. In this connection two general rules may be observed.

First, methods (such as taxes and subsidies) which alter relative prices and incomes in such a way as to induce citizens in an otherwise free market to change their actions in a desired direction are in general to be preferred to governmental quantitative regulations which require each individual to take certain specified acts. The former tax-subsidy-price-mechanism-market method allows much more freedom of personal choice than any prohibition-quantitative-licensing-direct-regulation method. Thus to tax the rich in order to subsidise the poor leaves much more individual freedom of choice than to rule that no man may own more than one car and that every man should receive a free bath and seven free loaves of bread a week.

Second, where direct regulations are unavoidable they should be based on principles and criteria which are as precise, as general and as impersonal as possible, rather than being left to the discretion and good judgement of the bureaucrat. The former give much greater security and equality of opportunity than the latter. For example, to rule that all concerns in certain clearly defined impoverished regions should receive certain clearly defined advantages is preferable to an arrangement whereby a governmental authority can at its discretion decide to help or hinder any concern which in its good judgement deserves encouragement or discouragement in order in the most general terms to help solve the problem of impoverished regions.

Our discussion will accordingly be designed ultimately to aid in the formation of a judgement between different policy measures, based upon more or less universally applicable principles and calculated to affect the distribution of income and wealth in certain well defined directions.

CHAPTER II

INTERPERSONAL COMPARISONS
OF WELFARE

It is impossible to go far with any discussion of the principles which should govern the distribution of income and wealth without raising the questions how far and by what means one can compare the needs and the welfare of one individual with those of another. If the psychologists had invented a utilitometer, all would be easy. By listening in to a man's heart beats or by recording his brain waves one could measure the total units of happiness which he was ticking up; and by feeding him extra marginal units of food or by putting extra marginal units of clothing on his back, one could discover the resulting increases in the quantity of happiness which he was producing. One could then compare A's happiness with B's.

But human beings are not simple happiness machines and the technicians have not yet invented an efficient utilitometer. Any comparison of A's welfare with B's welfare must necessarily take a much more rough and ready form. But we do in fact make some broad interpersonal comparisons. We can all agree that a man who is dying of thirst will get more happiness, welfare, utility – call it what you will – from a cup of water than will a man whose thirst is already quenched.

Fine distinctions may be impossible to make or, at least, impossible to make with any great confidence. But in principle any individual observer can ask himself the meaningful question: 'Would I prefer to be a person like A (e.g. with A's temperament and constitution) in A's situation (e.g. with A's level of income, etc.) or a person like B (e.g. with B's temperament and constitution) in B's situation (e.g. with B's level of income, etc.)?' Such questions are difficult to formulate precisely and to answer with confidence. But they are meaningful questions. If the answer to the question is 'Yes', then the observer is asserting that A's welfare or utility is greater than B's.

Different observers might answer this question differently simply because of the difficulty of putting themselves into A's and B's shoes both with respect to the differences between the temperaments and constitutions of A and B (e.g. differences in tastes) and also with respect to the differences in the situations of A and B (e.g. differences in the disagreeableness of their jobs). In this volume we are interested in governmental distributional policies. We shall not raise problems about the merits of different political arrangements for reaching decisions about distributional policies.[1] But we shall speak of those who do decide upon such policies simply as the policy-makers. The first and basic assumptions which we shall make in this volume is that the policy-makers are prepared, on the basis of the sort of question discussed in the previous paragraph, to compare A's and B's welfare at least to the extent of saying whether A's welfare is greater than, equal to, or less than B's.

Let us write[2]

$$\hat{U}_a = \hat{U}_a(\hat{C}_{xa}, \hat{C}_{ya}, \ldots)$$

and

$$\hat{U}_b = \hat{U}_b(\hat{C}_{xb}, \hat{C}_{yb}, \ldots) \ldots\ldots\ldots\ldots\ldots\ldots\ldots(2.1)$$

for the measure of A's and B's welfare or utility respectively, where $\hat{C}_{xa}, \hat{C}_{ya}$, etc., are the amounts of commodities X and Y being consumed by A; and similarly for $\hat{C}_{xb}, \hat{C}_{yb}$, etc. So far we are assuming simply that the policy-makers are prepared to decide whether, in their opinion, $\hat{U}_a > \hat{U}_b$, or $\hat{U}_a = \hat{U}_b$, or $\hat{U}_a < \hat{U}_b$.

The equations in (2.1) are written as if A's and B's welfare depended solely upon the amounts of the commodities X and Y which they are consuming. In fact welfare depends upon many other factors, such as the pleasantness or the disagreeableness of one's work, whether one is in good or bad health, and so on. One can allow for these other factors in either of two ways. First, one can add other factors (such as hours of work, conditions of work, state of one's health) to the $\hat{C}$'s as variables upon which welfare $\hat{U}$ is dependent. Secondly, one

---

[1] We hope to discuss such problems in a subsequent volume.

[2] Throughout this volume, as in the case of *The Growing Economy* and *The Controlled Economy*, we shall write a variable with a hat (e.g. $\hat{C}$) when we are considering a quantity per head (e.g. consumption per head or the consumption of a single individual).

could restrict the $\hat{C}$'s to the levels of consumption of different goods and services (as is done in (2.1)) and could allow for any other differences in the outcome simply by saying that A's $\hat{U}$-function differed from B's $\hat{U}$-function, because, for example, A had a less pleasant job than B. The ideal arrangement would be to include as causal variables together with the $\hat{C}$'s all those features of the external situation which affect A's or B's welfare and to relegate to differences in the $\hat{U}$-functions themselves only those internal personality differences of temperament or constitution between A and B which cause them to get more or less welfare out of any given external situation.[3] But such an ideal arrangement may often be impossible. One must relegate to differences in the $\hat{U}$-function all differences (whether of external situation or internal personality) which are not expressed by the $\hat{C}$'s or other similar variables which are expressly stated as arguments of the $\hat{U}$-functions.

Our policy-makers are the ultimate authorities in deciding whether or not $\hat{U}_a > \hat{U}_b$. But this does not mean that in other respects the economy must be an authoritarian one. Individuals A and B can be allowed to spend their incomes in whatever manner they please at current market prices in order to achieve what they regard as their highest possible utilities. A determines for himself what is the highest $\hat{U}_a$ that he can achieve with his own resources in his given situation and B determines for himself what is the highest $\hat{U}_b$ which he can attain. Thus by their own behaviour A and B can reveal whether they prefer one situation – i.e. one set of $\hat{C}$'s – to another, that is to say whether their $\hat{U}$ is greater in one situation than another. The policy-makers compare the resulting $\hat{U}_a$ with the resulting $\hat{U}_b$ and make the necessary interpersonal comparisons deciding whether $\hat{U}_a > \hat{U}_b$, $\hat{U}_a = \hat{U}_b$, or $\hat{U}_a < \hat{U}_b$.

The position which we have reached so far can be depicted in Figure 1 for the case in which A's and B's utilities, given A's and B's personal temperaments and constitutions, depend solely upon the amounts of their consumptions of two commodities, X and Y. In

[3] A fundamental difficulty with this distinction arises when one allows for the fact that a person's tastes – indeed his whole character and temperament – can be moulded by his experience of different external situations. Considerations of this kind raise very formidable issues of principle for the definitions of welfare. We intend to face these difficulties in a subsequent volume. In this volume we shall proceed in the main as if each individual had a set of tastes which were not necessarily constant over his life (an old man's needs are different from those of an infant), but which remained unaffected by his actual experiences in life.

Figure 1(i) we draw A's indifference curves between $\hat{C}_{xa}$ and $\hat{C}_{ya}$. A decides for himself what are the combinations of $\hat{C}_{xa}$ and $\hat{C}_{ya}$ which are indifferent to him in the sense that such combinations give him the same level of $\hat{U}_a$. As we move North East up any such ray as $O_a\hat{C}_a$, $\hat{U}_a$ increases. This simple fact can be depicted by giving a higher number to each $\hat{U}_a$-curve as we move up $O_a\hat{C}_a$. But for the limited purpose of saying no more than that $\hat{U}_a$ is increasing it does not matter what numbers we attach to each successive $\hat{U}_a$-curve provided only that these numbers rise as we move North East. An arbitrary set of numbers 1, 6, 29, 32 is illustrated on Figure 1 (i).

In Figure 1(ii) B similarly determines his own indifference curves. These may be of a quite different shape from A's indifference curves if B's personal temperament or constitution differs from A's. But the numbering of B's curves no longer has any degree of arbitrariness, if the policy-makers are prepared to compare A's and B's welfare. Thus in Figure 1 we suppose that the policy-makers attach the same number 6 to that particular indifference-curve of B which gives B the same welfare as A attains when A is on the A-indifference curve to which the number 6 has been arbitrarily allotted. And so on for the rest of B's indifference curves.

So far we have reached the following position: A can say, when his position changes, whether he is better or worse off; B can say, when his position changes, whether he is better or worse off; and the policy-makers are prepared to say whether A is better or worse off than B. But it is desirable to go a lot further than this. More information about the welfare of A and of B is necessary before it is possible for the policy-makers to take into account the effect of their policies on the total amount of welfare. Thus suppose that it is decided that A is better off than B and that it is desired for that reason to redistribute income in favour of B. A given redistributive policy reduces A's welfare and increases B's. But by how much does it reduce A's welfare and by how much does it increase B's welfare? Has A's welfare been decreased a great deal in order to increase B's welfare very little or has A's welfare fallen very little and B's risen a great deal? One's view as to the desirability of the policy might well be affected by the answer to this question. Or let us pose a different question. Regardless of the question whether A's or B's utility level is the higher, suppose we transfer a given amount of spendable income from A to B so that A's utility falls and B's rises. We may ask: 'Has A's utility fallen by more or by less than the rise in B's utility?'

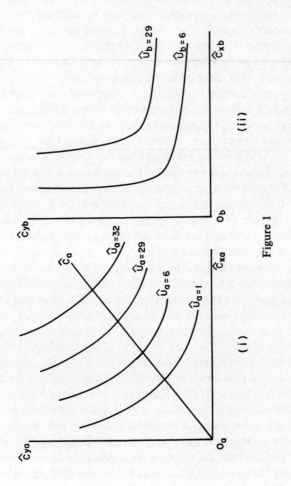

Figure 1

To answer these and similar questions it would be desirable to be able to allot a single set of numbers to the indifference curves of A in Figure 1 (i) which had no arbitrary element in them at all but which measured the amount of A's welfare or utility in an absolute manner as if it were pounds or kilograms of weight or inches or centimetres of length. If one could do this for $\hat{U}_a$ then by the basic process of interpersonal comparison of utilities one could allot the same absolute numbers to the corresponding levels of $\hat{U}_b$. For the purpose of developing such an absolute measure one needs to take two further steps. First, one must decide the base level for a zero amount of welfare (to correspond to a zero weight or a zero length). Second, having decided arbitrarily upon a unit of measurement for utility (corresponding to the decision whether to use pounds or kilograms for weight or whether to use inches or centimetres for length) one must be able to distinguish between equal additional amounts of welfare above the zero level of welfare.

One can think of a zero-level of welfare for A in the following way. If an individual's consumption level falls below a subsistence level, he will actually be unable to keep body and soul together. But before that ultimate subsistence level is reached, he may well sink to a level of misery at which it is just not worth while living. We may regard this level of consumption as providing a zero level of utility. The question may be raised whether this zero level should be judged by A himself (in which case it is the level at which A says: 'I wish I had never been born') or whether it should be judged by the policy-makers on A's behalf. The answer to this question (important though it may be for a general appraisal of the moral worth of society) need not be given here for our present purely economic analysis. We assume that the policy-makers have fixed a zero level for A's utility or welfare, whether it be that they have taken this from A's own decision or whether in a paternalistic authoritarian manner they have themselves decided it on his behalf.

We are left then with the problem of measuring equal increments of A's utility above this zero level. This can be tackled only along the lines which have been given in *The Growing Economy* (pages 212–19 and 419–25). We repeat here only the bare outline of the argument which is necessary for our present purpose.

In Figure 2 we draw along the horizontal axis the ray $O_a\hat{C}_a$ of Figure 1. Up the vertical axis we measure $\hat{U}_a$. We are attempting in Figure 2 to give non-arbitrary numbers to A's indifference curves instead of the arbitrary numbers 1, 6, 29, 32 which we allotted to A's indifference curves in Figure 1. In other words in Figure 2 we are trying to measure the actual height of the hill of utility as A moves along the ray $O_a\hat{C}_a$, whereas Figure 1 was simply a map giving the contour lines without specifying the actual heights which each contour line represented. In Figure 2 the broken lines for $\hat{C}_{xa}$, $\hat{C}_{ya}$,

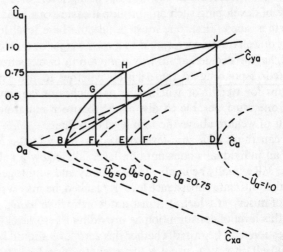

Figure 2

and the resulting A-indifference curves show the flat contour map of the hill of utility, the absolute height of which we are measuring in Figure 2 along the uphill path corresponding to the ray $O_a\hat{C}_a$ of Figure 1.

The level of consumption on the ray $O_a\hat{C}_a$ which corresponds to a zero level of $\hat{U}_a$ is no longer arbitrary. It is that level at which life is just worth living for A. Let this level of $\hat{C}_a$ be represented by the length O_aB in Figure 2. We take another much larger, but otherwise arbitrarily chosen, level of $\hat{C}_a$ equal to O_aD in Figure 2 and we choose units of measurement for $\hat{U}_a$ (corresponding to the choice of inches or centimetres for height) which makes $\hat{U}_a = 1$ when $\hat{C}_a = O_aD$.

We can now subject A to two kinds of test to discover the levels of utility which he would ascribe to various levels of consumption between the values for $\hat{U}_a$ of zero at $\hat{C}_a = O_aB$ and unity at $\hat{C}_a = O_aD$.

Test 1   We ask A: 'What is the level of $\hat{C}_a$ which, if you had it for certain, you would regard us of equal utility to you as a 50 per cent chance of living like a millionaire at $\hat{C}_a = O_aD$ plus a 50 per cent chance of living like a pauper at $\hat{C}_a = O_aB$?' If A had no particular enjoyment from gambling as such and if equal additional units of $\hat{C}_a$ resulted in equal additional amounts of $\hat{U}_a$ (i.e. if the marginal utility of real consumption did not decline), A would presumably answer 'O_aF'', where F' lay halfway between B and D on the line $O_a\hat{C}_a$. In this case in which the marginal utility of consumption did not decline, the $\hat{U}_a$-curve would be the straight line BKJ (equal additions to $\hat{C}_a$ giving the same constant equal addition to $\hat{U}_a$). With $\hat{C}_a = O_aF'$ the level of $\hat{U}_a$, namely $F'K$, would be halfway between its level of zero at B and of unity at D, so that $\hat{U}_a = 0.5$ when $\hat{C}_a = O_aF'$. A would be indifferent between a level of consumption half way between B and D and a 50–50 chance of consumption at B or consumption at D.

But if A's marginal utility of consumption fell as A's consumption increased, the $\hat{U}_a$-curve would be of the kind depicted by the curve $BGHJ$ where equal successive additions to $\hat{C}_a$ cause smaller and smaller increments of $\hat{U}_a$. In this case a consumption level of only O_aF would give a level of $\hat{U}_a$ halfway between $\hat{U}_a$ at B and $\hat{U}_a$ at D. A would be indifferent between a guaranteed consumption level of O_aF and a 50–50 chance of consumption at B or of consumption at D.

One could then go on to ask A further questions such as: 'What is the level of $\hat{C}_a$ which, if you had it for certain, you would regard us of equal utility to you as a 75 per cent chance of O_aD combined with a 25 per cent chance of O_aB?' With his utility curve $BGHJ$, A would answer 'O_aE' where EH was 75 per cent of JD – provided once again that A took no special delight in gambling.

But if A positively enjoyed the thrill of gambling and of not knowing whether he was to be a pauper or a millionaire, he might be prepared to give up a certain income of more than O_aF for a 50–50 chance and of more than O_aE for 25–75 chance as between pauperism and millionairism. This might be so even though the curve $BGHJ$ truly represented the increments of enjoyment which he would get out of successive increments of a guaranteed riskless income.

Test 2   Can one devise an alternative test which does not confuse a test of the rate at which the underlying marginal utility of consumption declines with a test of a man's enjoyment of gambling as such? One can ask A: 'What is the level of $\hat{C}_a$ which, if you had it all the year round, you would regard as of equal utility to spending 50 per cent of your days as a millionaire at O_aD and 50 per cent of your days as a pauper at O_aB?' In this case A would answer 'O_aF' (since half his days at $\hat{U}_a = 0$ and half at $\hat{U}_a = 1$ would be the equivalent of all his days at $\hat{U}_a = 0.5$) – provided in this case that A did not positively dislike changing his habits from day to day. But if A disliked change as such and longed for stability, then he might prefer a stable level of consumption less than O_aF instead of half-time at O_aD, even though the curve *BGHJ* truly represented the additional increments of utility which he would enjoy from additional increments to a stable level of consumption.

If A had no positive love or dislike of gambling as such or of stability in the level of his consumption as such, then Tests 1 and 2 should both reveal the same utility curve *BGHJ* of Figure 2 for the relationship between A's consumption and his utility. The starting level O_aB is not arbitrary, since it represents the level of consumption at which life is just worth living for A. The only arbitrary element is the choice of the unit in which utility is measured. Thus if one were to define units of measurement for $\hat{U}_a$ such that $\hat{U}_a$ was to be 20 instead of 1 when $\hat{C}_a$ was equal to O_aD, then the only difference would be that the numbers 0.5, 0.75, 1.0 up the vertical scale would all be multiplied by 20. It is equivalent to measuring height in a new unit, such as changing from the yard to the metric measure of the metre.

The problem would then be completely solved:

(i) A and B could themselves freely choose their preferred combinations of $\hat{C}_x$, $\hat{C}_y$, etc., i.e. decide upon their own indifference curves.

(ii) Taking A as a representative of a particular class of individuals, the policy-makers would decide (with or without A's guidance) the level of his consumption at which $\hat{U}_a$ was to be regarded as zero, i.e. at which life was just worth living for A.

(iii) The policy-makers choose an arbitrary unit for the measurement of all $\hat{U}$'s for all citizens by deciding in A's case what value $\hat{U}_a$ shall be deemed to have for some arbitrarily chosen high level of $\hat{C}_a$.

(iv) A then reveals the shape of his utility curve by means of Tests 1 and 2.

(v) The policy-makers then make the basic interpersonal comparisons between A's welfare and the welfares of B, of C, of D etc. at different levels of consumption for these representatives of other classes of individual.

As a result the policy-makers would know in every situation what was the utility level and what was the marginal utility of consumption for every individual citizen.

Even if it were possible (which it is not) to devise utility tests which were not confused with tests of attitudes towards risks and instabilities of consumption levels, it would not be possible in the real world to carry out such a systematic analysis of individual utilities. In spite of this the rest of this volume will be written 'as if' the policy-makers had carried out such a systematic analysis. Is there any justification for proceeding on so unrealistic an assumption? The procedure is not in fact as outrageous as may at first sight appear to be the case. The result of the systematic analysis (if the policy-makers could carry it out) would simply be that they would allot to different citizens two basic numbers: first, a number which represented the policy-makers' estimation of the weight to be put upon the total utility ($\hat{U}$) enjoyed by different citizens; and, second, a number which represented the policy-makers' estimation of the weight to be put upon the increments of utility which would be enjoyed by different citizens by giving them a increment of money income to spend at the ruling prices for $\hat{C}_x$ and $\hat{C}_y$ (i.e. a measure of the marginal utilities of consumption to different individuals); the marginal utility of spendable money income to A and B we will express as μ_a and μ_b.

Our contention is simply that any systematic consideration of distributional policies implies tacitly or expressly that the policy-makers do have in mind something corresponding to relative valuations both of the total utilities and also of the marginal utilities of the members of different classes in society. The policy-makers may have to determine these relative utility weights (the $\hat{U}$'s and the μ's) in a rather arbitrary manner, since the systematic analysis necessary for a less arbitrary determination is not possible. We shall proceed as if these weights have in fact been determined by whatever political mechanism exists for such determination, however arbitrary such a determination may be. To proceed on this assumption is not so unrealistic. It is merely to bring into the open certain underlying assumptions about the relative weights which must be put upon the welfare of different citizens if a given policy for the redistribution of income and wealth is to be justified on any given set of moral principles.

CHAPTER III

THE DISTINCTION BETWEEN EFFICIENCY AND DISTRIBUTION

We have spoken in Chapter I as if it were easy to distinguish between the efficiency aspects and the distributional aspects of any economic change caused by a given act of governmental policy. It seems only natural common sense to make some distinction. It seems natural to comment, for example, on certain policies that they may make the economy more efficient but that they bear hardly and unfairly on a particular group in society. Yet on looking more carefully into the question, the definition of the distinction between the efficiency and the distributional aspects of a given change raises great difficulties.

It is not very difficult to define perfect efficiency in an economic system. A stationary economy may be said to be in a perfectly efficient state if it is impossible to move to another feasible state in which someone is better off without any one else being made worse off. A growing economy may be said to be moving on an efficient time path if it is impossible to shift it on to another time path on which someone over his life span would be better off without anyone else being made worse off over his life span.[1]

On these lines an economy might be said to have been made more efficient, though not necessarily perfectly efficient, if some change had occurred which made one or more persons better off without making anyone worse off. Policies which have this effect might be said to be efficient policies. The view is sometimes expressed that the economist as such should be concerned only with efficiency, so defined. That is to say, it would be no business of an economist to pronounce on the desirability or otherwise of policies which made some people better off and others worse off. He should be concerned only with the devising of efficient policies whereby everyone can be

---

[1] We have used these definitions in Chapter XII of *The Stationary Economy* and Chapter XXIII of *The Growing Economy*.

made better off simultaneously or, at least, some can be made better off without anyone being made worse off.[2]

Such an attitude is surely too restrictive. It puts an immense premium on whatever happens to be the original distribution of income. The economist as such may have no more status than anyone else in deciding the ethical question as to what is a better or worse distribution of income, but it is surely part of his function to consider how a given redistribution of income (if it were desired by the political policy-makers) could be achieved with a minimum sacrifice of economic efficiency. Moreover, practically every conceivable change of policy will in fact be to someone's detriment as well as to others' benefit; and the economist would have virtually no contribution to make if he were strictly to confine himself to the consideration of policies which made no one worse off.

Can the economist say anything about the efficiency aspect of a policy which makes some people better off and others worse off? Is it possible to distinguish between the case in which the change marks an improvement in general economic efficiency (in spite of the fact that some particular individuals will be hurt) and the case in which it marks a general loss of economic efficiency (though a few special interests will gain from the change)?

One criterion which has been suggested for making such a distinction is of the following kind. A policy causes some people to be better off; we will call these 'the gainers'. It makes some others worse off; we will call these 'the losers'. Suppose that it is possible for the gainers out of their gains fully to compensate the losers for their losses and yet to remain better off by the change; then, it has been argued, the change may be regarded as an efficient one. Whether or not the gainers do in fact compensate the losers is another matter which concerns distributional policy. The fact that there are net gains to be distributed proves that the policy increases economic efficiency, whether the redistribution of these gains does or does not take place. The policy has so increased real income that the gainers could be made better off even if the losers were fully compensated.

---

[2] Not everyone would necessarily agree that all efficient policies were desirable. In an economy with great inequalities of income a change which made the very rich still richer without improving the welfare of the poor might be considered positively undesirable by policy-makers who were concerned with the general pattern of inequality as well as with the standard of living of individuals. We return to this possibility in Chapter IV.

And, conversely, of course, the change may be considered to be an inefficient one if the gainers could not fully compensate the losers out of their gains without themselves being worse off than before.

This way of attempting to distinguish between the efficiency and the distributional aspects of a policy change is open to two objections. The first objection is of a technical nature, namely, that in spite of its apparent simplicity it does not in fact manage in all cases to give a clear and decisive answer to the question whether a policy increases economic efficiency or not. The second objection, which is of much greater importance, is that the criterion simply fails to address itself to the question which is of real importance to the policy-makers.

Consider first the simple technical flaw. Let us describe the economic state of affairs as Situation I before the change of policy and Situation II after the change of policy, on the assumption that the gainers from the movement from Situation I to Situation II do not in fact compensate the losers. If they could in fact have done so and still preserved some part of their gains, the change from Situation I to Situation II would then be defined as an efficient change.

In some cases it may at the same time be true that if one started from Situation II and moved to Situation I the gainers from this change could have compensated the losers from this change and yet retained part of their gains. If this were so, then the move back from Situation II to Situation I, as well as the move from Situation I to Situation II, would be defined as an efficient move. In other words the criterion would break down; it would not give consistent answers.

The sort of case in which this criterion of economic efficiency gives inconsistent results is illustrated in Table I. Consider a simple economy with only two factors of production, land and labour, producing only two products, food and clothing. All land is owned by one class of persons, the landlords, and all labour is undertaken by another class of persons, the workers.[3] Suppose that the production of food is land-intensive and that of clothing is labour-intensive. Suppose further that there is a very marked difference between the high ratio of land to labour needed to produce food and the low ratio of land to labour needed to produce clothing, and that the elasticity of substitution between the two factors is low in both industries. In these circumstances a shift of demand from food to

---

[3] Such a society was defined as a Plantcap in Chapter III of *The Growing Economy*.

clothing will cause a very large redistribution of income from the landlords to the workers. The fall in the demand for food will release much land and little labour, while the increase in the demand for clothing will call for much labour and little land. There will be a marked excess demand for labour and excess supply of land; and if the elasticity of substitution between land and labour is low in both occupations the wage of labour will have to rise very greatly relatively to the rent of land before equilibrium is restored.

| | | Production programme encourages the output of | |
		Clothing	Food
Distribution of income favourable to	Landlords	1 Gainers from I compensate the losers	2 Situation II
	Workers	3 Situation I	4 Gainers from II compensate the losers

Table I

Finally, suppose that the consumption needs of workers and landlords differ and that at any given ratio of the price of food to the price of clothing landlords spend a markedly higher proportion of their income on clothing than do workers. The workers' consumption is food-intensive and the landlords' consumption is clothing-intensive.

Let us start with a governmental policy which subsidises the production of clothing and taxes that of food. We shall be in box 3 of Table I, which we call Situation I. In this situation the distribution of income is relatively favourable to the workers, since the labour-intensive clothing industry and thus the demand for labour is expanded and the land-intensive food industry and thus the demand for land is contracted. But the output of clothing (which suits best the tastes of the landlords) is high relatively to that of food (which suits best the tastes of the workers).

Suppose now that a new government comes in and in the interests of the landlords taxes the production of clothing and subsidises that of food. The result is to raise rents in food production and to lower the wages in clothing production and thus to redistribute income in favour of the landlords. But the output of food (which suits best the tastes of the workers) is now encouraged relatively to that of clothing (which best suits the tastes of the landlords). We are in Situation II, which is shown in box 2 of Table I.

In such a case it is very possible that the gainers from the move from Situation I to Situation II (i.e. the landlords) can compensate the losers (i.e. the workers) because in Situation II the things which the workers want (namely, food) are relatively plentiful. If this compensation did take place we would move from box 2 to box 4 of Table I. We would then have a production programme (high food output) which matched the distribution of income (namely, relatively high incomes of workers who want food). Since the compensation *could* take place, making both workers and landlords better off in box 4 than in box 3, the change from Situation I to Situation II would be described as an efficient one, *even if the compensation did not in fact take place*.

Suppose then that the compensation does not take place and we are in Situation II (box 2 of the Table). There is another change of government which, in order to encourage the demand for labour relatively to the demand for land and thus to redistribute income from rents to wages, once again subsidises the production of labour-intensive clothing and taxes that of land-intensive food. We move back from Situation II to Situation I.

By a process of reasoning exactly similar to that used to show that the movement from Situation I to II was an efficient one, it is possible that we can now also define the movement from Situation II (box 2 of Table I) to Situation I (box 3 of Table I) as an efficient one. The gainers in Situation I (the workers) could very probably compensate the losers (the landlords) because in Situation I the products (namely, clothing) which suit the tastes of the losers (namely, the landlords) are in exceptionally plentiful supply.

In fact in a real sense boxes 1 and 4 in Table I are both relatively efficient situations since the outputs are more suitable to the distributions of income than in boxes 2 and 3 in which the relatively plentiful goods are suitable to the tastes of those who are relatively impoverished. In this sort of case it is very probable that a move from Situation I to Situation II would be defined as an efficient move (because the gainers could compensate the losers, although in fact they do not do so) and at the same time for exactly similar reasons a move back from Situation II to Situation I would also be defined as an efficient one.

A more formal analytical demonstration of this possibility is shown in Figure 3. The horizontal dimension of each box in that

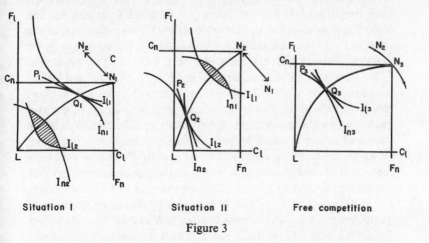

Situation I   Situation II   Free competition

Figure 3

Figure represents the total output of clothing (*C*) and the vertical dimension represents the total output of food (*F*). The points labelled *Q* within each box show the actual consumption of these amounts of *C* and *F* by the workers or labour (*L*) and by the landlords or owners of natural resources (*N*). The curves marked I_l are indifference curves for the workers, based on an origin of zero consumption for both products at the corners marked *L*; and similarly the curves marked I_n are indifference curves for the landlords based on origins at the corners marked *N*. The curves joining the points *L* to *N* are the relevant contract curves tracing out the points of tangency between an I_l-curve and an I_n-curve.[4]

In our example we are assuming a free competitive market for the purchase of whatever quantities of *F* and *C* are in fact produced. Workers and landlords will compete for purchases of *F* and *C* at a single market price for each product. The *Q* points will, therefore, always lie on the contract curve at which the slope of the workers' relevant indifference curve (I_l), and so the relative price paid by

---

[4] For a more complete description of this type of geometric construction see Chapter IV of *The Stationary Economy*.

workers for the two products, is the same as the slope of the land-lords' relevant indifference curve (I_n), and so the relative price paid by landlords for the two products. The fact that the workers' tastes are for F and the landlords' tastes are for C is shown by the curvature of the contract curves in Figure 3, which is such that the slope from the origin L to any one point Q is in all cases steeper than the slope from the origin N to that same point Q. This indicates that the ratio of F to C consumed by workers is always higher in any given market situation than the ratio of F to C consumed by landlords.

We start in Situation I as depicted in Figure 3. Much C and little F is produced. As a result landlords are relatively poor and workers relatively rich. If the factor intensities differ very much in the two industries and if, in addition, the elasticity of substitution between land and labour is small in both industries, then a very high level of wages relatively to rents will be needed to obtain the necessary high ratio of land to labour in both occupations in order to provide the labour needed to produce the large output of labour-intensive C.[5] In this case workers will be rich and landlords poor; the con-sumption point Q_1 will be near the origin N and far from the origin L (i.e. on a high I_l curve and a low I_n curve). The price of F relatively to the price of C will be very high (as shown by the very slight slope of the P_1-price-line), for the double reason (i) that the supply of F is relatively low and (ii) that the demand for F is high because the workers who have the favourable distribution of income demand F rather than C.

The change to Situation II is shown by the movement North West of the origin N from N_1 to N_2. More F and less C is produced. Rents go up considerably relatively to wages because factor intensities differ very much in producing F and C and because land and labour are not good substitutes for each other. The point Q_2 is, therefore, very near the L-origin and far from the N-origin because the land-lords are now rich and the workers poor. The price line P_2 is now very steeply sloped, the price of C now being very high because (i) the supply of C is low and (ii) the wealthy landlords demand C rather than F.

Consider now the way in which the curve I_{n1} moves relatively to I_{l1} as N moves North West from N_1 to N_2. If the slope of the gradient from N_1 to N_2 is steeper than the very gentle gradient of the P_1-price

5 See *The Stationary Economy*, Chapter VIII.

line, it is clear from the diagram in Situation I that as we move towards Situation II the I_{n1} curve will intersect the I_{l1} curve. At any point in the shaded area between these two curves in Situation II both landlords and workers would be better off than at the point Q_1 in Situation I. In other words moving from Q_1 in Situation I to Q_2 in Situation II the gainers (the landlords) could compensate the losers (the workers) by a redistribution of income which, with the production box of Situation II, moved Q_2 up into the shaded area between I_{n1} and I_{l1}.

Now start in Situation II and move to Situation I. If the movement of N down the gradient from N_2 to N_1 is less steep than the very steep P_2-price-line, it is clear that the I_{n2}-curve will come to intersec the I_{l2}-curve as one moves the N-origin from N_2 towards N_1. A any point in the shaded area in Situation I between the I_{l2}-curve and the I_{n2}-curve both landlords and workers are better off than at poin Q_2 in Situation II. This means that those who gained by the move ment from Q_2 to Q_1 could, while maintaining the production pro gramme of Situation I, compensate the losers by a redistribution o income which moved Q_1 down the contract curve to a point in th shaded area between the I_{l2}-curve and the I_{n2}-curve.

Thus Situation I would be defined as more efficient than Situatio II and at the same time Situation II would be defined as mor efficient than Situation I.

It is perhaps worth pointing out that this inconsistency can aris only if neither Situation I nor Situation II is perfectly efficient. Thi is an obvious result of the definition of perfect efficiency, namel that it is a situation such that it is impossible to move to anothe situation without making someone worse off. If Situation I wer perfectly efficient and one moved to Situation II it would by defin tion of perfect efficiency be impossible for any gainers to compensat the losers; and conversely if Situation II were perfectly efficient would be impossible for any gainers from a move to Situation I t compensate the losers.

In the greatly simplified example which we have been using, fre competition would result in such a perfectly efficient situatio although, of course, one might not like the distributional outcom This perfectly efficient situation is depicted by the outcome of tl competitive situation on the right-hand section of Figure 3. The will be some output combination shown by the origin N_3 which intermediate between the output N_1 (when F is taxed and C sul sidised) and the output N_2 (when F is subsidised and C taxed). The curve $N_1-N_3-N_2$ in fact shows the increasing-cost production-possibility curve resulting from the difference in factor proportions between the production of F and that of C.[6] In perfect competition the market demand prices of F and C must be the same as their marginal costs of production, or in other words the slope of the price line P_3 must be the same as the slope at N_3 of the curve $N_1-N_3-N_2$. If in these circumstances N_3 is moved South East towards N_1 or North West towards N_2, it can be seen that the I_{n3} curve must be drawn away from the I_{13} curve. Someone is bound to be worse off.

The inconsistency which we have examined at some length can occur because we defined efficiency in terms of a notional compensation test. We say that Situation II is more efficient than Situation I because the gainers from Situation II could compensate the losers, even though in fact no compensation takes place.

But this inconsistency does not always arise. Indeed as we have just argued, if Situation II were a perfectly efficient situation, it would not arise. But whether or not in any particular case this inconsistency exists, there is a second and much more basic objection to the definition of efficiency in terms of a notional compensation of losers by gainers. Let us consider a case in which the technical inconsistency which we have just examined could not occur. Suppose that there were only one product and then consider the two situations compared in Table II. There is an increase in total production between Situation I and Situation II and this can enable the gainers to compensate the losers as is shown by comparing box 4 with box 3. In this case if one moves back from Situation II to Situation I, since the total output of the single product has gone down it is not possible for the gainers to compensate the losers. In box 1 the workers are now worse off than in box 2, having compensated the landlords for the reduction in their income between Situation II and Situation I.

In this sort of case there is no problem in noting that as between Situation I and Situation II there is an increase in efficiency but that the distribution has moved against the workers. But in fact when we move from Situation I to Situation II, either compensation is paid (in which case we need to compare box 3 with box 4) or else

[6] See Chapter VIII of *The Stationary Economy*.

compensation is not paid (in which case we need to compare box 3 with box 2). If compensation is not paid and we are comparing Situation I with Situation II, box 4 is entirely irrelevant and we can forget about it. What we need to judge is whether or not Situation II is to be preferred to Situation I, taking into account the fact that

		Production of product	
		50	60
Distribution of income		1 Situation I with compensation of losers	2 Situation II
	Workers	10	20
	Landlords	40	40
		3 Situation I	4 Situation II with compensation of losers
	Workers	30	30
	Landlords	20	30

Table II

landlords' consumption has gone up from 20 to 40 and also the fact that workers' consumption has gone down from 30 to 20. We need a single criterion that tells whether the change is on balance for the good or the bad of society when one allows for the fact that some people have in fact gained and others have in fact lost.

Having designed such a criterion one can go on to ask whether it can be expressed in any way which distinguishes the efficiency and the distributional elements in the criterion. In other words, can one say that a given change has affected total social welfare by an amount ΔZ, but that a part ΔZ_1 of this is due to a change in the distribution of income and a part ΔZ_2 to a change in economic efficiency, where $\Delta Z = \Delta Z_1 + \Delta Z_2$?

Let us start the discussion of such a distinction by means of the simplest form of general comprehensive welfare criterion, namely that social welfare (Z) is to be measured by the sum of the economic welfares or utilities of individuals A, B, C, etc. $(\hat{U}_a + \hat{U}_b + \hat{U}_c + \text{etc.})$. This criterion will serve to illustrate the general problem and we shall discuss later the application of our analysis to certain other ways of formulating the criterion for general economic welfare.

We can now distinguish between the efficiency and the distributional effects of a change in the economic situation, if we confine our attention to small, marginal changes.[7] In order to illustrate this procedure let us assume that there are only two classes of persons, class a and class b, (e.g. workers and landlords), each individual having the same income and tastes as the other members of his class, but the individual members of one class differing in income and taste from the individual members of the other class. We will write N_a and N_b for the numbers of individuals in classes a and b respectively. Assume further that there are only two products, X and Y, the whole outputs of which are in a stationary economy consumed by the two classes of citizens, a and b. These products are available to all individuals at the same ruling market prices, P_x and P_y. The utility enjoyed by a member of class a depends solely upon the amounts of X and Y which he consumes.

We have then the following set of equations:

$$Z = N_a \hat{U}_a + N_b \hat{U}_b \quad \text{...........................(3.1)}$$

where $\hat{U}_a$ and $\hat{U}_b$ are the utility enjoyed by a member of class a and class b respectively. This equation simply defines social welfare as the sum of individual welfares.

$$\hat{U}_a = \hat{U}_a(\hat{C}_{xa}, \hat{C}_{ya})$$
$$\hat{U}_b = \hat{U}_b(\hat{C}_{xb}, \hat{C}_{yb}) \quad \text{...........................(3.2)}$$

where $\hat{C}_{xa}$ is the amount of X consumed per head in class a and similarly for $\hat{C}_{ya}$, $\hat{C}_{bx}$, and $\hat{C}_{by}$.

Let μ_a represent the marginal utility of money to an individual in group a and let P_x represent the money price at which X can be purchased for consumption. Then $\mu_a P_x$ will measure the marginal utility of a unit of X to a member of group a, since the individual will maximise his utility by purchasing X up to the point at which what it adds to his utility by consuming one more unit of X is equal to the utility of the money price which he has to pay for it. If this individual receives a small additional amount of X to consume (namely, $d\hat{C}_{xa}$), his utility will thus be increased by an amount equal to $\mu_a P_x d\hat{C}_{xa}$.

---

[7] This method has already been employed in Chapter XVI of *The Controlled Economy*.

We can, therefore, derive from (3.1) and (3.2) the expression

$$dZ = \mu_a N_a (P_x \, d\hat{C}_{xa} + P_y \, d\hat{C}_{ya})$$
$$+ \mu_b N_b (P_x \, d\hat{C}_{xb} + P_y \, d\hat{C}_{yb}) \quad \ldots\ldots\ldots\ldots (3.3)$$

where dZ measures the total sum of all the small increases in the utilities of all the members of group a and group b, when, because of some marginal change in economic policy, there are small changes $d\hat{C}_{xa}, d\hat{C}_{ya}, d\hat{C}_{xb}$, and $d\hat{C}_{yb}$ in the amounts of X and Y available for consumption by the individual members of the two groups.

We can rewrite this as

$$dZ = \mu N d\hat{C} + (\mu_a - \mu) \, N_a d\hat{C}_a + (\mu_b - \mu) \, N_b d\hat{C}_b \quad \ldots\ldots (3.4)$$

where: (i) $\qquad\qquad d\hat{C}_a = P_x d\hat{C}_{xa} + P_y d\hat{C}_{ya}$

which represents the change in the amounts of goods consumed by an individual member of class a, the different goods X and Y being valued at their ruling money prices P_x and P_y, so that $N_a d\hat{C}_a$ represents the change in the total amount of goods consumed by the N_a members of class a; and similarly for $N_b d\hat{C}_b$

(ii) $\qquad\qquad N d\hat{C} = N_a d\hat{C}_a + N_b d\hat{C}_b$

and measures the change in the total amounts of goods consumed by the community as a whole, the different goods being once again valued at their ruling market prices.

The expression for dZ in (3.4) is valid for any arbitrary value of μ. But for our purpose let μ be a weighted average of μ_a and μ_b, the weights being the total expenditures on consumption by the two classes a and b.

In this formulation[8] the term $\mu N d\hat{C}$ can be taken to represent

---

[8] In order to reach this simple formulation we have had to assume that the market prices (namely, P_x and P_y) are the same for all individuals whether they be in class a or class b. This means that we have to assume that trade is optimised (see page 185 of *The Stationary Economy*). Our simple model cannot, therefore, allow for any inefficiencies due to failures to optimise trade; but it can allow for inefficiencies due to failures to maximise or to optimise production. This limitation is removed in the more general model given in the Appendix (pages 220–42 below).

the efficiency element in the change in general economic welfare (dZ). This can be interpreted in either of two ways.

First, if the marginal utility of money were the same for all individuals both μ_a and μ_b would be equal to μ, which is simply a weighted average of μ_a and μ_b. We would then have:

$$dZ = \mu N d\hat{C}$$

In other words the term $\mu N d\hat{C}$ can be interpreted as an efficiency term in the sense that (given any arbitrary value for $\mu_a = \mu_b = \mu$) the change can be reckoned as desirable or undesirable according as $N d\hat{C} \gtrless 0$. This is in fact a very usual work-a-day way of regarding economic efficiency. Does a change cause the general index of quantities, weighted by their existing prices, to go up or down? This criterion rests essentially upon disregarding differences in the marginal utilities of income to different persons.

Second, the formula for dZ can be interpreted as giving a method for distinguishing between the efficiency and the distributional elements in the total effect on economic welfare of a change in those cases in which one is not prepared to disregard the difference between μ_a and μ_b. This can be seen in the following way.

Suppose that the total net increase in consumption $N d\hat{C}$ had been distributed between the two classes a and b in the same ratio as their existing consumption levels. We could define this as the case in which the change had no effect on distribution, so that any change in social welfare should be ascribed solely to the efficiency term $\mu N d\hat{C}$. And in fact this turns out to be the case, since the distributional term

$$(\mu_a - \mu)\, N_a d\hat{C}_a + (\mu_b - \mu)\, N_b d\hat{C}_b$$

would in this case be equal to zero.[9]

In other words the term $\mu \dot{N} d\hat{C}$ represents what the increase in economic welfare would have been if the distribution of the net

[9] $(\mu_a - \mu)N_a\, d\,\hat{C}_a + (\mu_b - \mu)N_b\, d\,\hat{C}_b = N d\hat{C} \left\{ \mu_a \dfrac{N_a d\hat{C}_a}{N d\hat{C}} + \mu_b \dfrac{N_b d\hat{C}_b}{N d\hat{C}} - \mu \right\}$

But if the increase in real consumption $N d\hat{C}$ has been distributed between $N_a d\,\hat{C}_a$ and $N_b d\hat{C}_b$ in the same proportion as the existing consumption levels of the two classes a and b, and if these same weights have been used to compute μ from μ_a and μ_b, then the above expression is equal to zero.

increase in consumption had been in the same ratio as the pre-existing levels of consumption. Suppose a small change in economic policy. This causes some changes in total real economic quantities (dX and dY). It is likely also to cause some changes in the distribution of these quantities among individual consumers. But suppose that by a system of lump-sum taxes and subsidies the individuals' purchasing powers were so controlled that, with these given changes in total quantities dX and dY, the values at current prices of the individuals' additional consumptions were maintained in the same ratio as their existing consumption levels; the resulting change in Z ($dZ = \mu N d\hat{C}$) would represent the efficiency effect of the real changes, dX and dY. Any further effect on Z would be due to the fact that, in the absence of these lump-sum taxes and subsidies, the distribution of the additional consumptions did not correspond to the existing consumption proportions. The term $(\mu_a - \mu) N_a d\hat{C}_a + (\mu_b - \mu) N_b d\hat{C}_b$ would measure this distributional effect, i.e. the addition to or subtraction from the efficiency effect $\mu N d\hat{C}$ due to the fact that a specially large or small part of the total net increase in consumption had accrued to the class where the marginal utility of income was above or below the average.

This volume is devoted to distributional effects so that we cannot neglect the fact that μ_a differs from μ_b. But the formula for dZ in this case becomes of operational significance only if one can give values to μ_a and μ_b. As we have argued in Chapter II, the marginal utility weights to be allotted to the spendable incomes of the various classes in the community (that is to say, the μ's) must ultimately be determined through some political process. On the basis of such political decisions about what may be called relative distributional weights, the economist can perform his technical task of applying the formula for dZ to determine whether the probable actual effects of a proposed policy change on various consumption levels will cause a net improvement in economic welfare.

The procedure is thus a mixture of the liberal and the authoritarian. Each individual, given his spendable income and the market prices of the various products, is free to decide for himself in what proportions he prefers to purchase the various goods and services. Within his own budget constraint he can climb his own peculiar hill of pleasure. But his budget constraint may be affected by the centralised decision of some political authority which is employing tax or other policies to redistribute spendable incomes.

CHAPTER IV

THE OBJECTIVES OF DISTRIBUTIONAL POLICIES

In the last chapter we proceeded on the assumption that the basic objective of economic policy was in some sense to maximise the sum total of individual utilities or enjoyments. But it is not at all obvious that this is a suitable criterion. One rather anomalous result of this procedure may serve to throw doubt upon it; the more the policy-makers make their interpersonal comparisons of utility in such a way as to emphasise inequalities in total utilities as between different individuals, the less importance does the criterion of maximising total utility attach to the redistribution of income. This paradoxical result is illustrated in Figure 4. Along the horizontal axis we measure an individual's consumption. Up the vertical axis we measure his total utility. Consider two individuals A and B with the same needs and tastes (i.e. the same utility functions) but with different consumption levels, $\hat{C}_a$ and $\hat{C}_b$. Let the height GH measure $\hat{U}_a$ i.e. the

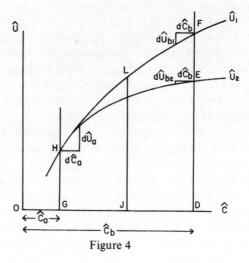

Figure 4

total utility of individual A when his consumption is equal to $\hat{C}_a$. Consider two utility functions passing through the point H, both with the same slope (i.e. the same marginal utility of consumption at this point H), but curve $\hat{U}_1$ having much less curvature than curve $\hat{U}_2$. For the higher level of consumption of $\hat{C}_b$ at the point D the total utility with curve $\hat{U}_1$ will thus be greater than the total utility of curve $\hat{U}_2$ $(FD > ED)$. Moreover the slope of the curve $\hat{U}_1$ is also greater than the slope of the curve $\hat{U}_2$.

We suppose individual B to have the same utility curve as A but to have $\hat{C}_b$ instead of only $\hat{C}_a$ units to consume. Consider now taking one unit of consumption from B and giving it to A $(d\hat{C}_a = d\hat{C}_b)$. With both curves A will gain the same amount of utility $d\hat{U}_a$; but with curve $\hat{U}_1$ B will lose much more utility than with curve $\hat{U}_2$ $(d\hat{U}_{b1} > d\hat{U}_{b2})$. The distributional effect, i.e. the possibilities of increasing total welfare through redistribution, will be much greater with curve $\hat{U}_2$ than with curve $\hat{U}_1$, i.e. much greater in the case where the inequalities in total utilities are less.

The criterion of the sum of individual utilities is not concerned with inequalities between utilities. It has nothing to choose between a policy which will result in a given addition to the utility of a poor man and a policy which will result in an addition of the same amount to the utility of a rich man, although the former policy will result in a less unequal and the latter in a more unequal society. This criterion simply regards a redistribution of income as a possible efficient measure for increasing the sum total of utilities.

Let us proceed with the analysis for the time being on the assumption that all individuals have the same utility functions, but that for each of them the marginal utility of consumption declines as their consumption increases. In this case an equal distribution of a given total amount of real consumption will be needed to maximise the sum of individual utilities. The transfer of £1 worth of consumption from a rich man (to whom the marginal utility of money is low) to a poor man (to whom the marginal utility of money is high) will always increase the sum total of utility. Equality is an efficient tool for raising total utility.

Consider now two economic situations. In Situation I there is a given total of consumption equally distributed. In Situation II there is a larger total amount of real consumption unequally distributed among the same population. But the inefficiency of inequality in Situation II is just offset by the higher total level of consumption in Situation II, so that the sum total of individual utilities is the same in Situation II as in Situation I. The criterion of the sum total of utilities would have nothing to choose between the two situations.

But if one is concerned with inequalities as such, one would presumably prefer Situation I with a given total utility equally divided to Situation II with the same total utility unequally divided. Indeed, one can go further. If the real income of Situation I were still further reduced so that Situation I had a smaller total of utility than Situation II but a more equal distribution of that smaller total, one might still prefer Situation I to Situation II. One would have some pay-off in one's mind between the total of utility and the equality in its distribution.

Any such pay-off is not, however, a simple matter. As we shall argue (See Chapter VII), there is no satisfactory unambiguous definition or measure of the degree of inequality in any distribution. All that one can say, and all that one needs to say for the present purpose, is that one may be interested in the general pattern of individual utilities rather than simply in their sum total.

In Chapter II and again at the end of the last chapter we noted the point that, since any direct comparisons of the utilities of various individuals were impossible, we must rely on the policy-makers to allot marginal utilities to the spendable money incomes of individuals. If the policy-makers wished (as was assumed to be the case) simply to maximise the sum total of personal utilities, these marginal utilities (μ_a and μ_b) would themselves constitute the 'distributional weights' which the authorities would apply to the spendable money incomes of the various classes of citizen in order to assess (on the lines of equation (3.4)) whether any given changes in the economic situation represented a rise or a fall in total economic welfare.

But there would be nothing to prevent the policy-makers from allotting distributional weights to the spendable incomes of various individuals which did not simply correspond to the marginal utilities of income to the individuals concerned but also took account of the desirability from a social point of view of changes in the distributional pattern of utilities. Thus a distributional weight which was low relatively to his marginal utility might be allotted to an individual who already enjoyed a high income and a distributional weight which was high relatively to his marginal utility might be allotted to a poor man with a low total utility. We will call such distributional weights 'pattern-modified distributional weights' and will express them as $\bar{\mu}_a$, $\bar{\mu}_b$ etc. in place of μ_a, μ_b etc. Thus if $\bar{\mu}_a/\mu_a$ is $> \bar{\mu}_b/\mu_b$ we are expressing the fact that the policy-makers put an extra value on increases in A's consumption because such an increase improves, in their view, the distribution of total utilities between the various individuals.

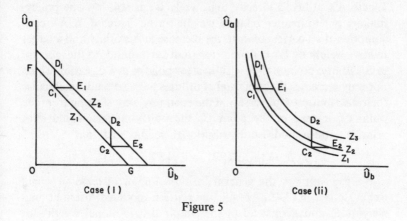

Figure 5

This distinction between the $\bar{\mu}$'s and the μ's can be readily understood from Figure 5 where we illustrate the case for a community which consists solely of two individuals, A and B. We measure A's utility $(\hat{U}_a)$ up the vertical axis and B's utility $(\hat{U}_b)$ along the horizontal axis. If, as in case (i) of Figure 5, it is desired simply to maximise the sum of utilities, namely $\hat{U}_a + \hat{U}_b$, then we can draw a series of straight lines such as Z_1 and Z_2 at an angle of 45° to the two axes to measure the social-welfare-indifference curves. Thus any combination of $\hat{U}_a$ and $\hat{U}_b$ on the line FG represents the same total utility, namely, $\hat{U}_a + \hat{U}_b = OF = OG$. Consider the two points C_1 and C_2 on the line FG. Let $C_1 D_1 = C_1 E_1 = C_2 D_2 = C_2 E_2$. Any one of these equal changes in either A's or B's total utility will raise the social welfare index by the same amount from Z_1 to Z_2.

Consider now the curved social welfare functions illustrated in case (ii) of Figure 5. Compare once again the two points C_1 and C_2 on a single curve Z_1, i.e. two distributions of $\hat{U}_a$ and $\hat{U}_b$ to which the policy-makers allot the same social value. Once again consider four equal changes in total utility, namely $C_1 D_1 = C_1 E_1 = C_2 D_2 = C_2 E_2$. The changes $C_1 D_1$ and $C_2 E_2$ raise social welfare only from Z_1 to Z_2, whereas the changes $C_1 E_1$ and $C_2 D_2$ raise welfare from Z_1 to Z_3. We can express this by allotting relative pattern-modified distributional weights such that at point C_1

$$\bar{\mu}_a/\bar{\mu}_b = (\mu_a/\mu_b)([Z_2 - Z_1]/[Z_3 - Z_1]).$$

Where A's utility is already high while B's is still low the policy-makers put a smaller relative weight on an increase in A's consumption than corresponds to the increase in A's utility and a larger relative weight on B's consumption than corresponds to the increase in B's utility, because they wish to steer policies in a direction which not only increases the sum total of utilities but also tends to equalise their distribution. Conversely, if the economy were starting from the point C_2 instead of the point C_1 the policy-makers would allot relative pattern-modified distributional weights such that

$$\bar{\mu}_a/\bar{\mu}_b = (\mu_a/\mu_b)([Z_3 - Z_1]/[Z_2 - Z_1]).$$

We can still use the general formula for an increase in social welfare given in (3.4) if we use the pattern-modified distributional weights $\bar{\mu}_a$ and $\bar{\mu}_b$ instead of the simple distributional weights or marginal utilities μ_a and μ_b. Thus (3.4) becomes

$$dZ = \bar{\mu}Nd\hat{C} + (\bar{\mu}_a - \bar{\mu}) N_a d\hat{C}_a + (\bar{\mu}_b - \bar{\mu}) N_b d\hat{C}_b \ldots\ldots (4.1)$$

where $\bar{\mu}$ is simply the weighted average of $\bar{\mu}_a$ and $\bar{\mu}_b$ which are in turn the distributional weights which the policy-makers now put upon the money expenditures on consumption of individuals in class a and class b respectively.

All that has happened is that the distributional weights, the $\bar{\mu}$'s, are now adjusted in the light of the policy-maker's views about the desirability of alterations in the pattern as well as the levels of individual utilities. $\bar{\mu}Nd\hat{C}$ represents the importance which the policy-makers would put on the changes in real quantities if the pattern of distribution of consumption levels were unchanged. The term $(\bar{\mu}_a - \bar{\mu})N_a d\hat{C}_a + (\bar{\mu}_b - \bar{\mu})N_b d\hat{C}_b$ represents the additional importance which is put upon redistributions which will change the pattern of utility-distributions in a desirable manner.

In Figure 5(i) we have the extreme case in which the objective of policy is simply to maximise total utility regardless of the degree of inequality between the utilities of different citizens. In Figure 5(ii) some weight is put upon increasing equality in the distribution of utilities as well as upon increasing the sum total of utilities. The more sharply curved are the Z-curves of Figure 5(ii), the greater the stress put upon equality of utilities relatively to the sum total of utilities.

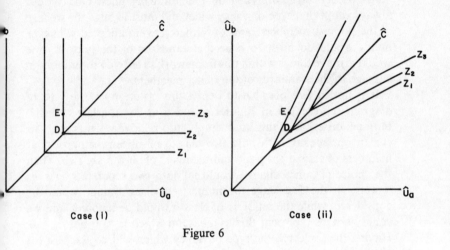

Figure 6

One could go to the extreme egalitarian criteria illustrated in Figure 6(i) and (ii). In both these Figures equal distributions of utility between A and B lie on the 45° line OC which shows the points at which $\hat{U}_a = \hat{U}_b$. Consider a movement from point D to point E which in both cases (i) and (ii) represents an increase in $\hat{U}_a$ without any change in $\hat{U}_b$. In case (i) of Figure 6 social welfare is regarded as unchanged at Z_2. This we may call the 'egalitarian' criterion. We reckon social welfare solely by the utility of the poorest member of society, and we do not count as a contribution to social welfare any rise in incomes that does not apply to the poorest member in society.

In case (ii) of Figure 6 we depict what may be called a 'super-egalitarian' criterion. In this case a rise of $\hat{U}_a$ from the point D to the point E, leaving $\hat{U}_b$ unchanged, is held to cause a reduction in social welfare from Z_2 to Z_1. Inequality is held to be so positively ugly that a community is considered to be a better place if the rich are reduced to equality with the poor even if the standard of the poor is not thereby raised. This would be equivalent to allotting a negative $\bar{\mu}$ to the spendable incomes of the rich.[1]

The criteria in Figure 6(i) and (ii) are unequivocally egalitarian. There is an alternative type of criterion which is not strictly egalitarian, but which simply puts all the weight on the welfare of the poorest members of society. This criterion, which we may call the 'anti-poverty' criterion, runs on the following lines. One should always adopt that type of policy which did most to raise the welfare of the poorest members; and only then, having adopted whatever policy would do most to raise the standards of the poorest, one would arrange things within this framework so as to do the minimum damage to the standards of the richer members.

It is not in fact possible to depict this criterion on the type of diagram represented in Figures 5 and 6 or to translate a distributional criterion of this kind simply into relative weights of $\bar{\mu}_a$, $\bar{\mu}_b$ etc. In our society with only two classes of citizens, suppose that members of class a are poor and members of class b are rich. Then the choice of policy change would fall into two separate stages, as it were. In the first stage the interests of class a alone would be considered, while the interests of class b would be ignored; and we could perhaps represent this as a case in which $\bar{\mu}_a > 0$ but $\bar{\mu}_b = 0$. Having then selected the type of policy which will do the best for class a, one may, in a second stage, be able to choose between variants of this policy all of which maintain the same improvement for class a but one of which is the best for class b. At this second stage one is giving $\bar{\mu}_b$ a positive value even though $\hat{U}_b > \hat{U}_a$.

The egalitarian and the super-egalitarian criteria of Figure 6, as well as the anti-poverty criterion which we have just discussed, all have one feature in common: a fall in the standard of living of the poorest member of society (however small) is judged unequivocally to represent a fall in social welfare even though there might be rises (however large) in everybody else's living standards. Do we really believe this? Consider its implications. Suppose that by reducing the consumption of one of the poor members of society by 1p one could raise the consumption expenditures of everyone else (including all the other members of the poorest class) by £1,000. Some persons would surely maintain that it was right and proper to demand the

---

[1] For different ways of interpreting this conclusion see the Note to this chapter (pages 61–7 below).

sacrifice from the single individual. Indeed, the individual himself might well be of the opinion that the policy should be adopted.

The case becomes more compelling if one puts it in its temporal setting. Suppose that in a stagnant undeveloped country in which no rise in living standards was occurring a small increase in savings (i.e. a small reduction in consumption standards) by the present population would, through the magic of compound interest, set in motion a process of economic growth which would lead to important and permanent improvements of standard for all future generations. Suppose that the only alternative would be perpetual stagnation at the existing poverty level; in this case, at least most people would agree that some moderate belt-tightening by the present generation was a proper sacrifice on the part of the present generation in order to improve the standards of future generations, even though this made the poorest (the present generation) somewhat poorer in order to improve the lot of others (the future generations).

Such a conclusion is in no way incompatible with a set of values which puts very much greater stress on the interests of the poorest members of society than on any other class. This sort of valuation can be obtained by the use of a set of distributional weights which involves a rapid decline in the value of $\bar{\mu}$ as one moves from the poorer to the richer members of society. The policy-makers can use distributional weights which correspond to Z-curves of the kind shown in case (ii) of Figure 5, but which are very sharply curved and thus give a large relative weight to equality of $\hat{U}$'s and a low relative weight to the sum total of all $\hat{U}$'s.

The case for using pattern-modified distributional weights which give some extra weight to increases in utility which will help to reduce inequalities as well as simply to increase the sum total of utilities is closely connected with the case for defining poverty in relative rather than in absolute terms. What does one mean by 'being in poverty'? Having a standard of living below some objective essential standard necessary to keep body and soul together? Or having a great deal less than most people in the society in which one is living?

In fact it is difficult to define an absolute standard of poverty.

In the first place, even if we limit essentials to what is needed to keep body and soul together, we are in difficulties. A diet may be sufficient to keep a person alive for the time being; but improvements in the diet may decrease the liability to disease and increase the expectation of life. What is the cut-off point in reduced diets and worsened expectation of life at which poverty begins? There is no absolute answer.

Secondly, suppose that being without warmth did not affect one's health but merely made one shiver miserably, incapable of enjoyable activity. Few people would assert that someone without any warmth was not in poverty simply because his life was not thereby endangered. But suppose the greater the warmth, the more the enjoyment. At what point in the scale of enjoyment does a man become poor?

The answers which would be given to questions of this kind in fact depend upon the general standards of the community in question. In a society in which everyone took it for granted that he had to shiver throughout the winter and in which everyone had learnt to make the best of life in these conditions, a shiverer might not be considered poor. But in a society in which everyone except Tom Jones lived with enjoyable central heating, while Tom Jones had to shiver, Tom Jones might well be considered to be living in poverty.

Poverty as we generally think of it has almost certainly a large element of the relative about it. People are poor if they are much worse off than the other members of the community in which they live.

But to give any precision to a definition of relative poverty we must ask at least two questions: first, how seriously short of the average must a man fall to be considered poor? and, second, what is the society against whose average this shortfall is to be reckoned? There can in the nature of things be no scientific, objective answers, independent of the states of mind and of the value judgements of the individuals concerned. Is a family to be regarded as being in poverty because it cannot afford a motor-car? In some countries in which cars are still the luxury of the rich the answer would be 'No'; but perhaps the answer would be 'Yes' in some communities in the United States. Is a family on a given housing estate poor because it cannot afford a TV set so that its children cannot discuss last night's programme with their playmates? Or must its children have to go to school in rags and tatters before it is regarded by its neighbours or by itself as being in poverty? A family which in a rich country is regarded as being in poverty may well have a real standard of living above the world average; it is regarded as poor because the frame of reference is that of a rich society, not of the world society. Certainly many of the poor in the United States of America would be regarded as affluent on the streets of Calcutta.

Defining people as being in poverty because their standard of living is greatly below that of their neighbours is comparable to allotting an exceptionally high pattern-modified distributional weight to their utilities for just this same reason.

So far in this chapter we have considered problems of inequalities which arise when all citizens have the same tastes and needs. We must now turn to some of the additional questions which arise when we allow for differences in individual needs and tastes.

If A and B have the same needs and tastes, so that they get the same utility from the same level of consumption, then an equal distribution of a given total amount of consumption will simultaneously equalise their utilities ($\hat{U}_a = \hat{U}_b$) and also maximise the sum total of utilities ($\hat{U}_a + \hat{U}_b$ maximised). Consider the utility curve marked $\hat{U}_1$ on Figure 4. If one takes the point J halfway between G and D (so that $OJ = \frac{1}{2}(C_a + C_b)$), then $\hat{U}_a = \hat{U}_b$ at a level JL. Since the $\hat{U}$-curve has some curvature, the vertical distance from H to L is greater than the vertical distance from L to F; or, in other words, because of the diminishing marginal utility of consumption, if $\hat{C}_a$ moves from G to J and $\hat{C}_b$ moves from D to J, poor A gains more than rich B loses. Equality of distribution thus maximises the total sum of utilities as well as equalising total utilities.

If redistributional policies had no adverse effect upon the size of the cake available for distribution, equality of distribution would in this case be the desirable outcome whatever the pay-off between the sum total of utility and equality of distribution of utilities. Problems of the pay-off would arise only in so far as redistributional policies had some disincentive effects upon the total output of goods and services available for consumption.

But where needs and tastes differ the maximisation of the sum total of utilities may well be in direct conflict with the equalisation of utilities. Let us give two examples.

In case (i) of Figure 7 we consider two individuals. A is an unfortunate cripple who because of his disability has little total enjoyment from a given level of consumption and also restricted opportunities for using additional consumption goods in order to increase his enjoyments. B is well and active with a keen interest in some rather expensive hobbies. If A and B have the same level of consumption (depicted by $O\hat{C}_1$), then the total utility of B will be greater than the total utility of A ($\hat{C}_1D > \hat{C}_1E$) and the marginal utility of B will be greater than the marginal utility of A ($\mu_b > \mu_a$, since the slope of $\hat{U}_b$ at D is greater than the slope of $\hat{U}_a$ at E). The maximisation of total utilities from a given level of available consumption goods would require that more be given to B and less to A until $\mu_b = \mu_a$. In case (i) of Figure 7, if $\hat{C}_1\hat{C}_{b2}$ is given to B and an equal amount $\hat{C}_1\hat{C}_{a2}$ is taken from A until the slope at J and the

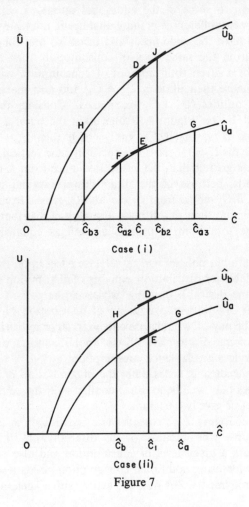

Case (i)

Case (ii)

Figure 7

slope at F are equalised, then $\hat{U}_a + \hat{U}_b$ will be maximised. Consumption has been transferred to the person who can get the keenest enjoyment from additional units of consumption; but inequalities between total utilities have been increased. If utilities are to be equalised, then an additional amount $\hat{C}_1\hat{C}_{a3}$ must be given to A and an equal amount $\hat{C}_1\hat{C}_{b3}$ must be taken from B until the height $\hat{C}_{a3}G$ is equal to the height $\hat{C}_{b3}H$. In such a case the policy-makers' judgement of the desirable pay-off between the maximisation of total utilities and the equalisation of utilities becomes of decisive importance.

Case (ii) of Figure 7 gives another less extreme, but significant example. A and B are now persons with the same tastes and needs, but A is working in an unpleasant job and B in a pleasant job. If, as is depicted in case (ii) of Figure 7, we include only the consumption of actual goods and services in the arguments of $\hat{U}_a$ and $\hat{U}_b$, then we must depict A as enjoying a smaller total of utility than B, when A and B are consuming the same amount of goods at $\hat{C}_1$. Case (ii) differs from case (i) of Figure 7 in that we now assume that at the equal level of consumption, $\hat{C}_1$, the marginal utility of consumption is the same for A and for B ($\mu_a = \mu_b$, since the slope of $\hat{U}_b$ at D is the same as the slope of $\hat{U}_a$ at E). Both A and B can get the same kick out of additional units of consumption, but A is worse off than B because his job is unpleasant.

If A and B had the same utilities and training as each other and if mobility between jobs were free and costless, A would need to be paid more than B in order that he should stay in the unpleasant job. Competitive equilibrium would then give a situation in which A was paid, say, $O\hat{C}_a$ and B was paid $O\hat{C}_b$ so that the utilities of both jobs were the same ($\hat{C}_bH = \hat{C}_aG$). This outcome would to most people (including the author of this volume) appear fair and desirable. It does, however, serve to illustrate once more the fact that the maximisation of total utility is not the sole criterion of social welfare. In the case of Figure 7 the slope of $\hat{U}_b$ at H is greater than the slope of $\hat{U}_a$ at G (i.e. $\mu_b > \mu_a$) and the sum of utilities could be increased by equal wages for jobs of unequal disagreeableness.

We have given these two examples in order to emphasise the fact that where needs and tastes differ the conflict of principle between the maximisation of total utilities and the equalisation of utilities becomes much more acute than in the case where all citizens have the same utility functions. But quite apart from the greater importance of this pay-off between total utility and equal utilities, differences in needs and tastes greatly increase the difficulty for the policy-makers in making their basic interpersonal comparisons between utility levels. If needs and tastes are the same for all citizens, then the policy-makers can at least say that if $\hat{C}_a > \hat{C}_b$, then $\hat{U}_a > \hat{U}_b$. Even this simple indicator of relative utility levels is absent if the $\hat{U}$-functions differ from individual to individual.

The two examples already given in Figure 7 illustrate this point. By how much does the utility of A fall below that of B at equal consumption levels, $\hat{C}_1$? Or, to put the question the other way round, how much consumption must be taken from B and given to A to make $\hat{U}_a = \hat{U}_b$? The policy-makers must struggle with these difficult questions on the lines discussed above in Chapter II in order to know how great the inequalities are between the various $\hat{U}$'s before they are ready to apply any given welfare criterion which expresses a given pay-off between total utility and equal utilities.

The following are a few further examples of cases in which the question arises whether equal levels of consumption should be treated as giving rise to equal levels of utility and, if not, by how much the utilities should be considered to differ.

First, consider two citizens A and B with the same basic endowments for earning income. Suppose A to put much greater weight on a carefree leisured life than B, who works hard and seriously to earn a high income to finance a high level of consumption expenditure. Should the policy-makers regard B as being better off than A because B's consumption level is higher or should they try to include leisure and the tea-break attitude to work as a form of enjoyable consumption? If so, how much enjoyment should they ascribe to it?

A rather similar problem arises when one considers the problems of risk-taking. Suppose A and B to start with the same resources and needs and to have the same tastes, including the same willingness to enter into risky undertakings. A happens to succeed, while B happens to fail. Should A be treated as better off than B, since in fact A has been luckier than B? Or should A and B be treated as equal for distributional purposes, since both started with the same resources and both chose to enjoy the same gamble?

The problem is even more obvious if A and B have different attitudes to risks. A likes a gamble; B values security above all else. A goes in for a risky career as a professional musician; B takes a safe job as a civil servant. If A succeeds, he will be much better off than B; if he fails, he will be much worse off than B. He chooses his career with his eyes open. If he succeeds, should he be treated for distributional purposes as better off than B? If he fails, should he be treated as worse off than B? Or should their relative positions be judged for distributional purposes from the point of view of the average utility which each expected at the time when the choice was made between a risky and a safe use of equal resources? Their expected utilities may well have been equal.

Differences in taste can appear in another way. Suppose that A and B have the same spendable incomes but that A has very simple tastes, while B has very expensive tastes. A, for example, wants only to be left alone to read and re-read his cheap paperback edition of the works of Dickens; but B is unhappy unless he can be travelling round the world to study the flora and fauna of every continent. Does B 'need' a higher income than A in order to make the distribution of welfare more equal?

One of the most important reasons why needs may differ is differences in the composition of the family unit. Consider a single adult living alone with an income of £20 a week. Compare this with a family of three persons – father, mother and child aged one year. Must we consider that family as being worse off if it receives a lower income per head, i.e. less than £60 a week? The needs of a baby are less than those of an adult, and the expenses of a couple living together are less than twice those of one person living alone. A large family will need more than a small family; but the need per head is almost certainly less. However, there is no easy objective test to determine how much lower is the need for spendable income per head in a three-person family than for a single adult living alone.

This raises a further basic question. How does one define the consumption unit? Is it the individual, the nuclear family, the extended family, the household, or some other form of community? Suppose that Granny has no income at all but lives with her wealthy son and daughter-in-law. Is Granny poverty stricken or wealthy? If a rich man marries a poor wife, is the woman still poor? If a rich man lives with a poor woman without the legal bond of marriage, is the woman still poor? What if he sleeps with her occasionally?

These problems of the family or other social unit raise many problems. In what way should we be concerned with inequality between the sexes? Clearly if an unmarried, self-supporting spinster is poor and an unmarried self-supporting bachelor is rich, there is a real inequality. But suppose that they now marry each other. The wife owns no property; and the husband owns much property. Compare this with a married couple with the same total property, but owned in equal shares between man and wife. To what extent are we concerned with inequality between men and women who make up a single family unit? Should steps be taken to equalise the ownership of property within families as well as between families? And if so, how much should the problem worry us?

Family life illustrates yet another basic conundrum. So far we have spoken as if there were no difficulty in defining consumption – apart from the question raised on page 56 above as to whether the amount of leisure should count as an item of real consumption. But consumption is not easy to define. Consider the wife who goes out to work and hires a housekeeper to do the housework in her place. There is presumably some increase in the family's utility; otherwise the change would not have been made. But the net advantage may have been quite minimal; the wife may have seen the advantages and disadvantages of the change as being quite evenly balanced. It is clearly an exaggeration in this case to count the whole of the expenditure on domestic services as an increase in the family's real consumption. Yet in the case of a family which, without any increase in effort on its own part, finds that it can afford to hire domestic service in order to attain a higher standard of living, the whole of the expenditure on the new service represents a net increase in consumption. This example is only one among many of the difficulties in deciding whether an item of expenditure is a business expense (the domestic servant being needed to enable the wife to carry on her outside job or business, the director's chauffeur-driven car being necessary in order to enable him to do his job efficiently) or whether expenditure represents a net improvement in one's standard of living or whether, as is so often the case, it is partly the one and partly the other.

Yet a further consideration that the policy-makers must have in mind is whether a recent change in the level of consumption should affect the distributional weight which is given to a current level of consumption. Compare three citizens, A, B and C, all of whom enjoy a current consumption level of 100. But A's consumption has recently fallen from 200 to the current 100 level; B's has recently risen from 50 to his current 100; while C's level has been, and still is, at the 100 level.

Consider the position of A whose consumption standard[2] has just fallen from 200 to 100. On the one hand one can argue that he will for a time be better off than C who has permanently lived at the 100 level, since consumption cannot be rigidly separated from capital investment. The man who was rich will possess a good stock of clothes, furniture etc. This phenomenon can, of course, be explained by saying that it is not the purchase of clothes, furniture and other durable goods, but their daily use, which represents true consumption. The rich man's consumption has not, therefore, yet fallen to its new level until his old stock of durable consumption goods has been reduced. But this does not cover the whole of the case. The rich man will have a stock of good health (due to past good nourishment) and a stock of memories (of good nights at the opera) on which he can live for a time.

On the other hand, it is arguable that a man whose standard has recently abruptly fallen will be worse off immediately after the change than he will ultimately be when he has become used to the new and lower standard. He will in fact take time to shake off legal and customary commitments to particular items of consumption which were undertaken when he was richer and to discover the most effective way of using his new and lower level of consumption resources.

It could similarly be argued of a man who has recently been enriched, (i) that the immediate sensation of improvement will give him an additional but temporary excited enjoyment from the higher level of consumption or, alternatively, (ii) that he will not obtain the full benefit of the change until he has by experience learned the best way to make use of his new resources.

The policy-makers will have to decide whether they wish to make any allowances in their distributional weights for recent changes in standards of living and, if so, in which direction the adjustments should be made.

There remains one further basic question. Should the policy-makers allot lower distributional weights to persons simply because they are more distant in time or in space? Whatever may be the

[2] It is to be emphasised that we are considering fluctuations in consumption, not fluctuations in income.

answer to this ethical question, there is little doubt that policy-makers as well as individual citizens do give less weight to those who are more distant. A governmental authority in London is likely to give more weight to the interests of a citizen of the United Kingdom than to a citizen of another member of the European Economic Community, or of the British Commonwealth. But this does not mean that zero weight is given to the latter. Indeed the United Kingdom authority is likely to give more weight to a citizen of other countries in the European Economic Community or the British Commonwealth than to a citizen of some other foreign land. Similarly governmental authority is likely to give more weight to the interest of a citizen of this generation than to one of the next generation and a still lower weight to a citizen of a still more remote generation in future time.

This phenomenon is marked among individuals as well as among public authorities. A man will give first thought to himself and his family, then to his close friends and more distant relatives, then to his acquaintances in the neighbourhood, then to the citizens of his own town, his county, his own country, and so on in descending order of concern. Similarly, he will be more directly concerned with the interests of his children than of his grandchildren, of his grand-children than of his great-grandchildren, and so on in an order of concern that diminishes with distance in future time.

We have in this chapter covered very many reasons for policy-makers deciding to allot differences in distributional weights to the spendable incomes of various classes of person. To put them all together into a set of objectives for distributional policies is a question of political choice. That is not the subject matter of this volume. We proceed on the basis that the choice is made. We are concerned with (i) the factors which cause inequalities to be what they are and (ii) the nature and other consequences of policies which will affect distribution in whatever manner the political process has decided to be desirable.[3]

---

[3] In this chapter we have considered different patterns of unequally distributed levels of consumption without raising the question whether one distribution was more or less unequal than another. The problem of devising a measure of the degree of inequality is discussed in Chapter VII.

Note to Chapter IV

ENVY, SYMPATHY AND EGALITARIANISM

Consider a society composed of N individuals, and in which there is only one consumption good with a constant money price of unity. Each citizen's utility may be affected not only by his own consumption standard but also by the consumption standards of his fellow citizens. In this case we can write the individuals' utility functions in the following general form:

$$\hat{U}_1 = \hat{U}_1(\hat{C}_1, \hat{C}_2, \ldots \hat{C}_n)$$
$$\vdots \qquad \vdots \quad \vdots \quad \vdots \qquad \vdots$$
$$\hat{U}_n = \hat{U}_n(\hat{C}_1, \hat{C}_2, \ldots \hat{C}_n) \qquad\qquad (4.2)$$

If we differentiate these functions, we obtain

$$d\hat{U}_1 = \mu_{11}d\hat{C}_1 + \mu_{12}d\hat{C}_2 + \ldots + \mu_{1n}d\hat{C}_n$$
$$\vdots \qquad\quad \vdots \qquad\quad \vdots \qquad\qquad \vdots$$
$$d\hat{U}_n = \mu_{n1}d\hat{C}_1 + \mu_{n2}d\hat{C}_2 + \ldots + \mu_{nn}d\hat{C}_n \qquad\qquad (4.3)$$

where $\mu_{12} = \partial\hat{U}_1/\partial\hat{C}_2$ and similarly for the other μ's in (4.3). μ_{11} expresses the increment of utility which citizen 1 gets out of a marginal rise in his own standard of living, while μ_{12} expresses the increment of utility which citizen 1 gets out of a marginal rise in the standard of living of his neighbour, citizen 2. If $\mu_{12} < 0$, we may say that citizen 1 is envious of citizen 2. If $\mu_{12} > 0$, we may say that he is sympathetic towards citizen 2. And similarly for the other μ's in (4.3).

If the policy-makers were pure utilitarians and wished to maximise total utility, taking into account the individual utility changes which result from interactions of sympathy and envy, we would have

$$dZ = d\hat{U}_1 + d\hat{U}_2 + \ldots + d\hat{U}_n$$

where the $d\hat{U}$'s have the values given in (4.3). We would then have

$$dZ = (\mu_{11} + \mu_{21} + \ldots + \mu_{n1})\,d\hat{C}_1$$

$$\vdots \qquad \vdots \qquad \qquad \vdots$$

$$+ (\mu_{1n} + \mu_{2n} + \ldots + \mu_{nn})\,d\hat{C}_n \quad \ldots\ldots\ldots\ldots \text{ (4.4)}$$

This would give us the following pattern-modified distributional weights:

$$\bar{\mu}_1 = \mu_{11} + \mu_{21} + \ldots + \mu_{n1}$$

$$\vdots$$

$$\bar{\mu}_n = \mu_{1n} + \mu_{2n} + \ldots \mu_{nn} \quad \ldots\ldots\ldots\ldots\ldots \text{ (4.5)}$$

But the policy-makers may not be pure utilitarians for either of two reasons. First, even though they may accept the fact that they should pay as much attention in their weightings to a man's utility whatever its source (i.e. whether it arises from the enjoyment of his own standard of living or from seeing a friend prosper or from seeing an enemy suffer), yet they may make a pattern-modification in the simple sense of not putting as much weight on the utility of an individual with a high $\hat{U}$ as on the utility of an individual with a low $\hat{U}$. Second, for the calculation of the $\bar{\mu}$'s they may modify some of the individual μ's in (4.5); for example, they may refuse to enter into their calculus any utilities or disutilities which arise from envy.

Let us next consider an egalitarian application of the above analysis. Consider a society in which the individual citizens have an egalitarian outlook. The rich are 'sympathetic' with the poor, in the sense that the pleasure which they get from a rise in their own standards is partly offset by a feeling of discomfort at the increased disparity between their own standard and that of the poor, and in the sense that the rich get a positive pleasure from an improvement in the standard of the poor. The poor are 'envious' in the sense – which is not necessarily pejorative – that they take some pleasure from a narrowing of the gap between themselves and the rich, whether this comes from a reduction in the standard of the rich or a rise in their own standards. In this case, as we have defined the μ's in our discussion of (4.3), everyone (both rich and poor) is sympathetic to the poor and envious of the rich.

Let us illustrate this case by assuming that our N citizens are divided into two groups of which N_a are rich citizens and N_b are poor citizens, with $N_a + N_b = N$. The rich citizens are all identical in standard of living ($\hat{C}_a$) and in tastes, including their 'envy' towards each other and their 'sympathy' with each poor man. The poor citizens are also similarly identical in standard of living ($\hat{C}_b$) and in their 'envy' of each rich citizen and their 'sympathy' with each other.

We will now consider two cases of redistribution.

In the first case a small amount of consumption goods (dC) is transferred from the rich to the poor, the fall in the standard of the rich being evenly spread over the rich population and the rise in the standard of the poor being evenly spread over the poor population. In this case we have

$$dC = -N_a d\hat{C}_a = N_b d\hat{C}_b \quad \ldots\ldots\ldots\ldots\ldots (4.6)$$

From (4.3) we can now obtain

$$d\hat{U}_a = \{\mu_{aa} + (N_a - 1)\,\mu'_{aa}\}\, d\hat{C}_a + N_b\mu'_{ab}d\hat{C}_b$$
$$d\hat{U}_b = \{\mu_{bb} + (N_b - 1)\,\mu'_{bb}\}\, d\hat{C}_b + N_a\mu'_{ba}d\hat{C}_a \ldots\ldots\ldots (4.7)$$

where μ_{aa} is the marginal utility to a citizen in group a of an increase in his own consumption while μ'_{aa} (which will be negative) is the increase in his utility from a rise in the standard of another rich man; and μ'_{ab} (which will be positive) is the marginal utility to a rich man of a rise in the standard of a poor man. And similarly for μ_{bb} (which will be positive), μ'_{bb} (which will be positive) and μ'_{ba} (which will be negative).

Let us write μ'_a for $\mu_{aa} - \mu'_{aa}$ and μ'_b for $\mu_{bb} - \mu'_{bb}$. If we suppose that a rich man is as disturbed by the inegalitarian consequences of a rise in his own consumption as he is by the inegalitarian consequences of a rise in the consumption standard of any other rich man, $\mu'_a \equiv \mu_{aa} - \mu'_{aa}$ will measure the marginal utility which a rich man would get from a rise in his own consumption if there were no disturbing external effects through his distaste for inequalities.

From (4.6) and (4.7) we can then obtain

$$d\hat{U}_a = \left\{-\frac{\mu'_a}{N_a} + (\mu'_{ab} - \mu'_{aa})\right\}dC$$

and

$$d\hat{U}_b = \left\{ \frac{\mu'_b}{N_b} + (\mu'_{bb} - \mu'_{ba}) \right\} dC \dots\dots\dots (4.8)$$

With the purely utilitarian criterion of social welfare we have

$$dZ = N_a d\hat{U}_a + N_b d\hat{U}_b$$

or from (4.8)

$$dZ = \{\mu'_b - \mu'_a + N_a(\mu'_{ab} - \mu'_{aa}) + N_b(\mu'_{bb} - \mu'_{ba})\} dC \dots (4.9)$$

Let us now consider a second case in which there is the same total distribution of consumption from the rich to the poor, but that, while the bounty to the poor is divided equally among the poor, the reduction of consumption is concentrated on a single rich citizen (citizen 1). In this case we have

$$dC = -d\hat{C}_1 = N_b d\hat{C}_b \dots\dots\dots\dots (4.10)$$

We then have from (4.3)

$$d\hat{U}_{a=1} = \mu_{aa} d\hat{C}_1 + N_b \mu'_{ab} d\hat{C}_b$$
$$d\hat{U}_{a\neq1} = \mu'_{aa} d\hat{C}_1 + N_b \mu'_{ab} d\hat{C}_b$$
$$d\hat{U}_b = \mu'_{ba} d\hat{C}_1 + \{\mu_{bb} + (N_b - 1)\mu'_{bb}\} d\hat{C}_b \dots\dots\dots (4.11)$$

From (4.10) and (4.11) we then have

$$d\hat{U}_{a=1} = \{-\mu'_a + (\mu'_{ab} - \mu'_{aa})\} dC$$
$$d\hat{U}_{a\neq1} = (\mu'_{ab} - \mu'_{aa}) dC$$
$$d\hat{U}_b = \left\{ \frac{\mu'_b}{N_b} + (\mu'_{bb} - \mu'_{ba}) \right\} dC \dots\dots\dots\dots (4.12)$$

With the purely utilitarian criterion of social welfare we have

$$dZ = d\hat{U}_{a=1} + (N_a - 1) d\hat{U}_{a\neq1} + N_b d\hat{U}_b$$

so that from (4.12)

$$dZ = \{\mu'_b - \mu'_a + N_a(\mu'_{ab} - \mu'_{aa}) + N_b(\mu'_{bb} - \mu'_{ba})\} dC \dots (4.13)$$

A comparison of (4.9) and (4.13) shows that for a small transfer it does not matter from the point of view of total utility whether the transfer is spread over all the rich or whether it is concentrated on one rich man. The direct loss in utility (disregarding the elements of envy and sympathy) will be the same whether the consumption loss is a small loss for many rich men or a larger loss for one rich man, provided that it is on a sufficiently small scale. And the degree of inequality which will be removed will be the same whether it is achieved by a small reduction in the standards of many rich men or a larger reduction in the standard of one rich man.

But a comparison of the two cases enables us to say something about the motivation for redistribution.

A single rich man will, from the point of view of his own ease of mind, be willing alone to redistribute (i.e. to give some of his money to the poor) if $d\hat{U}_{a=1}$ in (4.12) is positive, that is to say, if

$$\mu'_{ab} - \mu'_{aa} > \mu'_a \dots\dots\dots (4.14)$$

where μ'_a measure his 'selfish' loss in utility, μ'_{ab} measures his greater ease of mind in seeing the position of the poor improved and μ'_{aa} measures his greater ease of mind at the thought that he, a rich man, has a more moderate standard.

But one rich man's unselfish charity will have made other rich men more comfortable as they see the gap between riches and poverty thereby diminished. For this reason if all the rich men got together and planned a simultaneous redistribution of some of their wealth, they would have a greater incentive to redistribute. Citizen 1 would gain ease of mind from the increase in equality caused not only by his own sacrifice but by the sacrifices of all other rich men. There would be a motive for such joint redistribution if

$$N_a(\mu'_{ab} - \mu'_{aa}) > \mu'_a \dots\dots\dots (4.15)$$

In a large society such joint action could not readily be organised by a voluntary club; but in these circumstances the rich as well as the poor would be willing to vote for governmental action for a redistributive policy.[4]

---

[4] The administrative difficulties of organising a voluntary charitable club of all rich men might not be the only reason why compulsory governmental action was necessary. In the first place, there might be serious bargaining difficulties, since one

But for the maximisation of total utility one must be concerned not only with the happiness of rich men (even if they are sufficiently unselfish to put some weight on greater equality), but also on the happiness of poor men, whether that happiness be derived from their selfish utility or from their joy at contemplating a more equal society. Total utility will be increased by a redistribution if dZ in (4.9) and (4.13) is positive, that is to say, if

$$\mu_b' + N_b(\mu_{bb}' - \mu_{ba}') + N_a(\mu_{ab}' - \mu_{aa}') > \mu_a' \ldots\ldots (4.16)$$

If we make use of (4.7) and write $d\hat{C}_b = 0$, we obtain

$$dZ = N_a d\hat{U}_a + N_b d\hat{U}_b$$
$$= (\mu_a' + N_a\mu_{aa}' + N_b\mu_{ba}')\, N_a d\hat{C}_a$$

Similarly if we write $d\hat{C}_a = 0$, we obtain

$$dZ = (\mu_b' + N_a\mu_{ab}' + N_b\mu_{bb}')\, N_b\, d\hat{C}_b$$

In other words, if the policy-makers were pure utilitarians and wished to maximise dZ as given in (4.9) and (4.13) they would in fact be using the following pattern-modified distributional weights:

$$\bar{\mu}_a = \mu_a' + N_a\mu_{aa}' + N_b\mu_{ba}'$$

and

$$\bar{\mu}_b = \mu_b' + N_a\mu_{ab}' + N_b\mu_{bb}' \ldots\ldots\ldots\ldots\ldots (4.17)$$

In a society with an equalitarian outlook both μ_{aa}' and μ_{ba}' would be negative. It is not impossible, therefore, that $\bar{\mu}_a$ should be negative.

But it is not necessary either that the policy-makers should wish merely to maximise the sum of individual utilities (even though these include the individual's own utilities from greater equality) or

---

rich man might hope to gain ease of mind from the redistributive actions of all other rich men without himself joining the club and making any sacrifice of his selfish utility. In the second place, not all rich men might have the same distaste for inequalities. Those who did desire to see a reduction in inequalities might consider it unfair that they should make a sacrifice of their selfish utility for this purpose, while other unconcerned rich men made no sacrifice. They might be willing to act only if all rich men were made to act.

that the policy-makers should accept the individual's own attitudes of sympathy and envy. Policy-makers' weights can differ from individuals' weights even in a free democratic society, since individuals are in fact quite capable of voting at the ballot box for political action which is based on criteria which differ from those adopted in their own private lives both for their market transactions and for their private charitable acts.[5] A rich man may vote for fiscal redistribution to be guided by $\bar{\mu}$'s which differ from those given in (4.17). For example, a rich man may vote for a lower $\bar{\mu}_a$ and a higher $\bar{\mu}_b$ than those which would result in (4.17) from the employment of the μ'_a, μ'_{ab} and μ'_{aa} which would guide his private charity in (4.14).

[5] See J. E. Meade, 'Preference Orderings and Economic Policy' in Ashok Mitra (ed.), *Economic Theory and Economic Planning: Essays in Honour of A. K. Das Gupta*.

CHAPTER V

DEMOGRAPHIC CHANGES

In Chapters III and IV we illustrated the distinction between efficiency and distribution in a stationary setting with, among other things, a given and constant population. There was no discussion of the desirability of adopting policies which might affect the size of the population – a decision which might involve a conflict of interest between the born and unborn.

In the first part of the present chapter we shall start to repair this omission by discussing the criterion by which, in any given stationary economy of the kind discussed in Chapters III and IV, one would consider that an increase in the population would be desirable or undesirable. This will enable us to consider some of the basic ideas which must inform any population policy. But the story remains incomplete and unrealistic until we discuss population policies together with other distributional policies in a dynamic setting in which demographic changes, together with savings and capital accumulation, the using up of exhaustible resources and technical progress, are occurring over time in conditions in which there is uncertainty about future developments. These dynamic developments will be considered in the last part of the present chapter and in Chapter VI.[1]

We start then with the assumption made in Chapter III, that we are dealing with a stationary competitive economy, with only two classes of individuals, a and b, and only two products, X and Y, the whole outputs of which are being consumed. As in Chapter III we assume that there is some small once-for-all change in governmental policies which causes some once-for-all small changes in the

---

[1] A more complete dynamic model is to be found in the Appendix (pages 220–42 below).

amounts of X and Y consumed by the individuals in the two classes, a and b. We now assume – and this is the only change in our assumptions – that these once-for all changes in governmental policies also cause a once-for-all change in the numbers of the individuals in each of the two classes. We now ask by what criterion do we judge whether the changes are desirable or not when we allow for the changes in the sizes of the populations in classes a and b as well as for the changes of the levels of consumption of the existing individuals in each class.

There is a long-standing controversy as to whether the optimum population should be defined as that which maximises total welfare or that which maximises welfare per head. This debate has usually been conducted on the open or tacit assumption of an equal distribution of income and welfare. It is not, therefore, directly applicable to our problem, since it is an essential feature of our analysis to allow, simultaneously with a change in the size of the populations of the various classes, for an interest in the effect on the pattern of inequalities as between the various classes of citizen. But there remains real substance in the distinction between the criterion of total welfare and the criterion of welfare per head even when one allows for an interest in the pattern of inequalities as between different classes in society. Does one think that the absolute scale of the population should have any influence on the welfare function? Consider two societies which are exactly similar in incomes and utilities per head and in their pattern of inequalities, but in one of which all elements of the population are twice as large as in the other. Does one prefer the large-scale to the small-scale population? Or does one consider that absolute size is irrelevant and that the worth of a society depends solely upon its pattern of income per head and utilities per head?

If the policy-makers were pure utilitarians in the sense that their objective was simply to maximise the sum total of all individual utilities, then an increase in numbers which caused an increase in the sum total of utilities would have to be considered as an addition to social welfare. In this case if dN_a were the increase in numbers in group a and $\hat{U}_a$ were the total utility enjoyed by an individual in group a, there would be an increase in total utility equal to $\hat{U}_a dN_a$ as a direct result of the increased numbers in group a; and similarly for the term $\hat{U}_b dN_b$. Thus equation (3.4) (page 41 above) would have to be modified by the addition of the terms $\hat{U}_a dN_a + \hat{U}_b dN_b$ so that it became

$$dZ = \qquad \mu N d\hat{C} \qquad\qquad\qquad\qquad\qquad \text{(i)}$$
$$+ (\mu_a - \mu)N_a d\hat{C}_a + (\mu_b - \mu)\,N_b d\hat{C}_b \qquad \text{(ii)}$$
$$+ \hat{U}_a dN_a + \hat{U}_b dN_b \qquad\qquad\qquad\qquad \text{(iii)}$$
$$\dots\dots(5.1)$$

The term marked (i) is once more the term which allows for the efficiency effects of the changed situation; that is to say, it measures the extent to which the general average level of consumption per head has been affected by the change and would thus raise total utility in the absence of any redistribution of consumption. The terms marked (ii) once again represent the additional effect on total utility of the redistribution of real consumption per head between the two groups a and b. The term marked (iii) is the new term which represents the change in total utility due to the fact that there are simply more people with given utilities per head.

There is no conceptual difficulty in introducing into (5.1) the idea of pattern-modifications of utilities of the kind discussed above (pages 46–51) in connection with the derivation of (4.1). We can rewrite (5.1)

$$dZ = \qquad \bar{\mu} N d\hat{C}$$
$$+ (\bar{\mu}_a - \bar{\mu})N_a d\hat{C}_a + (\bar{\mu}_b - \bar{\mu})N_b d\hat{C}_b$$
$$+ \bar{U}_a dN_a + \bar{U}_b dN_b \dots\dots\dots\dots\dots\dots\dots\dots \text{(5.2)}$$

The $\bar{\mu}$'s differ from the μ's exactly in the way discussed in connection with (4.1). They represent the distributional weights which the policy-makers put on the spendable money incomes of the individuals concerned when they take into account not only the relative height of the marginal utilities of money to the different individuals concerned, but also the desirability of giving extra weight to increased spendable incomes in those cases in which it is desirable so to alter the distribution of utilities themselves.

The distinction between the $\bar{U}$'s of (5.2) and the $\hat{U}$'s of (5.1) is very similar. The policy-makers may wish to weight any increase in the numbers in a particular group not simply by that group's utility per head, but by something more or less than this because of the additional desirability of affecting the distribution of utilities among the total population.

It is of importance to note the fact that the pattern-modification $(\bar{\mu}/\mu)_a$ of the marginal utility of money to an individual in group a

may not be the same as the pattern-modification $(\bar{U}/\hat{U})_a$ of the total
utility of an individual in group a. It is perfectly possible for the
policy-makers to hold the view that a 1 per cent increase in total
utility brought about by a 1 per cent increase in the numbers in each
group of the population with utility per head unchanged in each
group should be given only half as much weight in any calculation
of social welfare as a 1 per cent increase in total utility brought about
by a 1 per cent increase in utility per head in each group of the population with the numbers unchanged in each group. In this case we
would have

$$(\bar{\mu}/\mu)_a = 2(\bar{U}/\hat{U})_a \text{ and } (\bar{\mu}/\mu)_b = 2(\bar{U}/\hat{U})_b.$$

The modifications would be such as to double the importance of
raising utility per head in any group relatively to the importance of
achieving a similar increase in utility simply by raising the numbers
in each group. In other words even though one may recognise a
scale factor in social welfare in the sense of regarding two identical
communities as being twice as valuable as one of these communities
taken alone, yet one may regard as even more desirable a doubling
of welfare per head in one only of these communities.

The efficiency term $\bar{\mu}Nd\hat{C}$ in (5.2) measures the average value to
society $(\bar{\mu})$ of any change in the average level of real consumption
per head which may have resulted from the economic changes under
consideration. But this change in the average level of consumption
per head may now be due to either or both of two very different
kinds of factor.

In the first place, as in the case discussed in Chapter III when
there were no changes in the sizes of the populations in the community, the policy changes which we are considering may cause the
existing resources of the community to be used in a more efficient
manner, for example by causing labour or some other factor to
move from an occupation in which the value of its marginal product
is low to an occupation in which the value of its marginal product
is high. Changes of this sort will be a main concern of *The Efficient
Economy*, the next volume in this series. Let us at this point simply
denote them by a general term, $\bar{\mu}\Delta$, where Δ represents the general
increase in total real consumption made available by this sort of
increase in efficiency. [2]

[2] A more detailed description of the elements in Δ is to be found in the Appendix.

But now with changes in the population (dN_a and dN_b) there is a second additional type of efficiency effect which may occur. If the addition of one more member to any class has caused output to increase by more than the existing consumption of a member of that class, there will be some net residue of additional output which would enable consumption per head to be raised somewhat in that class or in some other section of the community. We may express the value to the community of this effect upon the level of real consumption per head by the term

$$\bar{\mu}\{(\hat{V}_a - \hat{C}_a)dN_a + (\hat{V}_b - \hat{C}_b)dN_b\}$$

where $\hat{V}_a$ is the money value of the marginal product of the work of a member of class a and $\hat{C}_a \equiv P_x\hat{C}_{xa} + P_y\hat{C}_{ya}$ is the money value of the consumption of a member of that class so that $\hat{V}_a - \hat{C}_a$ is the excess of what he puts into the community by his production over what he takes out of the community by his consumption. And similarly, for $\hat{V}_b - \hat{C}_b$.

Splitting the efficiency effect up into these two sorts of term we can write

$$\bar{\mu}Nd\hat{C} = \bar{\mu}\Delta$$
$$+ \bar{\mu}\{(\hat{V}_a - \hat{C}_a)dN_a + (\hat{V}_b - \hat{C}_b)dN_b\}$$

Using this expression we can write (5.2) as

$$dZ = (\bar{\mu}_a - \bar{\mu})N_a d\hat{C}_a + (\bar{\mu}_b - \bar{\mu})N_b d\hat{C}_b \qquad \text{(i)}$$
$$+ \{\bar{U}_a + \bar{\mu}(\hat{V}_a - \hat{C}_a)\}dN_a \qquad \text{(ii)}$$
$$+ \{\bar{U}_b + \bar{\mu}(\hat{V}_b - \hat{C}_b)\}dN_b \qquad \text{(iii)}$$
$$+ \bar{\mu}\Delta \qquad \text{(iv)}$$
$$\ldots\ldots (5.3)^3$$

In (5.3) line (i) represents the distributional effect of the change, lines (ii) and (iii) represent the population effects of the change (these effects being the combination of the utilities of the new members of society and the addition to, or subtraction from, the utilities of others

---

[3] See section VI of the Appendix for a more formal derivation of this equation.

which their presence entails), and line (iv) represents what may be called 'the pure efficiency effect' of the change.

So far we have considered only a social welfare function which does put weight upon the scale of the population. Let us now consider what modifications would have to be made to the formula in (5.3) if the policy-makers put no weight upon the scale of the community but merely upon the average welfare per head in the community. Let us suppose that the Z-function which we have analysed in (5.1), (5.2) and (5.3) is of a kind which allows for constant returns to the scale of the population or, in other words, is such that a doubling of every group in the population with utilities per head constant will cause Z itself to double.

We can then compare this with a social welfare function Z^* where

$$Z^* = Z/N \dots\dots\dots\dots\dots\dots (5.4)$$

In other words we are now dealing with a function which measures total welfare in the same way as Z but is interested not in total welfare (Z) but only in welfare per head (Z/N).[4]

From (5.4) we obtain the expression

$$dZ^* = \frac{1}{N} \{dZ - \bar{U}dN\} \dots\dots\dots\dots (5.5)$$

In other words in order to remove the population scale effect from the measure of the change in social welfare given by dZ in (5.3) we must make two modifications.

In the first place we must divide the expression for dZ by the numbers in the total population, N. This modification speaks for itself. We are simply interested in the change in welfare per head, and not in the change in total welfare.

In the second place, we must deduct a term equal to $\bar{U}$ multiplied by the change in the total population, dN, from dZ before we average it over N to obtain dZ^*. This modification needs a little more consideration.

---

[4] We can in this case also express Z^* by the term $\bar{U}$, which is the weighted average of the pattern-modified utilities per head of the various groups in society. The common sense is clear. Z^* is a measure of average welfare per head which is a measure of average pattern-modified utility per head. For a more formal treatment see the Appendix, equations (A.16) and (A.17).

Suppose that we add dN_a and dN_b individuals to classes a and b respectively without any change in standards of living in either class. Then total welfare is increased by $\bar{U}_a dN_a + \bar{U}_b dN_b$. But if we are interested in the welfare per head $(\bar{U})$ of the existing population rather than in total welfare $(\bar{U}N = N_a\bar{U}_a + N_b\bar{U}_b)$ we will want to abstract from the effect of $dN_a + dN_b$ upon the scale of the population. This could be done by taking $dN = dN_a + dN_b$ individuals out of the population on a representative basis (i.e. out of both classes a and b in existing proportions of individuals in classes a and b). This representative subtraction from the population would leave the weighted average welfare per head $(\bar{U})$ unchanged but it would reduce the scale of the population back to its previous level N and it would reduce total welfare by $\bar{U}dN$.

The net effect upon total welfare would be $\bar{U}_a dN_a + \bar{U}_b dN_b - \bar{U}dN$. This is the increase in total welfare due to a change in the *proportions* between N_a and N_b after disallowance for any increase in welfare due to a change in the *absolute scale* of the total population. If we are interested only in welfare per head, this is the increase in total welfare which must be spread over the existing population N in order to calculate dZ^*. The terms $\bar{U}_a dN_a + \bar{U}_b dN_b$ are already included in the expression for dZ in (5.3). We must, therefore, subtract $\bar{U}dN$ from dZ to remove the scale effect before we average dZ over N to obtain dZ^*.

To illustrate in the starkest possible form the distinction between the demographic criteria in the case of a Z-function and in the case of a Z^*-function, let us suppose that in our stationary economy all individuals are identical (so that the distributional factor disappears) and that there are no pure economic inefficiencies. Then from (5.3) we have

$$dZ = \{\bar{U} + \bar{\mu}(\hat{V} - \hat{C})\}dN \dots\dots\dots\dots\dots(5.6)$$

and from (5.5)

$$dZ^* = \frac{1}{N}\bar{\mu}(\hat{V} - \hat{C})dN \dots\dots\dots\dots\dots(5.7)$$

In the stationary economy in which all output is consumed, output per head equals consumption per head. Equation (5.7) now expresses the obvious relationships that to maximise welfare per head one needs to maximise consumption per head, and to maximise consumption per head one needs to maximise output per head, and to maximise output per head one needs to increase the population until output per head is a maximum, and to raise output per head to its maximum one needs to add to the working population so long as the marginal product of labour is greater than output per head (i.e. so long as $\hat{V} > \hat{C}$).

The criterion in (5.6) for the maximisation of total welfare rather than welfare per head is a little more complicated. Suppose that one more individual is added to the population. The direct gain will be the welfare of that individual, $\hat{U}$. There will clearly be a net gain in total welfare unless there is some offsetting loss to the rest of the community. There will be an offsetting loss to the rest of the community only if they have to give up some of their consumption in order to supplement the newcomer's consumption in order to bring it up to the society's average level; and this will be the case to the extent that the newcomer adds less to the community's output than the average level of consumption of the community, i.e. to the extent that $\hat{C} > \hat{V}$. This loss must be measured at its marginal social valuation $\bar{\mu}(\hat{C} - \hat{V})$. There is a net gain in total welfare, therefore, from an increase in the population so long as $\hat{U} > \bar{\mu}(\hat{C} - \hat{V})$.

These relationships can be shown in a very simple set of diagrams. In Figure 8 we measure horizontally on both parts of the diagram output per head or consumption per head in real terms. On the top half of the Figure we measure vertically downwards the total size of the population (N). The horizontal distance of the curve AP then measures output per head which (as a result of the operation of increasing returns to scale) rises at first as N increases from zero to the value N_1; and output per head then falls as N increases beyond N_1 as more and more labour is applied to a fixed quantity of other productive resources. The marginal product of labour, measured by the horizontal distance of the curve MP, is greater than the average product of labour so long as the average product is rising with an increased labour force, equal to the average product of labour at the highest point of the latter, and is less than the average product of labour when the latter is falling as a result of an increased labour force.

In the lower half of the Figure we measure up the vertical axis the marginal utility of a unit of consumption, μ, so that the area under the curve marked MU measures an individual's total utility, $\hat{U}$, when he is consuming an amount equal to the consumption per head measured along the horizontal axis. But we suppose that there is a minimum level of consumption per head equal to $\hat{C}_0$ which is necessary to make life worthwhile. Total utility per head, $\hat{U}$, is negative if $\hat{C} < \hat{C}_0$ and only becomes positive as $\hat{C}$ becomes $> \hat{C}_0$. We can now use Figure 8 to illustrate the expressions for dZ and dZ^* in (5.6) and (5.7) above.

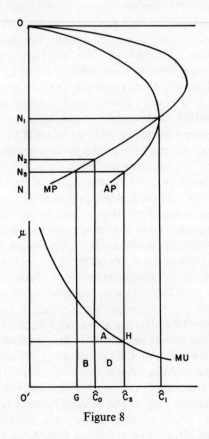

Figure 8

The case of dZ^* is almost trivial. The population ON_1 will maximise output per head and so consumption per head at a level $O'\hat{C}_1$; and this will maximise utility per head at a level equal to the area under the MU-curve between $\hat{C}_0$ and $\hat{C}_1$. Any increase in population up to the level N_1 will increase Z^*.

The case of dZ is a little more complicated. Consider the population

ON_3. In this case output per head and consumption per head is equal to $O'\hat{C}_3$ while the marginal product of labour is equal to $O'G$. If the population were increased by one individual, his marginal product of $O'G$ would have to be supplemented by an amount equal to $G\hat{C}_3$ in order to bring his consumption up to the ruling average $O'\hat{C}_3$. If this amount were subtracted at the margin from all the existing consumers the utility loss to the existing consumers would be $G\hat{C}_3$ multiplied by the marginal utility of $\hat{C}_1$, namely, $\hat{C}_3H$; or in other words the loss to existing consumers would be equal to the sum of the two areas marked $B + D$. But the positive gain in utility to the new citizen would be equal to the areas under the MU-curve between $\hat{C}_0$ and $\hat{C}_3$, i.e. to the sum of the two areas marked $A + D$. Thus there would be a net gain or loss equal to $A - B$.

It is not until N has grown beyond N_2 (at which point the marginal product of labour is equal to the minimum consumption level, $\hat{C}_0$), that the negative area B begins to make its appearance. As N is increased beyond N_2 the area A is reduced and the area B is increased. At some point A equals B, and at this point Z is maximised. It is to be noted that at this optimum level of N the size of the population will be sufficiently great to have reduced the marginal product of labour ($O'G$) not merely below output per head and so the average consumption level in the population ($\hat{C}_3$), but actually below the basic subsistence level of consumption ($\hat{C}_0$).

If we accept the definition of the optimum population as that which would maximise satisfaction per head (the Z^*-criterion illustrated by the population N_1 in Figure 8) rather than that which would maximise total satisfaction (the Z-criterion illustrated by the larger population N_3 in Figure 8), there is one very troublesome implication which is normally overlooked.[5] Apparently we would have a very simple method for judging whether the population were too big or too small to maximise output per head and so satisfaction per head. If the marginal product of labour is greater than average product per head, an increase in population would raise average product and the population is, therefore, below the optimum. Conversely if the marginal product were less than the average product of labour, a reduction in the total population would raise output per head. The test for an optimum population would, therefore, be as

---

[5] I stressed this implication in Chapter II of Part IV of my *Economic Analysis and Policy* published by the Clarendon Press in 1936. But no one seems to have taken any notice of it.

follows: if the payment of wages to labour, equal to the marginal product of labour, would not absorb the whole national product, then the marginal product of labour must be lower than the average product of labour and the population must be too big. If, on the other hand, the total national product is insufficient to pay wages equal to the marginal product of labour, then the average product of labour must be below the marginal product of labour and the population is too small.

This principle does not imply that there is too large a population simply because in a *laissez-faire* economy the whole of the national product is not being paid out in wages. For if the population were of the optimum size, there would be pervasive monopolistic conditions throughout the economy and labour would be paid less than the value of its marginal product. Suppose that the population were of the optimum size. Then a 1 per cent increase in the supply of labour would cause a 1 per cent increase in total product, so that output per head remained constant. In this case a 1 per cent increase in the supply of land and capital as well as of labour would cause total output to increase by more than 1 per cent. In other words, at the optimum population there are pervasive economies of large scale throughout industry; and at this optimum point output per head remains constant simply because the advantages of a larger scale of production are just offset by the reduction in the amount of land and capital equipment per head when the labour force is increased. But pervasive economies of large scale imply pervasive monopolistic conditions, since economies of large scale can persist only if demand is not sufficiently great to allow a large number of competing enterprises of a sufficient size to have enjoyed to the full all existing opportunities of cutting costs by expanding their sales.

It follows that an economy in which population is of the size necessary to maximise output per head will be an economy in which *laissez-faire* would not lead to competitive conditions and in which the control of monopoly, a subject which we intend to take up in *The Efficient Economy*, would be an exceedingly acute problem.[6]

[6] Suppose, for example, that the State were to socialise all monopolistic industries in order to run them on pricing principles which resulted in the payment to labour of a wage equal to the value of its marginal product. The managers of the nationalised industries might well not be able to finance their wage bills out of their sales proceeds. For it does not follow that, because the population is at the optimum, the wage paid in every individual industry would just absorb the total product of that industry. In some industries in which economies of large scale are unimportant, the marginal

The formulae for dZ and dZ^* which we have so far discussed in this chapter are of a completely static character. We can only interpret them, in so far as their demographic components are concerned, as telling us what would be the effect on social welfare in a completely stationary economy if the populations were greater than in fact they are by certain given amounts equal to dN. These populations must all be of a given age composition, working with a given equipment of capital goods with unchanging productivities.

But demographic changes must in fact be treated dynamically. Changes in population come about through changes in fertility and mortality rates. An increase in fertility, for example, increases the number of babies who consume without producing anything for the years of their childhood, who then produce goods for a period, and who later in their retirement will once again consume without producing. The direct economic effect of these new births will thus be a change which affects the future course of events in a fluctuating manner over a large number of future years. Moreover, according to future levels of fertility and mortality rates, these initial new births will in due course lead to further new births as the new babies grow up and become parents.

For these reasons the social valuation of demographic changes can be considered only in a dynamic system. In a fully dynamic context the analysis of the demographic effects of today's changes in policy would have to allow for the uncertainty of future events, for future redistributions of income between various types of person, for future inefficiencies in the economy, for future prospects of capital accumulation in the economy, for the future prospects of involuntary unemployment for various types of person, and so on. In the Appendix an attempt is made to put the demographic factors into a more or less complete dynamic context of this kind.

---

product of labour may be less than output per head and these industries (in which competition would be possible) will earn some surplus over and above their wage bills. In other industries in which large scale economies are very important (and these will be the industries which would be nationalised on monopolistic grounds), the marginal product of labour will be much above output per head, so that losses would be incurred if labour were paid the value of its marginal product. But if the population were at its optimum level the payment to labour in all occupations of a wage equal to the value of its marginal product would just absorb the whole national product. The State would somehow have to lay its hands on the total surplus above wages in the competitive industries in order to finance the deficits in the monopolistic, nationalised industries.

But in the remainder of this chapter, merely in order to emphasise one or two of the most important of the purely demographic considerations, we will consider an economy of the following restricted kind moving through time. We assume:

(1) that there is always full employment of all available labour;

(2) that there is only one product and only one exhaustible resource.

(3) that there is no uncertainty about future events;

(4) that there is only one type of citizen, individuals at any one time differing only in their age;

(5) that there are no economic inefficiencies of the kind comprehended in the term $\bar{\mu}\Delta$ in (5.3);

(6) that there are no governmental expenditures on goods and services; and

(7) that the amount of work done by each citizen of any given age is constant and unaffected by any policy changes.

We will, however, allow for the fact that the policy changes which we are considering may have direct or indirect effects upon the rate at which exhaustible resources are used up and upon the amount of real goods which are saved from consumption and are invested in real capital equipment from one year to the next, so that (see Chapter VI) there may be some real transfer of consumption from one generation of the population to another.

In these conditions we will write our formula for dZ in this case in the form

$$dZ = \sum_T dZ_T \dots\dots\dots\dots\dots\dots(5.8)$$

where

$$
\begin{aligned}
dZ_T = \sum_t N_t \lambda_{tT} &\left[(\bar{\mu}_{tT} - \bar{\mu}_T) d\hat{C}_{tT} \right. & \text{(i)} \\
&+ \left(\frac{\bar{U}}{\bar{U}}\right) \hat{U}_{tT} \frac{dN_t}{N_t} + \left(\frac{\bar{\mu}}{\mu}\right)_t \hat{U}_{tT} \frac{d\lambda_{tT}}{\lambda_{tT}} & \text{(ii)} \\
&\left. + \bar{\mu}_T (\hat{V}_{tT} - \hat{C}_{tT}) \left(\frac{dN_t}{N_t} + \frac{d\lambda_{tT}}{\lambda_{tT}}\right) \right] & \text{(iii)}
\end{aligned}
$$

$$+ \bar{\mu}_T \{(1 + i_{T-1}) dI_{T-1} - dI_T\} \qquad\qquad \text{(iv)}$$

$$+ \bar{\mu}_T P_{eT} dE_T \qquad\qquad\qquad\qquad\quad \text{(v)}$$

$$\dots\dots\dots(5.9)^7$$

---

[7] See Section VII of the Appendix for a more formal derivation of this equation.

We consider the change in the total future social welfare of the economy (dZ) as being composed of the sum of the increases or decreases in social welfare which the society will clock up as it passes through each future year. Thus dZ_T is the additional welfare clocked up in the year T as a result of the small changes which we are examining.

The year t is the date of birth of the persons whose welfare we are considering in the year T. We are thus concerned with persons aged $T - t$. N_t is the number of persons born in the year t; and λ_{tT} is the proportion of persons born in the year t who are alive in the year T. Thus λ_{tT} is the probability of a person born in the year t reaching the age of $T - t$. In the year T there will therefore be $N_t \lambda_{tT}$ citizens aged $(T - t)$ years. λ_{tT} will, of course, be zero for all values of $t > T$ since there is zero expectation of being alive before one's birth. It will also diminish as $T - t$ increases, until it again is always zero for values of $T - t$ beyond the greatest human age-span.

The distributional weight $\bar{\mu}_{tT}$ measures the importance which the policy-makers put upon increasing the amount of money which can be spent on consumption in the year T by a person who is aged $(T - t)$. These are the basic distributional weights, which will presumably depend *inter alia* upon the levels of consumption which the policy-makers foresee will be enjoyed by different age groups at different dates. But for the purpose of the formulae in (5.8) and (5.9) this basic comparison of one $\bar{\mu}_{tT}$ with another is broken down into two operations, by means of the intermediate term $\bar{\mu}_T$ which is the weighted average of all the $\bar{\mu}_{tT}$'s ruling at the date T for all values of t. In other words the term $\bar{\mu}_T$ is the weighted average at date T for the distributional weights allotted to all the various age groups at that date T. Thus if $t = 1950$ and $T = 1970$, a comparison of $\bar{\mu}_{t+1, T}$ with $\bar{\mu}_{t-1, T}$ is a comparison of the distributional weight to be allotted to a 19-year-old with the distributional weight to be allotted to a 21-year-old in the year 1970. A comparison of $\bar{\mu}_{T-1}$ with $\bar{\mu}_{T+1}$ is a comparison of the average distributional weight to be allotted to income in 1969 with that to be allotted to income in 1971.

Item (i) in (5.9) then measures any increase or decrease in welfare at time T due to a redistribution of consumption between the age groups at time T.[8] If the policy-makers consider that at time T the distributional weight to be attached to the consumption of those

---

[8] See the discussion of intertemporal redistribution on pages 107–9 below.

in the age group $T - t$ is exceptionally high, then $(\bar{\mu}_{tT} - \bar{\mu}_T)$ will be positive; a redistribution of consumption from some other age groups at time T to age-group $T - t$ will raise social welfare. If, however, any net increase in total real consumption at time T is in fact distributed among the various age groups at time T in the existing ratios of their consumption, then the terms in item (i) of (5.9) will add up to zero. There will be no gain from the effects of this change on the redistribution of consumption as between the various age groups at time T.[9]

Any social-welfare effects of a redistribution between one date and another date[10] will be caught in items (iv) and (v) of (5.9), where item (iv) refers to the amount of goods which are saved from current consumption for investment for future use and item (v) refers to the rate at which exhaustible resources are currently being depleted. We will consider these two items in the following chapter.

Items (ii) and (iii) of (5.9) represent the more strictly demographic factors.

Item (iii) represents the net contribution (positive or negative) which an increase at time T in the population of the age group $T - t$ can make to the supply of consumption goods available to others. If $\hat{V}_{tT}$ represents the marginal product of the work done by a person aged $T - t$ at time T and $\hat{C}_{tT}$ represents his consumption level, then $\hat{V}_{tT} - \hat{C}_{tT}$ represents his net contribution to the raising of the general average consumption level at time T. For young age groups of pre-working age and for old age groups of retired persons $\hat{V}_{tT}$ will be zero. They will be making a net drain on consumption. In working age groups $\hat{V}_{tT}$ will be positive, but it may or may not be greater than $\hat{C}_{tT}$. This demographic factor is the same whether the increase in the population aged $T - t$ at time T is due to a previous increase in births at time t (i.e. to $\mathrm{d}N_t$) or whether it is due to the survival of a greater number of persons from their year of birth t to the age of $T - t$ (i.e. to $\mathrm{d}\lambda_{tT}$). In both cases there will be at time T the same net drain on, or contribution to, the pool of consumption resources.

While item (iii) represents the contribution to others made by an increase in the population, item (ii) represents the value to themselves, as it were, of any additional number of citizens. But here the policy-makers draw a distinction between the social value to be put upon

---

[9] Cf. the discussion on pages 41–2 above of the measurement of these redistributional terms.

[10] Cf. the discussion of intergenerational distribution in the following chapter.

an increased population due to an increase in births (dN_t) and an increased population due to a decrease in deaths ($d\lambda_{tT}$). This can be done by distinguishing the pattern modification to be applied to a citizen's total life-time utility ($\bar{U}/\hat{U}$) and the pattern modification to be applied to a marginal increase in his utility ($\bar{\mu}/\mu$).[11] The former is relevant to the social valuation to be put upon one more soul born into the world and the second is relevant to any small increase in the life-span utility of an individual resulting from a small improvement in his expectation of life. If ($\bar{U}/\hat{U}$) < ($\bar{\mu}/\mu$) for any given individual, then the policy-makers will in fact be putting less weight on an increase in population brought about by an increase in fertility than on a similar increase brought about by a decrease in mortality.

The distinction between the weight to be put upon an increase in fertility and a reduction in mortality will be still greater if the policy-makers adopt for their criteria of social welfare a function of the kind Z^* (where the scale of numbers counts for nothing) rather than of the kind Z (where a doubling of numbers at unchanged standards is assumed to double social welfare). From (5.5) it is clear that the measure of welfare must be modified by subtracting from dZ in (5.8) the term $\hat{U} \sum_t dN_t$. In other words an increase in births at a particular date t is not to be reckoned as having any direct effect at all upon the social welfare function Z^* unless the life-cycle pattern-modified utility of an individual born at t exceeds the average life-cycle pattern-modified utility of all the individuals concerned over the whole of the planning period which is under discussion. But on the other hand an increase in the life-cycle pattern-modified utility of any individual due to a longer expectation of life (i.e. the term $[(\bar{\mu}/\mu)_t \, \hat{U}_{tT} \, (d\lambda_{tT}/\lambda_{tT})]$) is allowed to retain its full effect in raising Z^*.

In the formulae for dZ in (5.8) and (5.9) the mortality rate at time T for the persons aged $T - t$ is given by $\lambda_{t,T} - \lambda_{t,T+1}$, which represents the reduction between time T and time $T + 1$ in the proportion of persons born at time t who are still alive, but the formulae in (5.8) and (5.9) do not show fertility rates in the same way; they simply show the total number of births at any date, e.g. N_t births at date t. But these births depend upon fertility rates. We may write

$$N_t = \sum_\theta \lambda_{\theta t} N_\theta \beta_{\theta t} \quad\quad\quad (5.10)$$

[11] See pages 70–1 above.

where $\beta_{\theta t}$ is the probability of a person born at date θ bearing a child at date t. N_θ is the number of potential parents born at date θ; $\lambda_{\theta t} N_\theta$ is the number of these potential parents still alive at time t; and $\lambda_{\theta t} N_\theta \beta_{\theta t}$ is the total number of children actually born at time t by potential parents aged $t - \theta$. The total number of births at time t is the sum of the numbers born by potential parents of all ages at time t.

Equation (5.10) shows how the births at any one date depend upon past births, past and current death rates, and present fertility rates. If one knows the initial numbers of persons of different ages and if one knows the future of mortality and fertility rates, one can then forecast the number of births and deaths for all future dates by a repeated operation for each successive date t of the formulae in (5.10).[12] In order, therefore, to consider how any change in policy would affect the demographic elements of items (ii) and (iii) in (5.9) it would be necessary to assess how the changes would affect the future course of the λ's and the β's and, by the application of (5.10), to determine what the effect would be upon the N's for future dates, t.

The sort of policies which might most directly affect rates of fertility are government programmes for family planning or government programmes affecting the distribution of income as between families with a small and families with a large number of children. The sort of policies which might most directly affect mortality rates are governmental programmes for improved health services. In so far as family planning or health services involve governmental expenditures on real resources the formulae in (5.8) and (5.9) would be incomplete. Any value of the demographic effects in those formulae would have to be set against the value of the resources used up to finance the governmental programmes which have been omitted from (5.9). In so far as fertility was affected by the redistribution of income between large and small families any value of the demographic effects would have to be considered in conjunction with the redistributive effects.

We will return to some of these issues in later chapters of this volume.

---

[12] A simple exercise of this kind is given in the Note to Chapter X of *The Growing Economy*.

CHAPTER VI

DISTRIBUTION OVER TIME

In the preceding chapter we discussed the demographic problems which arise in a dynamic economy and which involve what one may call the problem of justice as between the born and the unborn. But there is a second basic distributional problem which arises in a dynamic economy and which involves distribution as between one generation and another.

This basic problem is illustrated in items (iv) and (v) of equation (5.9) in the preceding chapter (page 80). Consumption can be transferred from one point of time to a future point of time in two ways. First, productive resources may be used today to produce machines or other capital goods instead of consumption goods, and the use of the machines or other capital goods tomorrow will enable more consumption goods to be produced tomorrow. Thus at the expense of a reduction in today's consumption, tomorrow's consumption standards can be raised. Second, a similar effect can be produced by postponing the consumption of an exhaustible resource. Thus if there is a given stock of oil in the ground, a reduction in consumption today of products which rely on the using up of part of the finite stock of oil will make possible a higher level of consumption of such products at some future date.

The first of these two phenomena is illustrated in item (iv) of equation (5.9). The terms dI_{T-1} and dI_T stand for the values (at the current money prices of goods ruling at dates $T - 1$ and T respectively) of any addition to the goods put aside, at time $T - 1$ and time T respectively, out of consumption for addition to the productive capital stock. If the money rate of return on the additional investment at time $T - 1$ is i_{T-1}, then at time T there will be an additional amount of goods available equal to $(1 + i_{T-1}) \, dI_{T-1}$ (valued at the money prices ruling at time T). But if at time T there is an additional investment of real goods in capital investment equal to dI_T then the net addition to the goods at time T available for consumption will be $(1 + i_{T-1})dI_{T-1} - dI_T$. If this is valued by the policy-makers at the average distributional weight for time T of $\bar{\mu}_T$ then the net addition to social welfare at time T due to the changes in real capital investment is given in item (iv) of (5.9).

But this change can be regarded in another way. We may ask not what is the net addition to consumption at time T of the investment decisions at time T and of time $T - 1$, but what are the effects on consumption at time T and time $T + 1$ of the investment decision of time T. The term dI_T which appears with a negative effect on the goods available for consumption at time T will reappaear with the positive effect of $(1 + i_T)dI_T$ in the item (iv) of (5.9) for the year $T + 1$. The loss at time T must be valued at $\bar{\mu}_T$ and the gain at time $T + 1$ at $\bar{\mu}_{T+1}$. Thus the net gain in social welfare over time of the additional investment decision is $dI_T\{\bar{\mu}_{T+1}(1 + i_T) - \bar{\mu}_T\}$. This is positive if

$$i_T > (\bar{\mu}_T - \bar{\mu}_{T+1})/\bar{\mu}_{T+1} \quad\dots\dots\dots\dots\dots (6.1)$$

In other words an additional transfer of consumption from time T to time $T + 1$ will be worth while if the money rate of yield on the investment of capital needed for the transfer is greater than the rate at which the pattern-modified marginal utility of money income is falling over time. On the one hand, one can get a greater value of consumption goods by postponing consumption, this gain being measured by the rate of return on capital, i. On the other hand, an increase in expenditure on consumption may have a lower social marginal utility in the future; and this rate of decline is measured by $(\bar{\mu}_T - \bar{\mu}_{T+1})/\bar{\mu}_{T+1}$. The desirability or otherwise of the change depends upon the balance between these two influences.

A similar criterion governs the use of the exhaustible resource, illustrated by item (v) in (5.9). Consider the desirability of postponing the use of a small amount of E, namely dE, from time T to time $T + 1$. Suppose that the money price of E (namely P) which producers will pay for its use at any one time measures the money value of its marginal product at that point of time. Then $\bar{\mu}_T P_T$ measures the loss of social welfare due to the reduced use of E at time T and $\bar{\mu}_{T+1} P_{T+1}$ measures the increase in social welfare due to its use at time $T + 1$. The net change in welfare is, therefore, $(\bar{\mu}_{T+1} P_{T+1} - \bar{\mu} P_T) dE$; and this is positive if

$$P_{T+1}/P_T > \bar{\mu}_T/\bar{\mu}_{T+1} \dots\dots\dots\dots\dots\dots (6.2)$$

which implies simply that it is desirable to conserve E if the value of its marginal product is rising more quickly than the social marginal utility of money is falling.

Suppose now that there were an optimal capital investment programme under item (iv) of (5.9). This, as can be seen from (6.1), implies that

$$i_T = (\bar{\mu}_T - \bar{\mu}_{T+1})/\bar{\mu}_{T+1} \text{ or } \bar{\mu}_T/\bar{\mu}_{T+1} = 1 + i_T$$

It follows, therefore, from (6.2) that in this case it is desirable to postpone the using up of E if

$$P_{T+1}/P_T > 1 + i_T \dots\dots\dots\dots\dots\dots (6.3)$$

that is to say, if the price of E is rising more rapidly than the current rate of interest.

The common sense of this is clear. To some extent the use of capital goods and the use of exhaustible resources will be substitutable for each other. Suppose that the rate of return on real capital is 5 per cent. This means that giving up 100 units of consumption this year enables one to accumulate capital goods which will be worth 105 units of consumption goods next year. If the marginal productivity of an exhaustible resource were 6 per cent greater next year than this year, then by accumulating 100 units less capital this year but postponing the use of the exhaustible resource so as to offset the effect on this year's output, one could obtain 1 more unit of output next year without any loss of output at any other time. Conversely if the marginal productivity of an exhaustible resource were only 4 per cent greater next year than this year, by accumulating 100 units more capital this year and offsetting the effect on this year's output by using more of the exhaustible resource this year instead of next year, one could gain 1 unit of output next year without any loss of output at any other time.

Efficiency, therefore, demands that the marginal productivity of the exhaustible resource should be rising at a rate equal to the current rate of return on real capital. If the market price offered for the use of the exhaustible resource is equal to the value of its marginal product, this means that the price of the exhaustible resource will be rising at a rate equal to the rate of interest.

There will be forces in the market which tend to produce this appropriate rate of use of the exhaustible resource. Persons can invest in holding an idle stock of an exhaustible resource as well as in installing a new machine. If the rate of interest were 5 per cent and the rate of rise of the price of the exhaustible resource were 6 per cent, a profit could be made by holding more of the exhaustible resource in an idle stock; money could be borrowed at 5 per cent to purchase units of the resource which would otherwise be sold for productive use this year; these units could be sold at a 6 per cent higher price next year for productive use next year; and thus a profit would be made on the investment. Such additional purchases of idle stocks would go on until the increased scarcity of supplies for productive purposes this year so raised this year's price, and the prospect of decreased scarcity of supplies for productive purposes next year so depressed next year's price, that the price rise was reduced from 6 per cent to 5 per cent. On the other hand, if the rate of rise of the price were only 4 per cent, anyone who held an idle stock of the resource might sell at the current price and earn 5 per cent on lending the resulting money in the capital market. The increased supply of the resource for productive use this year and the prospect of its increased future scarcity would tend to raise the rate of price increase to 5 per cent. The result would be a spreading of the use of the resource over time in more and more economical ways as it became scarcer and scarcer, with the result that the value of its marginal product rose at the same rate as the real return on capital equipment.

There are thus two possible reasons why governmental intervention may be desirable in order to improve distribution over time. First, the general level of investment in new capital goods may not be on a sufficient level to reduce the real rate of return on capital equipment to the correct level indicated in (6.1); and, second, the market forces which we have just described may, for one reason or another, fail to cause the distribution of the use of an exhaustible resource over time to be such as to satisfy the optimal rate of rise in its price as indicated in (6.3). Let us for the time being assume that the distribution of exhaustible resources over time does correctly follow the rate of interest as indicated in (6.3) – we shall return to the question later – and start by considering the possible need for control over the level of total investment and the method by which such control might best be exercised.

The obvious general method of control over the general level of savings and investment is through a combination of budgetary and monetary policies. Suppose that $i_T > (\bar{\mu}_T - \bar{\mu}_{T+1})/\bar{\mu}_{T+1}$ and that in consequence the government wishes to increase investment in real capital. With full employment this means that current resources must be shifted to produce more capital goods and less goods for current consumption. The reduction in consumption can be achieved by higher rates of taxation of a kind which leave people with less purchasing power to spend on consumption goods. But to induce business to invest more funds on the purchase of additional capital goods, particularly at a time when there is a smaller total demand for any consumption goods which these capital goods may help to produce, the rate of interest at which monetary funds can be borrowed must be reduced to give a sufficient extra incentive to instal new machinery etc. Thus public savings in the form of a budget surplus resulting from higher taxation must be combined with an easy monetary policy which will reduce interest rates to a degree necessary to give an incentive for the increased rate of accumulation of real capital goods.

If the market for exhaustible resources is operating in the way which we have indicated above, then the reduction in the rate of interest will induce people to borrow funds not only for the purchase of additional machines and other real capital goods, but also for additional investment in the purchase of idle stocks of the exhaustible resource. As a result the present price of such resources will be driven up and, with the prospect of less scarcity of such resources in the future, the future price of the resource will tend to fall, until the rate of rise of the price over time has declined to an equality with the new and lower rate of interest. Both the holding of increased idle stocks of the exhaustible resource and the production of additional capital goods at the expense of current consumption goods would restrict current levels of consumption and raise future supplies of consumption goods.

Conversely if the government wished to reduce the level of current investment in new capital goods, it could by reducing tax rates allow consumers to have more disposable income to spend on consumption goods, and could combine this with a tighter monetary policy to raise interest rates which would have the double effect of reducing investment in real capital goods and reducing the incentive to hold idle stocks of the exhaustible resource. Both these developments would boost current consumption levels at the expense of future consumption levels.

By a proper combination of budgetary policy and monetary policy the government could thus shift productive resources from use for current consumption to use for future consumption and *vice versa*. But would it ever need to use these controls? There are in fact a number of reasons which may make the level of total savings which will result from uncontrolled personal decisions diverge from the level which the policy-makers consider optimal. We will enumerate these under three headings.

(1) *Divergences between the Market Rate of Interest and the Return on Capital Investment*

Consider a representative individual. Suppose the marginal utility to him of money purchasing power to be μ_T this year and to be expected to be μ_{T+1} next year. Suppose that he can obtain a rate of interest on his money of i_T. Then by giving up £1 of consumption this year he will get £1 $(1 + i_T)$ worth of consumption next year. He thereby sacrifices £1 μ_T units of utility this year to obtain £1$(1 + i_T)$ μ_{T+1} units of utility next year. He will presumably make the sacrifice if $\mu_{T+1}(1 + i_T) > \mu_T$, i.e. if $i_T > (\mu_T - \mu_{T+1})/\mu_{T+1}$. Apparently his incentive to save will correspond to the social criterion indicated in (6.1).

But this will not be so if the rate of return which the saver can get in the market on his savings does not correspond to the return on the real capital investment which his savings will finance. Thus suppose that the saver can get only 4 per cent on his savings but that the resulting real investment will yield 5 per cent. The saver could in fact be made better off without anyone else being made worse off if he saved another £1 and received £1·05 next year to spend on consumption next year; he will in fact have stopped saving at the point at which £1 of consumption this year was worth only £1·04 of consumption next year, whereas he could in fact be given £1·05 next year in return for £1 more saving this year without any one else being thereby affected.

There are a number of reasons why the net rate of interest offered to the saver may diverge from the return on real capital investment.[1] For example, if the new capital equipment is to be employed in monopolistic productive enterprises, the market rate of return on

---

[1] Many of these possible causes of divergence are indicated by the δ-terms in the Appendix (pages 220–42).

such equipment may be determined by the marginal revenue obtained from the marginal product of the equipment rather than by the market price of that marginal product.

But there is one other very important effect which, while the market rate of interest may properly measure the rate of return on the real capital investment, may cause the net return to the saver to fall below the market rate of interest. This will be the effect of an income tax which taxes the interest earned on any funds which are saved. If the market rate of interest were 10 per cent but there were a tax of 50 per cent on all incomes, a man who saved £100 and obtained £110 gross next year would receive only £105 next year after paying in tax 50 per cent of his interest income of £10. He would receive a net return of only 5 per cent, although the market rate of interest is 10 per cent.[2]

(2) *Governmental Distributional Objectives*

A second and very important reason why the policy-makers may wish to influence the level of total investment is because they desire to carry out distributional objectives which differ from those of the individual citizen. In order to consider this possibility it is necessary to consider both the distribution of purchasing power at any one time between individuals of different ages at that point of time (cf. item (i) of equation (5.9)) as well as the distribution of purchasing power between one point of time and another (cf. items (iv) and (v) of equation (5.9)). We are concerned with intergenerational distribution and the generations overlap. In considering intergenerational distribution, therefore, we cannot ignore the distribution between the young and the old of today.

We will illustrate this interrelationship by means of the very simple model depicted in Figure 9.[3] The curves marked W_1, W_2, W_3, W_4 are the same on both parts of the figure. They represent the life-cycle pattern of earnings of one individual who enters the labour market at the beginning of period 1, 2, 3 or 4 respectively. His earnings are low during a first period of apprenticeship, rise during his second period, reach a peak during the third period of his life,

---

[2] This divergence between the market rate of interest and the net return to the saver would be avoided if the tax were levied on consumption and not on income. (See page 208 and 215–19 of Chapter XIII below.)

[3] The arithmetical assumptions on which this figure is based are described in the Note to this chapter (pages 110–11 below).

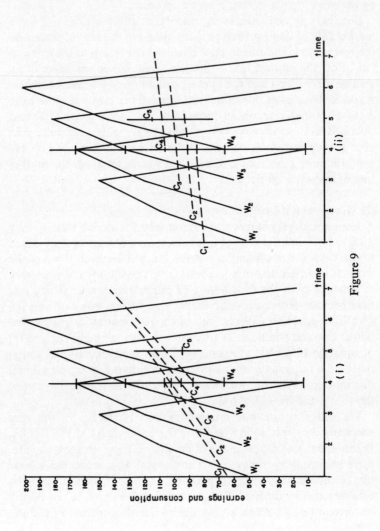

Figure 9

and fall to a low level during the fourth and last period of his old age and retirement. Figure 9 is drawn on the assumption that we are in a growing economy in which output per head is rising steadily by 10 per cent from one generation to the next.[4] This is indicated in Figure 9 by the fact that the W-curves are shown as being 10 per cent higher for an individual of generation 2 entering the life-cycle of earnings at the beginning of period 2 than for an individual of generation 1 entering the life-cycle of earnings at the beginning of period 1, with a similar 10 per cent growth of earnings for each succeeding generation.

An individual's standard of living does not depend directly upon his income, but rather upon his consumption; and his receipt of income is likely to fluctuate over his life-span much more than his level of consumption. This is true of short-run, random fluctuations. If a man does well in his business in some weeks and badly in other weeks, his standard of living will not fluctuate in the same manner; the good weeks will be used to help to finance the bad weeks. The same is true of the longer, more regular fluctuations of income over an individual's life span. He will save during his working years of relatively high earnings in order to finance his consumption during his old age after retirement. At the other extreme young persons in some occupations during the early years of training when their present earnings are low but their future prospects are good may live on their own or borrowed capital in order to finance an improvement in their immediate standard of living out of their future high income.

We have already discussed many aspects of these relationships between incomes and consumption in Chapters XII and XIII of *The Growing Economy*. If an individual could foresee his future income stream with certainty, if he were not shortsighted in his treatment of his future needs, and if he had ready access to the capital market to borrow or lend funds at the given market rate of interest, he could maximise his life-time utility by smoothing his consumption relatively to any fluctuations in his income.

But if the real rate of interest were constant and positive and if an individual's needs and tastes were constant over his life span,

---

[4] 'We assume, that is to say, that we have reached a steady state of growth in an economy in which technical progress is such as to cause output per head to rise steadily by 10 per cent per period. See *The Growing Economy*, Chapter VII.

then in order to maximise his life-time utility he would have to plan his consumption stream so that it rose steadily over his life. For, suppose that he planned a constant rate of consumption over the years. Then, with constant needs and tastes, the marginal utility to him of consumption would be constant. But with a positive real rate of interest if he reduced this year's consumption by a small amount, he could finance a larger increase in next year's consumption and thus gain more utility next year than he lost this year. The rate at which he would plan to raise his rate of consumption would be the greater, (i) the higher was the real rate of interest and (ii) the less quickly the marginal utility of consumption fell as his consumption increased (i.e. the more nearly his utility function were of the kind depicted as $\hat{U}_1$ rather than of the kind depicted as $\hat{U}_2$ in Figure 4).[5]

There are a number of reasons why in the real world individual consumption streams may not be planned in this ideal manner to maximise an individual's life-time utility level. First, an individual may not have free and costless access to a capital market; in particular an unknown young person with low present earnings will not be able to borrow all that he judges proper to finance his present consumption out of his prospective future high earnings. Second, individuals may be shortsighted and discount the future by giving greater weight to present utilities than to future utilities; but they may regret when they reach old age that they did not save more when they were at the height of their earning power. Third, there is the problem of uncertainty; individuals cannot tell for certain what their future incomes will be and cannot, therefore, make a precise life-time consumption plan.

In the real world, then, an individual's life-time consumption stream is likely to be a less smooth progression than a precise maximisation of his life-time utility would demand. On the other hand, it is unlikely to conform exactly to the life-time pattern of his income; his spendable income will be used to finance his life-time consumption in a manner which approaches to some degree the ideal smooth consumption progression. We will start with the assumption of perfect smoothing of consumption paths and will return later to the problems raised if smoothing is imperfect.

---

[5] He would as a result arrange his consumption so as to satisfy the equation $i_T = (\mu_T - \mu_{T+1})/\mu_{T+1}$ on page 90 above, where the rate at which the marginal utility of money spent on consumption is declining is equal to the rate of interest in the market.

In Figure 9 we illustrate the smoothing of the consumption stream which might occur on the assumption which we called that of 'perfect selfishness' in Chapter XII of *The Growing Economy*. That is to say, we suppose that the individual citizens plan to save and dissave over their life cycle in order to smooth out their life-cycle patterns of consumption, but that they plan to spend the whole of their earnings over their life cycle, receiving no inheritance of capital from their parents and leaving no capital to their children. The lines marked C_1, C_2, C_3, C_4 show the consumption streams which they could finance out of their earnings if they could borrow and lend freely at 20 per cent per period. In case (i) we assume that the marginal utility of consumption does not fall at all quickly, so that they choose a consumption stream which starts at a relatively low level but rises quickly over their life-cycle. This is due to the fact that the marginal utility of consumption does not fall rapidly so that, with a rate of interest of 20 per cent, they gain much future utility by giving up present consumption. In case (ii) we assume that the marginal utility of consumption falls rapidly, so that even with a consumption stream which is rising at only a very moderate rate, it is not worth while sacrificing much present consumption for future consumption even though one can obtain 20 per cent more consumption by postponing consumption for one period.

Suppose that all the individuals concerned do spread out their consumption on the steadily rising streams depicted by the C-curves in cases (i) and (ii) of Figure 9. At period 4 all the four generations which we have shown on the Figure will co-exist. But the pattern of inequalities in consumption levels at that point will be very different. In case (i) the ascending order of consumption standards will be C_4, C_3, C_2, C_1; and in case (ii) it will be exactly the reverse, namely C_1, C_2, C_3, C_4.

If the marginal utility of real income depends solely upon the individual's consumption level, then in case (i) we will have $\mu_{14} < \mu_{24} < \mu_{34} < \mu_{44}$ and in case (ii) $\mu_{14} > \mu_{24} > \mu_{34} > \mu_{44}$, where μ_{14} is the marginal utility of income at time 4 to an individual born at time 1, and so on for the other μ's.

We can now use this simple model to illustrate the relationships between item (i) and item (iv) of (5.9). We may calculate μ_4 and μ_5, i.e. the average of the individuals' marginal utilities at time 4 and time 5 respectively, as

$$\mu_4 = \frac{N_1\mu_{14} + N_2\mu_{24} + N_3\mu_{34} + N_4\mu_{44}}{N_1 + N_2 + N_3 + N_4}$$

and

$$\mu_5 = \frac{N_2\mu_{25} + N_3\mu_{35} + N_4\mu_{45} + N_5\mu_{55}}{N_2 + N_3 + N_4 + N_5} \quad \ldots\ldots\ldots \text{(6.4)}$$

where N_1 is the number of persons born and starting life at time 1 and similarly for the other N's. We can write these two expressions as

$$\mu_4/\mu_{14} = n_{14} + n_{24}\mu_{24}/\mu_{14} + n_{34}\mu_{34}/\mu_{14} + n_{44}\mu_{44}/\mu_{14}$$

and

$$\mu_5/\mu_{25} = n_{25} + n_{35}\mu_{35}/\mu_{25} + n_{45}\mu_{45}/\mu_{25} + n_{55}\mu_{55}/\mu_{25} \quad \ldots\ldots\text{(6.5)}$$

where $n_{14} = N_1/(N_1 + N_2 + N_3 + N_4)$ or the proportion of the total population existing at time 4 who were born at time 1 (i.e. the proportion of the population who are three years old at time 4); and similarly for the other N's.

We confine our attention to cases in which the parameters describing the distribution of marginal utilities between the various age groups remain unchanged between time 4 and time 5. The reason for this is as follows. We are concerned with the relation between item (i) of (5.9) which concerns distribution between age groups at one point of time and item (iv) of (5.9) which concerns distribution between one point of time and another. There will be a simple relationship between these two distributions only if the pattern of the distribution between age groups, considered in item (i), remains the same at both the points of time between which the transfer of resources is considered in item (iv).

There are two relevant sets of parameters which describe the pattern of distribution between age groups. First, the proportions of the total population in the various age groups must remain unchanged if the distributional pattern between age groups is to remain the same, and this implies that in (6.5) $n_{14} = n_{25}$, $n_{24} = n_{35}$, $n_{34} = n_{45}$, and $n_{44} = n_{55}$. Second, the ratios between the marginal utilities of consumption of an individual in one age group and an individual in another age group must remain unchanged, which implies that in (6.5). $\mu_{24}/\mu_{14} = \mu_{35}/\mu_{25}$, $\mu_{34}/\mu_{14} = \mu_{45}/\mu_{25}$, and $\mu_{44}/\mu_{14} = \mu_{55}/\mu_{25}$.

If the distributional pattern between age groups remains unchanged in this sense from time 4 to time 5, then from (6.5) we have $\mu_4/\mu_{14} = \mu_5/\mu_{25}$ so that

$$\mu_5(1 + i_4) - \mu_4 = \mu_4 \left\{ \frac{\mu_{25}(1 + i_4)}{\mu_{14}} - 1 \right\} \quad \ldots\ldots\ldots (6.7)$$

But if each individual born at time 2 is smoothing his consumption in an optimal manner over time we have $\mu_{25}(1 + i_4) = \mu_{24}$ (see page 90), so that

$$\mu_5(1 + i_4) - \mu_4 \gtrless 0 \text{ according as } \mu_{24} \gtrless \mu_{14} \quad \ldots\ldots (6.8)$$

In the steady-state model depicted in Figure 9 the distributional parameters will in fact remain unchanged over time. In case (i) of Figure 9 we have $\mu_{24} > \mu_{14}$, since at time 4 the consumption level of those elderly persons born at time 1 will be higher than that of their juniors who were born at time 2. In this case, therefore, we have $\mu_5(1 + i_4) > \mu_4$. In case (ii) of Figure 9 we have $\mu_{24} < \mu_{14}$ and, as a consequence, $\mu_5(1 + i_4) < \mu_4$.

We can summarise this result as follows. We start from a simple steady state with perfect selfishness in order to illustrate the connection between item (i) and item (v) of (5.9). We can conclude that, if in this case the authorities were pure utilitarians and accepted the μ's as the operative $\bar\mu$'s in (5.9), then with case (i) of Figure 9 item (i) of (5.9) would indicate the desirability of transferring purchasing power from the old to the young (i.e. $\mu_{24} > \mu_{14}$) and for the same underlying reasons item (iv) would indicate the desirability of increasing the level of savings and investment (i.e. $\mu_5(1 + i_4) > \mu_4$), whereas with case (ii) of Figure 9 item (i) of (5.9) would point to a redistribution from the young to the old (i.e. $\mu_{24} < \mu_{14}$) and item (iv) would at the same time point to a reduction in savings-investment, (i.e. $\mu_5(1 + i_4) < \mu_4$).

Starting from the position shown by the C-curves in Figure 9, there are in fact two distinct types of change which will lead to the maximisation of total utility over time (that is to say, which will make the greatest possible contribution to social welfare as indicated by (5.9) with the $\bar\mu$'s replaced by the relevant individual μ's).

The first is a change of heart of individuals from 'perfect selfishness' to 'perfect ultimism', that is to say, to a state of affairs in which at each point of time either the old help the young, if the old are then better off than the young as in case (i) of Figure 9, or the young help the old, if the old are worse off than the young, as in case (ii) of Figure 9. In case (i) at any given time parents would help their children; this implies a transfer of purchasing power from the old to the young; and since the young will be postponing the consumption of part of any addition to their purchasing power (in order to maintain the smooth upward movement of their consumption), this transfer from old to young will result in some increase of savings; if full employment is maintained by an appropriate monetary policy, the increased savings will be accompanied by an increased accumulation of real capital and a fall in the rate of interest; when the rate of interest falls, all individuals (as we have seen on page 94) will plan for a less steeply rising consumption curve over their life-time. This movement will go on until the rate of rise of the consumption curves over individuals' lives has fallen to such a degree that the consumption levels of the old and young coincide at each point of time, as is indicated in case (i) of Figure 10. We will then have $\mu_{14} = \mu_{24}$ so that from (6.8) $\mu_5(1 + i_4) = \mu_4$. The change to perfect ultimism will not only have optimised item (i) of (5.9); it will also incidentally have led to the optimal level of savings-investment as indicated by item (iv) of (5.9).

But this same result could be brought about without any surrender of their perfect selfishness by individual savers, if the government, through increased taxation and an increased budget surplus, combined with a monetary policy which reduced interest rates, brought about an increase in investment in order to optimise item (iv) of (5.9). The reduction in interest rates would once more cause individuals to plan for a slower rate of growth of their C-curves. In accordance with (6.8) when $\mu_5(1 + i_4)$ has been reduced to μ_4, we will have $\mu_{14} = \mu_{24}$ so that item (i) of (5.9) will also incidentally be optimised, as in case (i) of Figure 10.

If we start from case (ii) of Figure 9, we can once again reach a state in which total utility is maximised either by individual action based on optimising item (i) of (5.9) or by governmental action based on optimising item (iv) of (5.9). In the case of individual action, the transfer from young to old will involve a reduction in individual savings by the young, interest rates will rise, and the

C-curves will become more steeply sloped until they once again take the general pattern shown in case (i) of Figure 10. With governmental action, a reduced budget surplus will reduce total public savings with a similar result on the rate of interest and on individual C-curves.

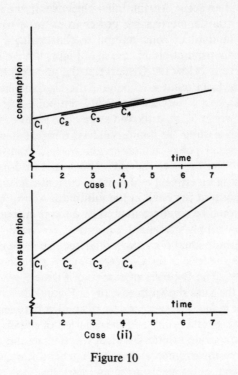

Figure 10

We have in the above simple model not only illustrated a possible interconnection between item (i) and item (iv) of (5.9), but have also illustrated a case in which governmental action to control the distribution of purchasing power between the generations may be desirable because the distributional policy objectives of the policy-makers do not correspond to the objectives of individual savers. Thus if individuals are perfectly selfish, whereas the policy-makers desire to maximise total utility, the policy-makers must promote public saving through a budget surplus in case (i) of Figure 9 or public dissaving through a budget deficit in case (ii) of Figure 9.

But this is not, of course, the only possible distributional objective which the policy-makers might adopt. They may not wish to maximise total utility, and they may replace the individual μ's with pattern-modified $\bar{\mu}$'s in (5.9). Suppose that the policy-makers had a very egalitarian set of distributional objectives in the sense that they desired to transfer purchasing power from those who had a high life-cycle standard of consumption to those with a low life-cycle standard of consumption. In case (i) of Figure 9 it is clear that, while the C_4-curve is below the C_1-curve at the point of time 4, yet over its life-cycle from point 4 to point 7 the C_4-curve lies higher than does the C_1-curve over its life-cycle from point 1 to point 4. The young are worse off than the old at any one point of time, but over their lives as a whole the young will have a higher standard than the old. Egalitarian policy-makers might wish to transfer purchasing power from the young to the old.[6] This would be done by means of a reduction in investment and a rise in current consumption so that the higher output per head in the future due to improved technical progress would be counterbalanced by a lower output per head due to a falling supply of capital equipment per head. Interest rates would rise, individual C-curves would become more steeply sloped, but the starting level of the C-curves of successive generations would be equalised. The C-curves of case (i) of Figure 9 would move to a pattern of the kind shown in case (ii) of Figure 10.[7]

We have in fact a very clear case of conflict between the criterion of maximising total utility and the criterion of equalising individual utilities. Equalising utilities involves transferring purchasing power from later to earlier generations, if the general standard of living is going up from one generation to another. But if the rate of interest is high and the marginal utility of consumption falls only slowly, a transfer of resources from the earlier generation may be so productive of future consumption goods for future generations for whom the marginal utility of consumption falls very slowly that the future

[6] This would be indicated in (5.9) by the fact that $\bar{\mu}_{14} > \bar{\mu}_{24} > \bar{\mu}_{34} > \bar{\mu}_{44}$ even though $\mu_{14} < \mu_{24} < \mu_{34} < \mu_{44}$ with the result that $\bar{\mu}_5(1 + i_4) < \bar{\mu}_4$ even though $\mu_5(1 + i_4) > \mu_4$.

[7] This pattern must be regarded in an impressionistic manner. With the falling level of capital per unit of effective labour we ought no longer to think in terms of a steady state. The general proposition of higher interest rates combined with more nearly equal starting points for the C-curves is, however, valid.

(rich) generations gain more than the present (poor) generation loses.[8]

So far we have considered only the case where technical progress is causing a rise in output per head and a general improvement in standards as the years pass. But this is not necessarily the case. If technical progress is slow but there is a very rapid rise of population being applied to an important fixed factor like land, there could be a steady state with a declining output per head.[9] This result may be intensified if some exhaustible resources are becoming scarcer and scarcer and more and more costly to acquire. In this case both the maximisation of total utility and the equalisation of utilities would require a higher level of savings than would result from the private savings of perfectly selfish individuals.[10]

(3) *Governmental Planning for an Uncertain Future*

Everything which we have said so far about the optimisation of items (iv) and (v) in (5.9) concerns the optimal rate at which the community's standard of consumption should be rising over time; it does not yet tell us what is the optimal absolute level for the starting point of this consumption path.

Suppose that item (iv) in (5.9) is optimised in the sense given in

[8] If we start from case (ii) of Figure 9 then both the maximisation of total utility and the equalisation of individual utilities requires a reduction in savings. But the equalisation of utilities requires a greater reduction of savings (in order to bring the C-curves to a pattern of the kind shown in case (ii) of Figure 10) than does the maximisation of total utility (in order to bring the C-curves to a pattern of the kind shown in case (i) of Figure 10).

[9] See equation (7.15) on page 99 of *The Growing Economy* with $r < Zl$.

[10] So long as the rate of interest remained positive, the maximisation of total utility would require a greater level of savings than would the equalisation of utilities. The equalisation of utilities might bring one to a pattern of C-curves like that in case (ii) of Figure 10. These curves would be sloping upwards if the rate of interest were positive; and still further savings would be needed to change the pattern to one like that shown in case (i) of Figure 10, where capital accumulation would have to be so great that the starting point of the C-curves would actually be rising, because improved capital equipment more than offsets the pressure of population on the land and the growing scarcity of other resources. It is, of course, possible that the marginal product of capital would fall to zero before this happy result were reached. Indeed, it might become negative because it cost real resources to store consumption goods to carry into the future. In this case the maximisation of total utility would require less saving than the equalisation of individual utilities. The C-curves of case (i) of Figure 10 would coincide with a falling instead of a rising slope, so that their starting points could be allowed to fall; but for the equalisation of individual utilities their starting points must not be allowed to fall.

(6.1), so that $i_T = (\mu_T - \mu_{T+1})/\mu_{T+1}$. The marginal utility of tomorrow's consumption will depend upon the level of tomorrow's consumption; but that in turn will depend upon the amount which it is planned to save instead of to consume out of tomorrow's income; and, if tomorrow's saving and investment is also to be optimised, that in turn will depend upon the relationship between the marginal utility of consumption tomorrow (μ_{T+1}) and the marginal utility of consumption the day after tomorrow (μ_{T+2}); but the marginal utility of consumption the day after tomorrow will in turn depend upon the amount which it is planned to save and invest instead of to consume the day after tomorrow – and so on *ad infinitum.* The optimal amount to save and invest instead of to consume today thus depends upon a future plan for savings and investment and consumption stretching out indefinitely into the future.[11]

The same relationship arises in the case of the use of an exhaustible resource, in which case the problem can be even more clearly expressed. Equation (6.3) tells us at what rate the price (i.e. the value of the marginal product) of the exhaustible resource should be rising over time, but it does not tell us what should be the absolute level of the present starting price for the resource. Suppose that equation (6.3) told us that today's price should be 10 per cent less than tomorrow's price. One cannot determine today's optimal price without forecasting tomorrow's price; but if that is to be optimal it must be 10 per cent below the price on the day after tomorrow – and so on *ad infinitum.* One cannot judge the absolute level of today's optimal price unless one knows the prices which will rule in the far-distant future. But the prices which will rule in the far-distant future will depend upon the scarcity of the then remaining supplies of the exhaustible resource in relation to the then ruling demands for the use of the resource. Thus the absolute level of today's optimal price, and thus the optimal rate of use of the resource today, will depend upon what is judged to be the need for the resource in the far-distant future.

We have discussed at length in Part 3 of *The Controlled Economy* why a free market mechanism cannot work perfectly to deal with this problem. Today's optimal prices would have to depend upon

[11] See pages 227–36 of *The Growing Economy* where this problem is treated with more technical detail of analysis.

forward markets for the use of goods and services for consumption and investment for every future period stretching out in theory till the end of time. We have discussed in *The Controlled Economy* why such a set of forward markets is impossible and how, for that reason, it may be desirable for the government to take part in a plan for the future use of the community's resources.

The future contains so many uncertainties that it is not practicable to extend the period of such a plan into the indefinite future. Suppose that for this reason the plan looks only five years ahead. Then in order to decide what is the proper starting point this year for the rate of investment in new capital goods and for the rate of use of exhaustible resources one must have some decision, probably of a rather arbitrary kind, as to the proper terminal conditions of the plan, that is to say, as to how much capital equipment and how large a remaining stock of exhaustible resources one must leave for the use of future generations at the end of the five-year plan.

All this can, of course, be left to the free play of competitive markets, the result of which will imply some tacit notion as to what the value of capital equipment and of exhaustible resources will be in five years' time. But the government may well feel called upon to intervene, not only (as in the case of the indicative planning discussed in Part 3 of *The Controlled Economy*) to provide some mechanism for the exchange of information between private producers and consumers of different goods and services about their future plans and expectations, but also positively to change the provision made for the future. The government, for example, may want to play safe against the possibility of future disasters for future generations to a greater extent than is implied in the plans of private producers and consumers. That is to say, it may wish to take steps to ensure that the terminal stocks of capital goods and of exhaustible resources at the end of the five-year plan will be greater than they would otherwise have been.

Nor is this a question only of the terminal conditions of any plan. Events during the course of the five-year plan are necessarily uncertain because of what in *The Controlled Economy* we called 'environmental uncertainties', and the policy-makers may wish to influence the reaction of the private market to such uncertainties.

Suppose, for example, that today's pattern-modified marginal utility of consumption is $\bar{\mu}_T$. But suppose tomorrow's weather is uncertain. If it is fine tomorrow, there will be a good harvest;

consumption goods will be plentiful; and the pattern-modified marginal utility of consumption tomorrow if the weather is fine $(\bar{\mu}_{T+1,F})$ will be low. But if it is wet tomorrow and food is scarce, tomorrow's pattern-modified marginal utility of consumption $(\bar{\mu}_{T+1,W})$ will be very high.

How should one react in order to invest for tomorrow's uncertain outcome? This must depend among other things upon the probability of fine or wet weather tomorrow. Suppose that the government judges that the probability of fine is ε_F and of wet is ε_W, where $\varepsilon_F + \varepsilon_W = 1$. Then if a unit of consumption is given up today in order to acquire $1 + i_T$ units of consumption tomorrow, the loss of social welfare today is $\bar{\mu}_T$ and the expected gain of social welfare tomorrow is $(1 + i_T)(\varepsilon_F \bar{\mu}_{T+1,F} + \varepsilon_W \bar{\mu}_{T+1,W})$. It follows that, in this case, current investment should be increased if

$$i_T > \frac{\bar{\mu}_T - (\varepsilon_F \bar{\mu}_{T+1,F} + \varepsilon_W \bar{\mu}_{T+1,W})}{\varepsilon_F \bar{\mu}_{T+1,F} + \varepsilon_W \bar{\mu}_{T+1,W}} \dots\dots\dots\dots (6.9)$$

The policy-makers may put a greater weight both on the probability of disaster (ε_W) and also upon the horrific effects on social welfare of disaster $(\bar{\mu}_{T+1,W})$ than does the private market. If this is so, the policy-makers will wish to cut down current consumption in order to increase investment for the future in order to be 'on the safe side' during the course of the five-year plan.

So much for the reasons why the policy-makers may wish to intervene to affect the proportion of the current national income which is devoted to savings and investment instead of to consumption. Suppose that the level of savings-investment is optimised so that the level of the rate of interest is also optimised in accordance with (6.9). The question then arises whether the rate of use of any exhaustible resources will follow an optimal time pattern as indicated by the relationship between the rate of interest and the rate of rise of the price of the resource given in (6.3). We can deal with this problem by using the same type of analysis as that which we have employed in the discussion of the optimal rate for savings and investment.

In the first place, there may be market divergences between the ruling market price of an exhaustible resource and its current market price.[12]

Second, as we have already argued, in their construction of a plan for an uncertain future the policy-makers may wish to play safe for future generations by taking action to ensure that adequate terminal stocks of the exhaustible resource will be left at the end of, say, a five-year plan for the use of future generations. It would be natural for the policy-makers to be even more concerned with the adequacy of the terminal stock of an exhaustible resource than with the adequacy of the terminal stocks of man-made capital equipment. If the latter turns out to be inadequate, future generations can take steps to build it up. If the finite stock of an exhaustible resource has been used up, there is nothing that future generations can do to replace it.

Third, as in the case of investment in man-made capital equipment, the policy-makers may wish to influence the reactions of the private market to uncertainties during the period of the plan in so far as the use of the exhaustible resource is concerned.

Consider the case in which there are no divergences between the rate of marginal products and the prices of the inputs concerned. Suppose P_T to represent today's price of an exhaustible resource. Suppose that the price tomorrow if tomorrow's weather is fine $(P_{T+1,\,F})$ will be low, because other resources will be plentiful, but that the price tomorrow if it is wet $(P_{T+1,\,w})$ will be very high. Then from the point of view of social welfare a unit of the resource used tomorrow if the weather is fine will add $\bar{\mu}_{T+1,\,F}P_{T+1,\,F}$ to social welfare, but will add $\bar{\mu}_{T+1,\,w}P_{T+1,\,w}$ to social welfare if the weather is wet.

If ε_F and ε_w are the probabilities with which fine and wet are expected, the expected social welfare from the use of a unit of the resource tomorrow will be $\varepsilon_F\bar{\mu}_{T+1,\,F}P_{T+1,\,F} + \varepsilon_w\bar{\mu}_{T+1,\,w}P_{T+1,\,w}$. It will be desirable to postpone the use of a unit of the resource from today till tomorrow, if this expected addition to social welfare is greater than $\bar{\mu}_T P_T$ which measures the social value of the unit of the resource in today's use. Thus the use of the resource should be postponed if

$$P_T < \frac{\varepsilon_F\bar{\mu}_{T+1,\,F}P_{T+1,\,F} + \varepsilon_w\bar{\mu}_{T+1,\,w}P_{T+1,\,w}}{\bar{\mu}_T} \quad ......(6.10)$$

---

[12] These are indicated by the δ-factors in item (x) of equation (A.25) on page 234 of the Appendix.

Suppose that the rate of savings and investment had been optimised, so that i_T had the optimal value indicated in (6.9). Using the
value of $\bar{\mu}_T$ which can in this case be derived from (6.9) and substituting for it in (6.10), we can see that the use of the exhaustible
resource should be further postponed from today to tomorrow if

$$1 + i_T < \frac{1}{P_T} \frac{\varepsilon_F \bar{\mu}_{T+1,F} P_{T+1,F} + \varepsilon_W \bar{\mu}_{T+1,W} P_{T+1,W}}{\varepsilon_F \bar{\mu}_{T+1,F} + \varepsilon_W \bar{\mu}_{T+1,W}} \quad \dots (6.11)$$

In other words the further postponement should take place if the
rate of interest is less than the rate of increase between today's price
and the weighted average of tomorrow's possible prices, the weights
being $\varepsilon_F \bar{\mu}_{T+1,F}$ and $\varepsilon_W \bar{\mu}_{T+1,W}$.

On the general principles outlined on pages 86–8 above, the
private market may be expected to postpone further the use of the
resource if the current rate of interest at which it can borrow money
to hold idle stocks of the resource is lower than the expected rate of
rise of the price of the resource. But in reckoning the expected rate
of rise of price in conditions of uncertainty, the market may use
weights which differ from the policy-makers' $\varepsilon_F \bar{\mu}_{T+1,F}$ and
$\varepsilon_W \bar{\mu}_{T+1,W}$. The policy-makers may wish to play safe by setting a
high probability on disastrous weather tomorrow (a high ε_W and
low ε_F) and by setting a high social weight on the horrific effects of
such disastrous weather (a high $\bar{\mu}_{T+1,W}$).

In this case the policy-makers will be concerned not only with
influencing (e.g. through budget surpluses or deficits combined with
appropriate monetary policies) the level of total savings and investment so as to optimise the rate of interest as indicated in (6.9). They
will in addition wish to influence the rate of use of exhaustible
resources in order to make the market follow this optimal rate of
interest with the optimal weighting of future expected prices of the
exhaustible resource, as indicated in (6.11). An appropriate policy
instrument for discouraging the current use of an exhaustible
resource would be the imposition of a high rate of tax on its current
use with the expectation that the tax would be lowered in the future
when the resource became very scarce. There would then be a tax
incentive to shift the use of the resource from the present high-tax
period to the future lower-tax periods.

Our analysis of the distribution of consumption over time has up
to this point been based upon the assumption that individual

citizens have smoothed their consumption over their life-cycle in the optimal manner indicated by the smoothed *C*-curves of Figure 9. But let us now return to the fact that they start with unsmoothed incomes, illustrated by the *W*-curves of Figure 9, and that the resulting *C*-curves will not be optimally smoothed.

Let us consider the extreme case. Suppose that individuals spent on consumption in each period what they earned in that period so that the *W*-curves instead of the *C*-curves depicted their consumption patterns. This could happen for either or both of two reasons. In the first place, they might be shortsighted and unable to look before or after in a rational manner. This cause would be most likely to operate as between periods of high earnings and the period of old age and retirement. People consume what they earn and forget about their old age. In the second place, it could be due to the fact that they have no access to a capital market. This cause would be most likely to operate as between the early period of low earnings and the later periods of high earnings. As apprentices they cannot borrow to supplement their current low earnings at the cost of mortgaging their future earnings.

The policy-makers may now wish to smooth out consumption streams in order to increase each individual's utility out of his own available resources in order to offset either the lack of private foresight or the inability of private persons to raise appropriate private consumption loans on reasonable terms. Such a policy would involve, for example, the taxation of persons in the prime of life to finance the payment of childrens' allowances at the end of life and old age pensions at the other end.[13]

Figure 9 has been discussed so far on the assumption that all individuals of any one single generation had the same levels of income and consumption. This overlooks the obvious inequalities between persons of the same generation but of different socio-economic classes – perhaps the most familiar distinction between

---

[13] Figure 9 gives a good example of the importance to the policy-makers in their distributional policies of considering standards of living in terms of consumption rather than of income. Suppose that people have adjusted their income streams in the way shown by the *C*-curves in case (i) of Figure 9. Then in period 4 the consumption of the individual of generation 1 will in fact be $7\frac{1}{2}$ per cent *greater* than that of an individual of generation 2, but the current income of the individual of generation 2 will be no less than $12\frac{1}{2}$ times that of the individual of generation 1. To devise a distributional policy on the assumption that A's standard of living is $12\frac{1}{2}$ times that of B when in fact it is somewhat less than B's would not be helpful.

rich and poor. In fact we must conceive of a revised Figure 9 in which for each generation there is an array of higher and lower W-curves with corresponding high and low C-curves. If we maintain for the moment the assumption that all individuals have the same needs and tastes, i.e. the same utility functions, the modification of such inequalities calls for a transfer of consumption from the rich to the poor of any one generation; this will both increase the sum total of utilities, since it will represent a redistribution from those with a low to those with a high marginal utility of income, and it will also serve to make more equal the total utilities of the different citizens.

When we allow for such interclass inequalities between rich and poor citizens of the same generation, we have yet another interconnection between the distributional objectives of policy to take into account. Suppose that according to (6.1) an increase in investment, leading to a general transfer of consumption from the present to future generations, would be to the advantage of society because $i_T > (\bar{\mu}_T - \bar{\mu}_{T+1})/\bar{\mu}_{T+1}$. The question who should do the additional saving and who should receive the fruits of the additional saving is not irrelevant to the final judgement of social advantage. Thus a decreased current consumption by the rich, the resulting capital from which was given to the poor for their future enjoyment of the income from the investment, would be doubly desirable: first, because with the existing patterns of distribution between the rich and the poor a general transfer of consumption from the present to future generations would be desirable; and, second, because it would improve the future pattern of distribution between rich and poor. But an increase in savings and investment which involved the poor saving for the future benefit of the rich might be on balance undesirable on grounds of the future worsening of the distribution between the rich and the poor, even though on the basis of existing distributional patterns between rich and poor a general transfer of consumption from the present to future generations would be desirable.

We have then three classes of distributional policy which we may call intergenerational, intertemporal and interclass; and we have to be careful about the interconnections between the three.[14]

---

[14] See pages 489–501 of *The Growing Economy*.

(1) *Intergenerational Distribution*

The policy-makers may take measures to increase (or decrease) the total savings-investment of the society (e.g. by raising or lowering the total level of taxation so as to achieve an appropriate budget surplus or deficit), in order to shift consumption from present to future (or from future to present) generations.

(2) *Intertemporal Distribution*

The policy-makers may take steps (for example, by taxing the middle-aged to subsidise the young and the old) to redistribute each individual's consumption from one period of his life to another in order to offset the intertemporally inefficient use of individual incomes due either to a citizen's shortsightedness or to his inability to borrow funds for personal consumption.

(3) *Interclass Distribution*

The policy-makers may take steps (e.g. by taxing the rich in order to subsidise the poor) to transfer consumption from the rich to the poor of any one generation.

This requires a nicely adjusted total set of policies which combines (1) the correct degree of total taxation or subsidy to give the level of budget surplus or deficit necessary to adjust total savings for intergenerational distribution, with (2) that distribution of taxes and subsidies between young and old which will smooth out intertemporal inefficiencies in consumption-stream patterns over the life-cycle and (3) that degree of progression in taxes and subsidies as between the rich and the poor of any given age at any given point of time which will give the desired degree of correction for interclass inequalities.[15]

---

[15] The above sketch of the type of policy needed to cope simultaneously with intertemporal, intergenerational and interclass redistribution makes no mention of two fundamental complications. In the first place, when we are dealing with distributions over time it is impossible to neglect the dynamic problems arising from the need to devise a current policy plan which will have effects over an uncertain future. In the second place, one cannot overlook the second-best problem, namely, that the tax or other instruments which are in fact available to deal with the distributional problems may have adverse effects in other directions – for example, on incentives or on other factors affecting the efficiency of the economic system. In the Appendix (pages 220–42 below) an attempt is made to put these distributional problems in the context of a dynamic second-best control plan.

Note to Chapter VI

A NUMERICAL EXAMPLE OF LIFE-CYCLE INCOME STREAMS AND CONSUMPTION STREAMS

Consider an economy in a state of steady growth of 10 per cent per period in which individuals have a four-period cycle of earning ability of the following kind:

Period	1	2	3	4
Labour power (a)	50	100	125	10
Output per unit of labour power (b)	1	1·1	$(1·1)^2$	$(1·1)^3$
Earnings (c) = (a) × (b)	50	110	151·4	13·3

In row (a) we assume that an individual has a period of apprenticeship with a relatively low labour power of 50; then two periods of full work at labour powers of 100 and 125; and then a period of old age with the very low labour power of only 10. But output per unit of labour power is growing at the steady rate of 10 per cent per period as shown in row (b); and the individual's actual earnings will be shown in row (c) as the product of his labour power and of output per unit of labour power.

The rows marked L and W in Table III show what will be the labour power and the consequential earnings in these conditions of workers born at four successive periods, with earnings improving relatively to labour power by 10 per cent in each period.

We suppose that each worker plans to spend the whole of his earnings over his four-period life-cycle.[16] We assume the following values of the underlying parameters, using the notation of *The Growing Economy*:

$$l' = 0·1$$
$$i = 0·2$$

case (i)	case (ii)
$\sigma = 0·9$	$\sigma = 0·1$
$\hat{c} = i\sigma = 0·18$	$\hat{c} = i\sigma = 0·02$

where l' is the underlying steady state growth of output per unit of labour power, i is the rate of interest, and $\hat{c} = i\sigma$ is the steady rate

---

[16] That is to say, we assume 'perfect selfishness' in the sense of Chapter XII of *The Growing Economy*.

Period	1	2	3	4	5	6	7
Output per unit of labour power	1	$(1 \cdot 1)$	$(1 \cdot 1)^2$	$(1 \cdot 1)^3$	$(1 \cdot 1)^4$	$(1 \cdot 1)^5$	$(1 \cdot 1)^6$
Generation 1							
L_1	50	100	125	10	—	—	—
W_1	50	110	151·4	13·31	—	—	—
$\hat{C}_1$ (i)	65·2	77·2	91·0	107·5			
$\hat{C}_1$ (ii)	80·0	81·6	83·2	84·9			
Generation 2							
L_2	—	50	100	125	10	—	—
W_2	—	55	121	166·5	14·6	—	—
$\hat{C}_2$ (i)	—	71·8	84·7	100·0	118·0		
$\hat{C}_2$ (ii)	—	88	89·8	91·5	93·3	—	—
Generation 3							
L_3	—	—	50	100	125	10	—
W_3	—	—	60·5	133·1	182·5	16·1	—
$\hat{C}_3$ (i)	—	—	78·8	92·9	109·7	129·5	—
$\hat{C}_3$ (ii)	—	—	96·8	98·7	100·7	102·6	—
Generation							
L_4	—	—	—	50	100	125	10
W_4	—	—	—	66·6	146·4	201·5	17·7
$\hat{C}_4$ (i)	—	—	—	86·8	102·5	121·0	142·6
$\hat{C}_4$ (ii)	—	—	—	106·5	108·6	110·8	113·0

Table III

of growth of an individual's consumption which would maximise his life-cycle utility. If the marginal utility of consumption falls quickly then σ (the elasticity of substitution between consumptions in period 1 and in period 2) will be low and $\hat{c}$ will be low.

The figures for $\hat{C}$ in Table III show the consumption streams which, growing at the steady rate of $\hat{c} = 0 \cdot 18$ in case (i) and of $\hat{c} = 0 \cdot 02$ in case (ii), the individual concerned can finance out of his earnings marked W, if he can lend and borrow freely at the market rate of interest of 20 per cent period ($i = 0 \cdot 2$).

CHAPTER VII

MEASUREMENTS AND PATTERNS
OF INEQUALITY

In Chapter IV we were concerned with the various types of distributional objective which the policy-makers may aim at achieving and in Chapters V and VI we applied this discussion of distributional objectives to the special cases of distribution between the born and the unborn and distribution between present and future generations.

In Chapters VIII to XII we shall go on to discuss some of the principal factors which cause standards of living to be unequal. But before doing so we shall digress in the present chapter in order to explain why, throughout our discussion of distributional objectives and in particular of the pay-off between economic efficiency and a more desirable distribution of income and wealth, we have not attempted to use any single quantitative measure of the degree of inequality in society.

We have argued above (page 53) that if all citizens had the same needs and tastes, then an equal distribution of spendable incomes would be desirable both to maximise the sum total of individual utilities and also to equalise utilities. Even in this case perfect equality of distribution might not be desirable because it might have disincentive effects which would lead to a reduction in the total size of the cake which would be available for distribution; but the degree of inequality of distribution (whether unnecessary or necessary for efficiency reasons) might in such circumstances be regarded as the measure of the degree to which the distribution of spendable income diverged from the distributional optimum.

Unfortunately it is not possible to think in terms of a single unambiguous measure of the extent to which any given distributional pattern diverges from that of perfect equality. There is in principle no difficulty in defining complete equality; such a state exists if and only if all incomes are of precisely the same size. But in a state of affairs in which there is not complete equality, difficulties do arise in defining the degree of inequality which exists in the actual distribution of incomes. It is the purpose of this chapter to explain some of the definitions which may be used to measure the degree of inequality in any given distribution of incomes, and to consider how different changes in the distribution of incomes may affect the degree of inequality as measured by the various methods. It will become apparent that the measurement of the degree of inequality is by no means a straightforward task. Indeed some changes in the distribution of incomes will be found to have a marked effect in reducing the degree of inequality according to one very reasonable measure of inequality and at the same time to have a marked effect in increasing the degree of inequality if some alternative but equally reasonable method of measurement is employed.

We will illustrate these points by means of the simple society depicted in Table IV.

	Poor	Middle class	Rich	Total population
Number	30	60	10	100
Income per head	£0·33	£1·00	£3·00	£1·00
Total income of the class	£10	£60	£30	£100

Table IV

We consider a simple society with three classes of persons – 30 poor, 60 middle class and 10 rich, making up a total population of 100. The middle class have an income per head of £1·00 which is also the average for the whole society. The poor, however, have an income per head of only one third of the society's average, while the rich have an income per head which is three times the society's average. As a result the total national income is £100, of which £10 goes to the poor, £60 to the middle class and £30 to the rich.

This pattern of distribution can be depicted most dramatically by arranging the citizens from left to right in ascending order of income per head, as is done with the solid lines in Figure 11. The height of the blocks measures income per head for the persons in the given class, and the area of the blocks shows the total income going to that class. The poor with an income per head equal to one third of the society's average are on the left; the rich with an income per head 9 times as high as that of the poor are on the right of the Figure.

We will now consider seven different ways of measuring the

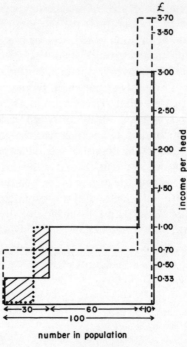

Figure 11

degree of inequality of incomes in the distribution given in Table IV
and in the solid blocks of Figure 11.

§1   *The Average Proportionate Deviation of Income*
In the given distribution, 30 per cent of the population have £0·66
less than the average of £1·00, 60 per cent have the average and
10 per cent have £2·00 more than the average. The average deviation
from the average income of £1 is, therefore, $0.3 \times £0.66 + 0.6 \times
£0.00 + 0.1 \times £2.00 = £0.40$. If this is expressed as a percentage of
the average income per head of £1·00, one can say that on the
average the citizens in our society have an income which is 40 per
cent more or less than the average income. We will call this measure
of inequality *the average proportionate deviation*.

This straightforward measure is, however, subject to one fatal
criticism. Suppose that in any given society income is transferred
from a richer man to a poorer man. One would want to have a

measure of inequality which in such a case invariably recorded a reduction in the degree of inequality as resulting from such a transfer. But this is not necessarily the case with the average proportionate deviation. A simple modification of Table IV will illustrate the case. Suppose that the 30 poor of Table IV each with an income of £0·33 were split into two groups – 20 having no income at all and 10 having now the average income of £1·00. The poor as a whole class would still have a total income of £10 (namely, 20 × £0·00 + 10 × £1·00). To move this situation back to the original situation in which all the poor had equal incomes of £0·33 should be registered as an increase in equality since it would be caused simply and solely by a transfer of income from those with £1·00 per head to those with £0·00 per head. But the average proportionate deviation would be unchanged. With the modification of Table IV it would be 0·2 × £1·00 + 0·7 × £0·00 + 0·1 × £2·00 = £0·40 instead of 0·3 × £0·66 + 0·6 × £0·00 + 0·1 × £2·00 = £0·40.

The point is illustrated in Figure 11 by the dotted lines which show the modification of the original distribution which occurs if 20 of the poor receive no incomes and the other 10 of the poor now receive the average of £1·00. The two crossed hatched areas are equal to each other; and with a simple arithmetic averaging of the degree to which the poor as a total class are below the average of £1·00, the change from the solid line to the dotted line of Figure 11 causes no change in the overall measure of inequality.

§2 *The Coefficient of Variation of Incomes*

The trouble with the average proportionate deviation is that it gives equal weights to every penny by which an income falls below the average whether the total fall be a large one or a small one and similarly it gives equal weight to every penny by which an income exceeds the average, whether the total excess be great or small. But one needs to give a greater weight to each penny by which a very poor man's income falls below the average than one does to each penny by which a moderately well-off man's income falls just below the average. If one does this, a transfer of a penny from the latter to the former will reduce the measure of inequality since it will count more as a reduction in inequality in its effect upon the very poor man than it will as an increase in inequality in its effect upon the moderately well-off man.

This sort of weighting can be obtained by using the squares of the deviations of each income from the average instead of the simple deviation themselves. Squaring a number gives a much bigger proportionate lift to a large number than to a small number. One can then use the square root of the weighted average of these squared deviations themselves and relate this modified measure of average deviation to the average income in the community. This measure is called the *coefficient of variation* of the incomes. In the case of the distribution given in Table IV (the solid line of Figure 11) this measure is given by

$$\frac{\sqrt{0\cdot3 \times (£0\cdot6)^2 + 0\cdot6 \times (£0\cdot00)^2 + 0\cdot1 \times (£2\cdot0)^2}}{£1\cdot00} = 0\cdot72.$$

In the case of the modification of Table IV shown by the dotted line in Figure 11 the measure is given by

$$\frac{\sqrt{0\cdot2 \times (£1\cdot00)^2 + 0\cdot7 \times (£0\cdot00)^2 + 0\cdot1 \times (£2\cdot0)^2}}{£1\cdot00} = 0\cdot78.$$

The squaring of the deviations of the incomes of the poor causes a greater weight to be put upon the poverty of the very poor; for this reason the measure of inequality has increased when the deviations below the average are all concentrated on a small group of very poor persons instead of being spread evenly over a larger number of moderately poor persons.

§3   *The Gini Coefficient for Income Distribution*

A third method of measuring the degree of inequality is depicted in Figure 12. We measure the percentage of the total population along the horizontal axis and the percentage of the total national income up the vertical axis. If the total national income were equally divided among all the members of the population, the distribution of income could be represented by the 45° straight line *AB*. The first 30 per cent of the population would receive 30 per cent of the total available income; and so on up the scale.

But suppose incomes not to be equally divided and arrange the population along the horizontal axis from left to right in an ascending order of income per head. The poorest 30 per cent of the population will now receive less than 30 per cent of the total available income; in Figure 12 in accordance with the distribution of Table IV we represent the poor by the solid line *AC* as making up 30 per cent of the population but receiving only 10 per cent of the total available income. We now can depict the distribution of income by a line like *ACDB*. This line will start off with a slope of less than 45°, as in the section *AC* which we have just described. The slope will increase as we move to the right because we have deliberately arranged the

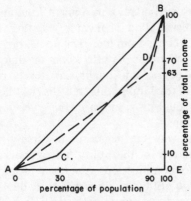

Figure 12

classes of the population in ascending order of their income per head. At point *C* we reach the middle class who have an income per head equal to the society's average. This means that the slope of the line from *C* to *D* will have a 45° angle, since the 60 per cent of the population (from 30 to 90) accounts for 60 per cent of the total income (from 10 to 70). The line *ACD* must, of course, eventually end up at the point *B*, since 100 per cent of the population must absorb 100 per cent of the total available income. The rich are represented by the line *DB* which has a steeper slope than the 45° slope of the line *CD*, since in this case 10 per cent of the population (from 90 to 100) accounts for 30 per cent of the society's income (from 70 to 100).

Since the straight 45° line *AB* depicts an equal distribution of income and the kinked line *ACDB* depicts the actual unequal distribution of income, the degree of inequality in the distribution of income is often measured by the ratio of the area *ACDB* to the area of the whole triangle *ABE*. This ratio is known as the *Gini coefficient*. In our numerical example the area *ACDB* is 32 per cent of the area *ABE*, and this is the measure of the degree of inequality.

§4   *The Degree of Proportionate Distributional Waste*

A quite different approach to the problem of measuring the degree of inequality in the distribution of incomes can result from the consideration that we are not basically interested in income, but in the welfare which income can give. Let us assume then that all income is spent on consumption.[1] Let us assume further that all citizens have the same needs and tastes. Then total utility will be maximised if income is equally distributed; a movement from an unequal to a completely equal distribution of income will thus increase total utility by shifting income from 'the rich (to whom the marginal utility of income is low) to the poor (to whom the marginal utility of income is high). The degree of inequality can thus be represented by the percentage loss of total utility caused by having the actual rather than a completely equal distribution of the given total income of the society in question.[2]

Measured in this way the degree of inequality will naturally depend upon the nature of the utility function of the individual citizen. In order to continue our numerical example we have, therefore, devised two utility functions which are depicted in Figure 13. Both functions have two points in common. In both cases utility is zero when consumption is £0·10, and in both cases utility is 1 when the average consumption per head of £1·00 is reached. But the curvature of the two functions is very different. In the case of $\hat{U}_1$ the marginal utility of the early units of consumption is not very high, but marginal utility falls off very gradually (the slope of $\hat{U}_1$ being only moderate at the outset but remaining little changed as consumption increases). In the case of $\hat{U}_2$ the marginal utility of consumption is very high at first but falls off very quickly. With $\hat{U}_1$ it is assumed that satiety is reached when consumption reaches a level of £10. Beyond that point any further consumption would actually cause a reduction in utility, though our examples will never in fact place even the rich within reach of this satiation level. $\hat{U}_1$ then rises to a maximum of 5·76 when consumption reaches a level of £10·00, but $\hat{U}_2$ approaches asymptotically a maximum level of

---

[1] Or alternatively let us assume that the figures in Table IV show not income per head and total incomes but consumption per head and total consumption and that we are interested in measuring the degree of inequality of consumption.

[2] See the Note at the end of this chapter for a justification of the procedure of measuring the loss in terms of utility.

only 1·11, which it reaches for all practical purposes at a much lower figure for consumption than £10·00.

We have so devised these two utility functions that utility per head is unity when consumption is at the average level of £1·00. Since there are 100 persons in the population, total utility would in both

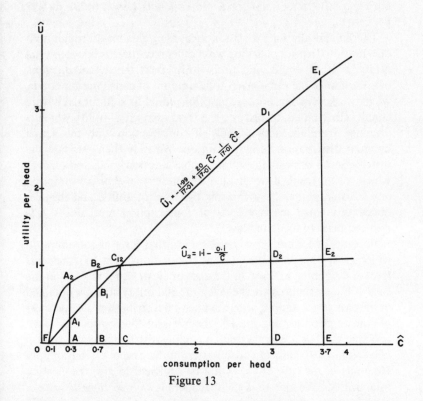

Figure 13

cases be 100 if the £100 of total national income were equally distributed among the 100 members of the population. In this case in Figure 13 the level of utility per head is equal to the height CC_{12} for both utility functions and total utility is $100 \times CC_{12} = 100$.

With the distribution of income given in Table IV the total utility with $\hat{U}_1$ would be $30AA_1 + 60CC_{12} + 10DD_1$ since 30 persons have an income per head of OA, 60 an income per head of OC and 10 an income per head of OD. But $30AA_1 + 60CC_{12} +$

$10DD_1 = 96.86$. As a result of the unequal distribution of incomes, there is therefore an absolute utility waste of 3·14 units or a *proportionate loss of utility* of 3·14 per cent of the total utility attainable with an equal distribution.

Similarly with the utility function $\hat{U}_2$ the total utility obtained with the unequal distribution of Table IV would be $30AA_2 + 60CC_{12} + 10DD_2 = 94.07$ or a *proportionate loss of utility* of 5·93 per cent.

There is an alternative way of measuring this loss through maldistribution. Instead of asking what difference there is between total utility with an equal, and total utility with the actual unequal, distribution of the same given total amount of consumption goods, we may ask what level of consumption would be sufficient, if it were equally distributed, to provide the total amount of utility which is obtained from the actual levels of consumption with the actual unequal distribution of consumption. We may then measure the distributional waste by the saving of consumption goods and services which would result if we divided the present level of consumption goods equally (thereby increasing the total of utility) and then reduced this equal average level of consumption until utility was reduced back to its actual level.

In terms of Figure 13 we need to find that level of consumption which gives a height of the relevant $\hat{U}$-curve such that 100 times this level of $\hat{U}$ is equal to 96·86 in the case of $\hat{U}_1$ or equal to 94·07 in the case of $\hat{U}_2$, since these are the levels of total utility actually obtained in the case of $\hat{U}_1$ and $\hat{U}_2$ with the unequal distribution of ₤100 units of consumption among the 100 members of the community given in Table IV. The answer is that an equally distributed consumption of a total of £97 units of consumption in the case of $\hat{U}_1$ but of only £65 units in the case of $\hat{U}_2$ would be sufficient to give the existing total utility.[3] We may thus say that there is a *proportionate waste of consumption* of 3 per cent in the case of $\hat{U}_1$ and of no less than 35 per cent in the case of $\hat{U}_2$.

With $\hat{U}_1$ the consumption waste is very small because the marginal utility of consumption to the rich is not much less than it is to the poor. With $\hat{U}_2$ one can economise greatly in consumption resources, since when one takes consumption goods from the rich (to whom

[3] These numbers are obtained from the solution of the equations $96.86 = 100\{-1.99 + 20\hat{C} - \hat{C}^2\}/17.01$ and $94.07 = 100\{1.i - (0.i/\hat{C})\}$ in the cases of $\hat{U}_1$ and $\hat{U}_2$ respectively.

their marginal utility is low) one need give only a fraction of these to the poor (to whom their marginal utility is high) in order to make up for the loss of utility at the richer end of the spectrum.

Thus, whether one uses the index of proportionate loss of utility or that of the proportionate waste of consumption there is less distributional waste with $\hat{U}_1$ than with $\hat{U}_2$ simply because the marginal utility of consumption is more nearly constant with $\hat{U}_1$ than with $\hat{U}_2$. These measures of inequality thus result for the same distribution of actual consumption in a *lower* degree of inequality with $\hat{U}_1$ than with $\hat{U}_2$ even though from Figure 13 it can be seen at a glance that inequalities in the distribution of utilities is much *greater* for $\hat{U}_1$ than for $\hat{U}_2$ ranging for $\hat{U}_1$ from AA_1 to DD_1 and for $\hat{U}_2$ only from AA_2 to DD_2.[4]

The argument in the preceding paragraph suggests that a measure of distributional waste is not really in any fundamental sense a measure of inequality at all. It is a measure of inefficiency or of the loss of utility[5] from a less than optimal distribution of the available income.

§5   *The Average Proportionate Divergence of Utility*

One can, of course, argue that one is not interested in inequalities of income but in inequalities of utility; and one can perfectly well apply a measure of the average proportionate divergence to the utilities of different persons (measured up the vertical axis of Figure 13) instead of to the incomes of different persons (measured along the horizontal axis of Figure 13) as we did in §1 above.

With the distribution of incomes given in Table IV above, we have seen that total utility in the case of $\hat{U}_1$ in Figure 13 would be 96·86 so that average utility per head would be 0·9686. Thus the *average proportionate divergence of* utility in the case of $\hat{U}_1$ would be

---

[4] Cf. the discussion of Figure 4 in Chapter IV.

[5] The measure of waste in the text has been conducted as if the social welfare function were simply a sum of individual utilities (the $Z = N_a \hat{U}_a + N_b \hat{U}_b$ of equation (3.1)). The argument could be conducted in terms of a social welfare function which took account of the pattern of distribution of utilities. In this case the waste would be in the shortfall of the Z from which (4.1) was derived below the maximum level which Z could attain if the existing total income were so distributed among the existing population as to maximise Z. But in this case also the measure is basically a measure of inefficiency due to maldistribution rather than a direct measure of inequality.

$$\frac{0 \cdot 3\,(0 \cdot 9686 - AA_1) + 0 \cdot 6\,(CC_1 - 0 \cdot 9686) + 0 \cdot 1\,(DD_1 - 0 \cdot 9686)}{0 \cdot 968}$$

and similarly in the case of $\hat{U}_2$. These measures work out at $43 \cdot 4$ per cent for $\hat{U}_1$ and $10 \cdot 4$ per cent for $\hat{U}_2$.

§6 *The Coefficient of Variation of Utilities*

Just as in §2 we replaced the average proportionate deviation of incomes of §1 with the co-efficient of variation of incomes, so in this §6 we can, for similar reasons, replace the average proportionate deviation of utilities of §5 with the coefficient of variation of utilities. These measures work out at $0 \cdot 737$ for $\hat{U}_1$ and $0 \cdot 116$ for $\hat{U}_2$.

Thus for both the average proportionate deviation of utilities of §5 and for the coefficient of variation of utilities of §6 the measures of inequality in utilities is much greater for $\hat{U}_1$ than for $\hat{U}_2$, as indeed is clear from a glance at Figure 13, whereas the measure in §4 of the loss of utility or of the wastes of consumption due to maldistribution gave the higher index to $\hat{U}_2$ and the lower index to $\hat{U}_1$.

§7 *The Gini Coefficient for Utility Distribution*

Just as in §3 we worked out a Gini coefficient for the inequality in the distribution of the incomes given in Table IV (i.e. for the incomes measured along the horizontal axis of Figure 13), so one could on exactly the same principle work out a Gini coefficient for the inequality in the distribution of the resulting utilities (measured up the vertical axis of Figure 13). Thus in §4 we showed that in the case of $\hat{U}_1$ the first 30 members of the population enjoyed a total utility of $30AA_1$, while the total utility enjoyed by the whole community amounted to $30AA_1 + 60CC_{12} + 10DD_1$. Thus the first 30 per cent of the population receives a proportion of the total utility enjoyed by the whole society equal to $30AA_1/(30AA_1 + 60CC_{12} + 10DD_1)$, and similarly for the 60 middle class and the 10 rich members of society. If we were to re-draw the lines AC, CD and CB in Figure 12 with these proportions of total utility instead of the proportions of total income which accrued to the 30 per cent poor, the 60 per cent middle class and the 10 per cent rich, we would obtain an area $ACDB$ which was $33\frac{1}{3}$ per cent of the whole triangle ABE. This then is the *Gini coefficient for the inequality in the distribution of utility* in the case of the distribution of income of Table IV and the $\hat{U}_1$ utility function.

The corresponding figure for $\hat{U}_2$ works out at 5·7 per cent. Once again the inequality in the distribution of utilities is much less in the case of $\hat{U}_2$ than in the case of $\hat{U}_1$.

We have now described a number of different ways in which the degree of inequality may be measured. All these measures would be zero if incomes were equally distributed.[6] But suppose now that we are considering two distributions, neither of which gives complete equality. It turns out that, if we apply the seven different measures described in §§1 to 7, some of these measures may say that the degree of inequality has increased, while others say that it has decreased.

	Poor and middle class	Rich	Total population
Number	90	10	100
Income per head	£0·70	£3·70	£1·00
Total income of the class	£63	£37	£100

Table V

Consider the distribution of incomes in Table V and compare it with that already given in Table IV. In both Tables there is a total population of 100 and a total national income of £100, giving an average income per head of £1. In both Tables there are 10 members of the rich class. But as between Table IV and Table V the middle class is worse off and the poor and the rich are both better off. The poor have an income of £0·70 instead of £0·33 per head, the middle class now has the same income per head as the poor, namely £0·70, instead of its previous income per head of £1·00, while the rich have an income per head of £3·70 instead of £3·00.

The new distribution of Table V is represented by the broken lines in Figure 11, which shows clearly how the poor and the rich have gained and the middle class has lost. The same comparison is made with the broken line on Figure 12, which shows how the 30 poor and the 10 rich both have a larger proportion of the total national income.

Has the inequality in the distribution of income become greater or less as a result of the change? On the one hand the levelling up of the income of the poor relatively to the middle class represents

[6] Assuming also, in the case of §§ 4, 5, 6 and 7, that all citizens had the same utility function.

	Distribution of Table IV with consumption per head of £0·33, £1·00 and £3·00 for poor, middle class and rich respectively	Distribution of Table V with consumption per head of £0·70, £0·70 and £3·70 for poor, middle class and rich respectively
§1 Average proportionate divergence of incomes	0·40	0·54
§2 Coefficient of variation of incomes	0·73	0·90
§3 Gini coefficient for income distribution	0·32	0·27
§4 Distributional waste (i) Proportionate loss of utility $\hat{U}_1$	0·031	0·048
$\hat{U}_2$	0·059	0·035
(ii) Proportionate waste of consumption $\hat{U}_1$	0·030	0·035
$\hat{U}_2$	0·352	0·245
§5 Average proportionate divergence of utilities $\hat{U}_1$	0·434	0·517
$\hat{U}_2$	0·104	0·024
§6 Coefficient of variation of utilities $\hat{U}_1$	0·737	0·866
$\hat{U}_2$	0·116	0·040
§7 Gini coefficient for utility distribution $\hat{U}_1$	0·333	0·260
$\hat{U}_2$	0·057	0·012

Table VI   Measures of Inequality

an equalisation of incomes. But on the other hand the increase in the incomes of the rich who already enjoyed an income which was three times as great as the national average must be regarded as a disequalising factor.

If we work out for the new distribution of Table V the measures of inequality which we calculated in §§1 to 7 for the old distribution of Table IV, we obtain the results given in Table VI.

The verdicts of the various measures are very diverse. The Gini coefficients both for the distribution of income and for the distribution of utilities tell us that there is less inequality (§§ 3 and 7), whereas the average proportionate divergence of income (§1) and the coefficient of variation of incomes (§2) both tell us that inequality has risen substantially.[7] The measures of distributional waste (§4), of the average proportionate divergence of utilities (§5) and the coefficient of variation of utilities (§6) all tell us that inequality will have increased if the utility function is of the $\hat{U}_1$-type but will have decreased if the utility function is of the $\hat{U}_2$-type. In fact there is no clear answer. What has happened is that equality is greater at the bottom end but smaller at the top end of the income scale. The policy-makers must simply decide, in the way discussed in Chapter IV, whether they prefer the distribution of Table IV to that of Table V or *vice versa*.

There can be no single, simple measure of inequality. But just as a given change in distribution of incomes (as between Table IV and Table V for example) may cause very different changes in the different measures of inequality, so also very different changes in the pattern of distributions can give rise to similar movements in any one given measure of inequality. We will illustrate this truth by considering six very different possible changes in the distribution of incomes as given originally in Table IV, all of which would cause a reduction in the degree of inequality as measured by the Gini coefficient for the distribution of incomes (as described in §3 above).

In Figures 14 to 19 we accordingly make in turn six simple modifications to the society described in Table IV. In each case the Table on the left of the Figure describes the change arithmetically; the new numbers are shown in italics with the original numbers in brackets for ease of reference. In the middle diagram in each Figure the solid lines illustrate the Gini coefficient for the original society and the broken lines illustrate the Gini coefficient for the new society. Similarly the diagram on the right gives an alternative presentation of the new society with the broken lines and of the original society with the solid lines, which reproduce the solid lines of Figure 11.

---

[7] These two measures need not move in the same direction. Suppose that the new distribution of the total national income in the right-hand column of Table VI had resulted in incomes per head of £0·76 for the 30 poor citizens, £0·76 for the 60 middle class citizens and £3·10 for the 10 rich citizens, the average proportionate deviation of income would have risen from 0·40 to 0·42 but the coefficient of variation of incomes would have fallen from 0·73 to 0·70.

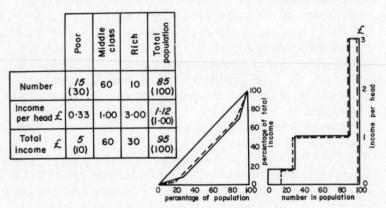

Figure 14   Contraction of the Poor.

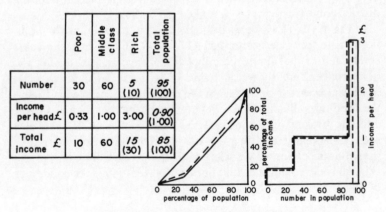

Figure 15   Contraction of the Rich.

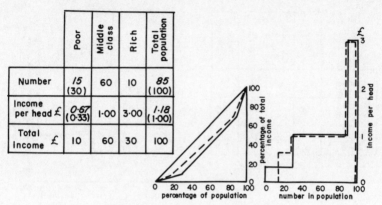

Figure 16   Dilution of Poverty.

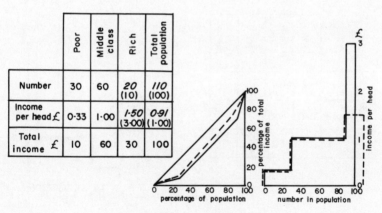

Figure 17   Dilution of Riches.

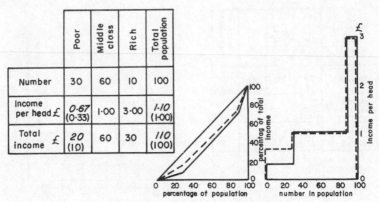

	Poor	Middle class	Rich	Total population
Number	30	60	10	100
Income per head £	0·67 (0·33)	1·00	3·00	1·10 (1·00)
Total income £	20 (10)	60	30	110 (100)

Figure 18   Enrichment of the Poor.

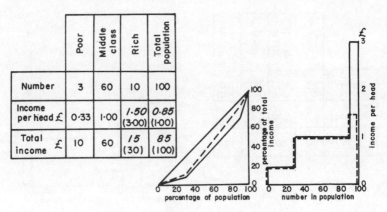

	Poor	Middle class	Rich	Total population
Number	3	60	10	100
Income per head £	0·33	1·00	1·50 (3·00)	0·85 (1·00)
Total income £	10	60	15 (30)	85 (100)

Figure 19   Impoverishment of the Rich.

Figure 14 illustrates what we will call a *Contraction of the Poor*. In this case the number of the poor is halved from 30 to 15 with its income per head unchanged at £0·33. The numbers and income per head of the other classes remain unchanged. The reduction in the number of the poor raises the average income per head for the whole community from £1·00 to £1·12, and it reduces the Gini coefficient of inequality from 32 to 27 per cent.

Inequality can be reduced by reducing the number of the rich as well as by reducing the number of the poor. In Figure 15 we illustrate what we call a *Contraction of the Rich*. In this case the number of the rich is halved from 10 to 5, the income per head in each class (including the rich class) remaining unchanged. The Gini coefficient of inequality is reduced once again from 32 to 27 per cent. But the average income per head for the whole community is now reduced from £1·00 to £0·90 by the disappearance of some of the richest citizens. The patterns of distribution in Figures 14 and 15 can be seen to be very different indeed, even though the effect on the Gini coefficient of inequality is similar.

In Figure 16 we assume, as in Figure 14, that the number of the poor is halved from 30 to 15. But in Figure 16 we now assume that this is combined with a doubling of the income per head of the poor from £0·33 to £0·66. The idea is that there is a certain total income, namely £30, available for the poor, which is now shared out among half the number of poor. We call this a *Dilution of Poverty*. The result is a rise in average income per head for the whole community from £1·00 to £1·18, since the total income of the community is unchanged but the total population is reduced. There is, moreover, a marked fall in the Gini coefficient of inequality from 32 to 22 per cent.

In Figure 17 we illustrate what we call a *Dilution of Riches*. In order to dilute poverty a *smaller* number of poor persons is needed to share a given total income. But in order to dilute riches a *larger* number of rich persons is required to share a given total income. In Figure 17 accordingly we represent the case in which the number of the rich is doubled from 10 to 20 while their income per head is halved from £3·00 to £1·50. The result is a fall in the average income per head from £1·00 to £0·91, due to the same total national income being spread over the larger population. The Gini coefficient of inequality falls from 32 to 23 per cent; but the pattern of distribution is very different from that resulting from a dilution of poverty as shown in Figure 16.

Figure 18 illustrates the very straightforward case where the only change is a rise in the income per head of the poor from £0·33 to £0·66, which we call an *Enrichment of the Poor*. Average income per head for the whole community is raised from £1·00 to £1·10 and the Gini coefficient of inequality is reduced from 32 to 23 per cent.

Figure 19 shows the corresponding *Impoverishment of the Rich* where all that has happened is a reduction from £3·00 to £1·50 in the income per head of the same number of rich persons. Average income for the whole community falls from £1·00 to £0·85 and the Gini coefficient of inequality falls from 32 to 22 per cent.

Consideration of Figures 14 to 19 shows how the same reduction in the Gini coefficient of inequality can be achieved by very different changes which have very different effects upon the pattern of distribution. One very clear and simple distinction is between those changes (Contraction of the Poor, Dilution of Poverty and Enrichment of the Poor) which operate to raise the average income per head of the community and to reduce poverty by reducing the importance of the bottom left-hand section of the lines which illustrate the Gini coefficient and those changes (Contraction of the Rich, Dilution of Riches and Impoverishment of the Rich) which operate to lower the average income per head of the community and to reduce riches by reducing the importance of the top right-hand section of the lines which illustrate the Gini coefficient.

It is, however, to be observed that in the latter class of cases in which the average income of the community falls there is some slight reduction in relative poverty in the sense that the slope of the bottom left-hand section of the lines illustrating the Gini coefficient is slightly raised. This represents a very simple fact, namely that in all these cases the *absolute* income per head of the poor remains unchanged (namely, £0·33 per head); but as the average income for the whole community is reduced because of the reduction of riches, the income per head of the poor relative to the average income per head of the community is raised.[8]

___

[8] In the case of the *Contraction of the Poor* we can observe the opposite effect. The absolute income per head of the poor is unchanged at £0·33, but there is a slight increase in relative poverty because the average income per head for the whole community has risen from £1·00 to £1·12.

Note to Chapter VII

THE MEASUREMENT OF PROPORTIONATE DISTRIBUTIONAL WASTE

In the Note to Chapter XII of *The Growing Economy* (pages 212–19) we outlined a method of measuring an individual's utility function through an examination of his preferences for various combinations of consumption levels. The resulting utility function depended upon the selection of two benchmark levels of consumption, namely a level of consumption at which we defined the level of utility as being zero and another higher level of consumption at which we defined the level of utility as being unity. In the numerical example given in *The Growing Economy* we took \$400 as the benchmark level of consumption for $\hat{U} = 0$ and \$100,400 as the benchmark level for $\hat{U} = 1$. The resulting utility function was shown by the curve MT in Figure 24 of *The Growing Economy* with $\hat{U} = 0$ at $\hat{C} = OM$ and $\hat{U} = 1$ at $\hat{C} = ON$.

In Figure 13 of the present volume we have taken for both our utility functions $\hat{U}_1$ and $\hat{U}_2$ a benchmark of $\hat{C} = 0.1$ for $\hat{U} = 0$ and a benchmark of $\hat{C} = 1$ for $\hat{U} = 1$. The utility curves over the section $FA_1B_1C_1$ or $FA_2B_2C_2$ correspond to the utility curve over the section MT in Figure 24 of *The Growing Economy*.

If these two benchmarks could both be arbitrarily selected for the purpose of defining units of utility, it would not be possible to employ the measure of proportionate loss of utility discussed in §4 of this chapter. The result of the calculations would itself become arbitrary. This can be shown in the following way.

Consider either of the utility functions $\hat{U}_1$ or $\hat{U}_2$ shown on Figure 13. Both have the same two benchmarks $\hat{U}(0.1) = 0$ and $\hat{U}(1) = 1$. Suppose one wished to construct a new index of this same utility function simply by taking two different benchmarks. Let $\hat{V} = 0$ when $\hat{C} = \hat{C}_0$ and $\hat{V} = 1$ when $\hat{C} = \hat{C}_1$ where $\hat{C}_0$ and $\hat{C}_1$ are no longer equal to 0.1 and 1 respectively but are arbitrarily chosen provided only that $\hat{C}_1 > \hat{C}_0$. Then $\hat{U}$ can be transformed into this new index of utility, $\hat{V}$, by means of two constants G and H such that

$$\hat{V}(\hat{C}) = G + H\hat{U}(\hat{C})$$

where

$$G = - \frac{\hat{U}(\hat{C}_0)}{\hat{U}(\hat{C}_1) - \hat{U}(\hat{C}_0)}$$

and

$$H = \frac{1}{\hat{U}(\hat{C}_1) - \hat{U}(\hat{C}_0)}$$

It will be seen from the above formulae that when $\hat{C} = \hat{C}_0$, $\hat{V}(\hat{C}) = 0$ and when $\hat{C} = \hat{C}_1$, $\hat{V}(\hat{C}) = 1$.

Suppose now that we make this redefinition of units. Let us compare the use of the new index $\hat{V}(\hat{C})$ with that of the old index $\hat{U}(\hat{C})$. Consider a society with a total amount of consumption, C, to be divided between two individuals A and B. Suppose that a fraction, a, of C is given to A so that A has aC and B has $(1 - a)C$ to consume.

With the old index total utility is $\hat{U}(aC) + \hat{U}\{(1 - a)C\}$, whereas with an equal distribution of C (i.e. with $a = \frac{1}{2}$) it would be $2\hat{U}(\frac{1}{2}C)$. The index of proportionate loss of utility would be

$$1 - \frac{\hat{U}(aC) + \hat{U}\{(1 - a)C\}}{2\hat{U}(\frac{1}{2}C)}$$

Suppose now that we employed the new index of utility. The measure of proportionate loss of utility would be

$$1 - \frac{\hat{V}(aC) + \hat{V}\{(1 - a)C\}}{2\hat{V}(\frac{1}{2}C)}$$

$$= 1 - \frac{2G + H\hat{U}(aC) + H\hat{U}\{(1 - a)C\}}{2G + 2H\hat{U}(\frac{1}{2}C)}$$

where $\hat{U}(aC)$, $\hat{U}\{(1 - a)C\}$, and $\hat{U}(\frac{1}{2}C)$ have the values for the corresponding heights of the $\hat{U}$-curves of Figure 13. It follows that the actual value of this expression depends upon the values of G and H which are themselves determined by the arbitrary choice of values for the two new benchmarks $\hat{C}_0$ and $\hat{C}_1$.

The measure would thus appear to be itself an indeterminate, arbitrary measure. But this difficulty disappears if we do not treat as arbitrary the benchmark value of $\hat{C}_0$ which gives both $\hat{U}$ and $\hat{V} = 0$. We have already argued that the value of $\hat{C}_0$ should not be treated arbitrarily, but should correspond to that level of consumption which just makes life worth living (see Chapter II, page 25).

Otherwise we could not begin to consider any of the issues concerning the optimal level of the population which we discussed in Chapter V. We must know whether an additional citizen has the prospect of a level of consumption which will give him a positive enjoyment of life rather than a negative misery.[9]

Suppose then that we have no arbitrary choice in our decision about $\hat{C}_0$ and that it must in fact be chosen at the value $\hat{C} = 0.1$ given in Figure 13, though $\hat{C}_1$ may still be chosen arbitrarily. Then we have

$$G = -\frac{\hat{U}(0.1)}{\hat{U}(\hat{C}_1) - \hat{U}(0.1)} = 0$$

and

$$H = \frac{1}{\hat{U}(\hat{C}_1) - \hat{U}(0.1)} = \frac{1}{\hat{U}(\hat{C}_1)}$$

It follows that G must be zero since $\hat{U}(0.1)$ must be zero, whereas H may be arbitrarily chosen since $\hat{C}_1$ may be arbitrarily chosen. In this case we can have

$$\hat{V}(\hat{C}) = H\hat{U}(\hat{C})$$

with H chosen arbitrarily.[10] But with only this degree of arbitrariness in the definition of units of utility it can be seen from the two formulae for the measure of proportionate loss of utility that both give the same results, since

$$1 - \frac{\hat{V}(aC) + \hat{V}\{(1 - a)C\}}{2\hat{V}(\tfrac{1}{2}C)}$$

$$= 1 - \frac{H\hat{U}(aC) + H\hat{U}\{(1 - a)C\}}{2H\hat{U}(\tfrac{1}{2}C)}$$

$$= 1 - \frac{\hat{U}(aC) + \hat{U}\{(1 - a)C\}}{2\hat{U}(\tfrac{1}{2}C)}$$

[9] Take, for example, the formula for dZ in equation (5.1). The terms involving $\hat{U}_a$ and $\hat{U}_b$ in this equation can be expressed as $\mu(\hat{U}_a/\mu)\mathrm{d}N_a + \mu(\hat{U}_b/\mu)\mathrm{d}N_b$. μ can then be chosen arbitrarily. If we double μ, we are simply calculating every term in (5.1) in twice the number of units of welfare which we were previously employing. But $\hat{U}/\mu$ cannot be arbitrarily selected. We must decide what actual level of $\hat{C}$ gives $\hat{U} = 0$.

[10] The arbitrary choice of H is comparable to the arbitrary choice between yards and metres for measuring length. See Chapter II, page 25 above.

The measurement of the proportionate waste of consumption, unlike the measurement of the proportionate loss of utility, would give a unique answer even if we could make an arbitrary choice of both benchmarks ($\hat{C}_0$ and $\hat{C}_1$) and so an arbitrary choice of both the constants G and H for the transformation of $\hat{U}$ into $\hat{V} = G + H\hat{U}$. Let us repeat our example where a total amount of consumption C is divided between two individuals A and B in the amounts aC and $(1 - a)C$ respectively. With the old index of utility, total utility is $\hat{U}(aC) + \hat{U}\{(1 - a)C\}$. In order to calculate the proportional waste of consumption we must find a single level of consumption per head for both A and B such that the sum of A's and B's utilities with this new equalised consumption level is the same as the sum of A's and B's utilities with the old unequal levels of consumption, aC and $(1 - a)C$. Let us call this equalised level of consumption per head, $\hat{C}^*$. It is to be found by solution of the equation

$$2\hat{U}(\hat{C}^*) = \hat{U}(aC) + \hat{U}\{(1 - a)C\}$$

The degree of proportionate waste of consumption is then equal to

$$1 - (2\hat{C}^*/C).$$

With the transformed utility function we have to find the value of $\hat{C}^*$ by the same process, i.e. by the equation

$$2\hat{V}(\hat{C}^*) = \hat{V}(aC) + \hat{V}\{(1 - a)C\}$$

i.e. by the equation

$$2\{G + H\hat{U}(\hat{C}^*)\} = G + H\hat{U}(aC) \\ + G + H\hat{U}\{(1 - a)C\}$$

Both G and H can now be eliminated from both sides of this equation, giving once more the equation

$$2\hat{U}(\hat{C}^*) = \hat{U}(aC) + \hat{U}\{(1 - a)C\}$$

Both the old and the new transformed utility function thus give the same value for $\hat{C}^*$ so that the calculation of the degree of proportionate waste of consumption is not affected by whatever values of G and H may result from an arbitrary choice of new benchmark values for both $\hat{C}_0$ and $\hat{C}_1$.

CHAPTER VIII

COMPETITION AND THE DISTRIBUTION OF INCOME

As we have already argued, competition tends to increase economic welfare through increasing the efficiency with which resources are used by attracting resources to activities in which the value of their marginal products are highest. But there is always the possibility of a clash between economic efficiency and a desirable distribution of income, since the result of this competitive process may give high rewards to one set of resources and low rewards to another.

This clash will not occur, and the forces of competition will tend to reduce inequalities in the distribution of income between individual citizens as well as to remove economic inefficiencies, provided that two conditions are fulfilled: first, that all citizens are equally endowed with the various factors of production; and, second, that there is easy mobility between the various activities.

If different citizens start with different endowments of factors of production, then the forces of competition can lead to greater inequalities. A simple example of this possibility would be an economy consisting of poor workers and rich landowners producing a single agricultural crop.[1] If there were only limited substitutability between land and labour, the elasticity of demand for labour would be less than unity. In this case the setting of the wage rate above the competitive level through trade union action or minimum wage legislation would (i) cause some reduction in employment and output but (ii) increase the total income of the wage earners, the landlord's rent being reduced by more than the reduction in total output. The reintroduction of competitive forces into the labour market would make the economy more efficient (in the sense that total output would be increased so that with an appropriate distribution of the gain everyone could be made better off simultaneously);

---

[1] We have already analysed this example in *The Stationary Economy*, Chapter XII, pages 189–91.

but in the absence of any governmental intervention to make the gainers compensate the losers it would cause a greater inequality in incomes, since the poor wage earners would lose absolutely and the rich landowners would gain more than the total increase in income. This clash between efficiency and distribution is due to differences in the patterns of initial endowments of the various citizens. If each citizen owned the different factors of production in the same proportion, then the distribution of income among the different factors of production would not affect its distribution among persons. Thus suppose Mr A to have twice the earning capacity of Mr B and at the same time to own twice as much land as Mr B. Mr A will in all circumstances have twice the income of Mr B. Any rise in rents and fall in wage rates that makes Mr A better off will also make Mr B better off, since A's income will always remain twice B's income.[2]

To revert to our example of workers versus landowners in a simple one-crop agricultural economy, suppose that all citizens owned earning capacity and land in the same proportions. In this case the reintroduction of competitive forces into the labour market would have made everyone better off without increasing any inequalities of income. Suppose that the citizens in such a community, in their capacity as workers, had exercised trade union pressure to keep the real wage rate above the competitive level. Such action would have reduced the profits of the competitive plantations in which, in their capacity as property owners, they had invested their capital, and would have caused some unemployment of labour and reduction of output. The introduction of competitive forces in the labour market would have caused a reduction in the real wage rate, but it would have led to an increase in total output. Thus each citizen would have gained more in his capacity as a property owner than he lost in his capacity as a wage earner.

If what we are interested in is the distribution of income among persons, we shall be concerned with the distribution of income between the factors of production (between the rent of land and the wages of labour in our example) only in so far as the ownership of

---

[2] An extreme case of such a balanced distribution of the ownership of resources is where Mr A and Mr B are both representative workers and representative land-owners in the sense that both own the same absolute amount of earning capacity and the same absolute amount of land. In Chapter III of *The Growing Economy* we called such a community a Propdem.

the factors of production (of property and of earning capacity) is divided in an unbalanced way among persons (in our example, only in so far as some classes own a higher ratio of property to earning capacity than do other classes in society).

Competitive forces may also lead to inequalities of income if factors of production are immobile. Suppose that, in an economy composed solely of farmers producing food and weavers producing clothing, the earnings of farmers and weavers are initially the same.[3] Suppose then that there is a permanent technological improvement in agriculture so that the total output of food is increased. If the demand for food is sufficiently inelastic, the price of food will fall so much that the real income of the farmers will fall, and the weavers will gain through the heavy fall in food prices more than the whole increase in the real income of the community. Total incomes would rise, but they would be less equally divided.

In such conditions a system of price controls which prevented the farmers in competition with each other from offering food at such low prices would help to equalise the incomes of farmers and weavers at the expense of some degree of economic inefficiency. At the high price for food the farmers would not be able to sell all the output which they could produce; some food would go to waste. However, the farmers would receive a larger total income than would otherwise be the case and the fall in their incomes relatively to the weaver's incomes would be mitigated.[4]

An outstanding example where mobility is impossible is from one generation to another. A man with a given ability in the middle of the nineteenth century could not choose to put off his existence until the middle of the twentieth century in order to take advantage of a better opportunity for the use of his ability. If we are concerned

[3] We have already analysed a situation of this kind in *The Stationary Economy*, Chapter IV, page 77.

[4] It is in some cases merely a question of definition whether one calls it a 'difference in factor endowment' or a 'factor immobility' which is causing an inequality of income. Thus suppose that all youths were identically endowed with earning capacity, but that some chose to train as farmers and some as weavers. Elderly farmers could not become weavers and elderly weavers could not become farmers because their training and experience did not give them the necessary skill. Do we call this a 'difference of factor endowment' (the elderly farmers being endowed with farming skill but not with weaving skill) or a 'factor immobility' (the elderly farmers being equally endowed with basic earning capacity, but not being able to move easily into the other occupation)? The reader is free to make his or her own choice of the use of words.

with the distribution of income and wealth as between the members of the present generation and the members of future generations, we cannot rely upon the forces of competition between them to equalise their incomes.

In the examples given earlier in this chapter we confined our attention to cases in which there were only two classes of citizens – workers and landlords in our first example, and farmers and weavers in our second example. Quite new considerations may arise when the possible clash of interests is between three or more classes of citizens.

We will illustrate the point by means of a development of our first example of a clash of interest between workers and landlords. In that example we considered the interests of the wage earners as a single class. Perhaps this was appropriate because of the existence of an extended family system such that the employed members of the family shared their wages equally with the unemployed members of the family. But suppose that the employed do not share their earnings with the unemployed. We now have two classes of workers, the employed and the unemployed. When the wage rate is pushed up by trade union action or by governmental minimum wage legislation, the landlords as before reduce output and employment; but now the unemployment is concentrated on certain unfortunate individual workers. The result is (i) some reduction in output below the full-employment level (this as before is the inefficiency aspect of the change), and (ii) a rise in the incomes of the employed workers at the expense of a fall in the incomes of the rich landlords and also of the impoverished unemployed. Is the distribution of income now more equal than before (the employed workers being better off and the landlords worse off than before) or is it now less equal (the workers who are now unemployed having lower incomes and the employed workers higher incomes than before)?

This is a straightforward example of the comparison which we illustrated by means of Table IV and Table V in the preceding chapter. Let Table V (page 123) represent now the initial situation in which 90 per cent of the population are workers earning £0·70 per head in wages and 10 per cent of the population are landlords receiving £3.70 per head in rents. The workers now push up the wage to £1·00; the number employed falls from 90 to 60, leaving 30 unemployed who receive only a social benefit of £0·33 each. The landlords now are squeezed and receive only £3·00 instead of £3·70 each. We have moved to the distribution shown in Table IV (page 113). The broken lines in Figures 11 and 12 (pages 114 and 117) represent the competitive situation and the solid lines the situation with the minimum wage fixed at £1·00. Whether or not we would say that the reintroduction of competitive conditions (i.e. a move from Table IV to Table V and from the solid to the broken lines of Figures 11 and 12) would cause an increase or decrease in equality raises all the issues discussed on pages 123–5 above. In fact we can only leave it to the policy-makers to decide which pattern of distribution is to be preferred.[5]

In our example we have assumed that those workers who are no longer employed by the landlords are unemployed. But Tables IV and V and Figures 11 and 12 can also be employed to illustrate conditions in which full employment is maintained, but the interference with the competitive system involves an inefficient reallocation of resources. Let our three classes now be rich owners of printing works, printing operatives and roadsweepers. Suppose that all workers have the same innate ability, and that the purely competitive system will lead to an equalisation of wage rates between printers and roadsweepers. We start with Table V and the broken lines in Figures 11 and 12 with roadsweepers and printers making up 90 per cent of the population and receiving 63 per cent of the total available income. The printers now by trade union action push up the printers' wage rate and restrict entry into the occupation; employment in printing is reduced; the unemployed flood the market for road sweeping and the wage there is pushed down, so that the situation is now depicted by the distribution in Table IV and by the solid lines in Figures 11 and 12[6] in which the

[5] The above application of Figures 11 and 12 and Tables IV and V of the preceding chapter to our present example is in one respect unduly favourable to the non-competitive situation. The holding of the wage rate above the competitive level would, as we have seen, somewhat reduce output and cause unemployment. The total real income available for distribution would therefore be lower in the non-competitive situation than in the competitive situation. Suppose output were reduced by 10 per cent, but that the effect on the distribution of the reduced income were as illustrated in Figure 12. Then all the quantities for income per head and for total income in Table IV and the height of all the solid blocks in Figure 11 should be reduced by 10 per cent to give a true comparison with the quantities in Table V and with the broken lines in Figure 11. Both the broken and the solid lines in Figure 12 would, however, remain unchanged, since that Figure deals only with the proportionate shares of income, and not at all with the absolute levels of income accruing to different classes.

road sweepers (making up 20 per cent of the population) have a very low wage which earns them only 10 per cent of the total available income, while the restricted number of workers in printing who make up 60 per cent of the population now receive 60 per cent instead of 42 per cent of the national income.

We can conclude this chapter with a consideration of the influence of competition upon some of the different objectives of policy discussed in Chapter IV. Consider the following five possible alternative objectives of distributional policy:

(1) The Equalisation of Opportunity.
(2) The Equalisation of Actual Income and Wealth.
(3) The Maximisation of the Minimum Level of Consumption.
(4) The Equalisation of Enjoyment.
(5) The Maximisation of Total Enjoyment.

Equality of opportunity results from free competition, but only if mobility is both unrestricted and costless. If in addition initial endowments are the same, then equality of opportunity will lead to equality of actual income and wealth, as people move from the less rewarding to the more rewarding activities. For equality to be the result it is not necessary that everyone should be identically endowed, but only that the supply of persons with different types of endowment should be matched to the demand for them. Thus unskilled brawn and skilled brain can both earn the same, if brawn and brain are in supplies which are matched to the needs for heavy manual work and for light desk work respectively.

If this is so, and if as a result incomes are in fact equalised, then the minimum income will already be as high as the maximum income, and the maximisation of the minimum income will already be achieved. There will be no exceptionally poor people to merit exceptional attention.

If needs and tastes were the same for everyone, then equality of actual income and wealth if it were achieved would lead to equality of welfare and enjoyment. But where needs are different, an unequal distribution of income may be needed to provide an equal welfare and enjoyment of life.

If everyone's needs and tastes were the same, an equal distribution of actual income and wealth would also lead to the maximisation of the sum total enjoyment or utility throughout the community. The

[6] Subject to any reduction in the absolute levels of income due to the reduction in the total output of the economy, as described in the preceding footnote.

marginal utility of income would be less to the rich than to the poor, and to transfer £1 from the rich to the poor would subtract less utility from the rich than it would add to the poor.

We may conclude then that (i) if people were equally endowed with income-earning assets, (ii) if they were free to move themselves and their property without cost from any low-reward to any high-reward occupation and (iii) if everyone had the same needs and tastes, then free competition would simultaneously achieve all the five distributional objectives enumerated above. But, alas, in the real wicked world these three basic conditions are not fulfilled. Hence the need for distributional policies, for choice between the various possibly conflicting objectives of different distributional policies, and for balancing the distributional against the efficiency effects of any set of policies.

CHAPTER IX

THE INTERGENERATIONAL TRANSMISSION OF ENDOWMENTS

We turn now to a consideration of the forces in society which cause inequalities of income and wealth. In Chapter VI (page 109 above) we drew a distinction between intergenerational inequalities, intertemporal inequalities and interclass inequalities. In this chapter we are primarily concerned with interclass inequalities; but we shall be examining the mechanisms by which such inequalities are developed and perpetuated as riches or poverty are transmitted from one generation to another in any given family.

In the preceding chapter we have argued that in a perfectly competitive economy, with complete mobility of the factors of production, inequalities in the distribution of income must be explained in terms of inequalities in the endowments of the various citizens with the various factors of production. We will start by considering the forces at work in a competitive society which lead to inequalities in factor endowments and thus to inequalities in personal incomes and properties. In order to isolate these factors we shall accordingly start off with the following three assumptions: first, that there is perfect competition; second, that there are no artificial barriers restricting the movement of factors of production from low-yield to high-yield activities; and, third, that there are no governmental policies designed to affect the distribution of endowments and of incomes and properties – in particular that there are no governmental expenditures on education and no redistributive taxes and social benefits.

A citizen in such a stylised *laissez-faire* competitive society would receive certain endowments from his parents which would help to determine the amount of income which he could earn and property which he could accumulate during his own life-time. This in turn would affect the endowments which he could hand on to his children.

The endowments with which we will be concerned may be enumerated under four heads.

First a citizen will be endowed with a certain genetic make-up. There is some genetic component in intelligence which may affect earning capacity. But it would be a mistake to forget other characteristics which probably have some genetic component and which may well exert a greater influence on earning capacity. Quite apart from straightforward bodily strength and health, there may be other relevant physical differences which have some genetic component; there may, for example, be some genetic influences affecting the vocal chords of Mr Fischer-Dieskau and Miss Janet Baker which help to explain their ability to earn income. There may also be genetic components in the determination of certain qualities of character which have an income earning potential, though it by no means follows that all of these are desirable in themselves. Thus a certain streak of ruthlessness and aggression may be helpful to the accumulation of wealth without being in any basic ethical or aesthetic sense good or desirable qualities in and for themselves.

Second, a citizen may inherit a certain amount of income-earning property of one kind or another from his parents.

Third, a citizen will have received as a child a certain education and training. In a strictly *laissez-faire* competitive society this education and training will have been provided and financed privately by his parents, though this is, of course, one of the fields in which our present neglect of governmental interventions and policies is especially significant.

Fourth, there are the rather less tangible advantages or disadvantages which accrue to a citizen through the social contacts which he makes with other persons, these social contacts being much affected by the social background into which he was born.

These two last elements of endowment – namely, education and social contacts – must together cover a very wide range of social phenomena. Education obviously covers an individual's formal education and training at school, university or similar institution. Social contacts obviously cover a citizen's range of acquaintances who through their particular brand of the old-boy network can or cannot get him a good job or provide him with a favourable investment opportunity. But there are many other factors to be taken into account which must be put into either the one or the other of the very general categories of 'education' and 'social contacts'.

The category of education may be thought of as covering a large range of the environmental influences which affect the development of an individual's knowledge, character and motivation. He will thus receive much of his so-defined education directly from his parents, as they bring him up in a certain way, and from the acquaintances he makes – to say nothing of the education which husband and wife receive from each other.

A citizen is thus fortunate or unfortunate according to whether he starts out in life with a helpful or unhelpful endowment of genes, inherited property, education and social contacts. But in addition to these initial structural elements of good or bad fortune which are determined by his family background, a citizen will also encounter many elements of good or bad luck in the course of his career. To take but one example, two men with the same inborn ability and the same initial advantages of education, property and social contacts may end up with very different incomes and properties, simply because they embarked on careers in different lines of economic activity, one of which prospered and the other of which declined. And yet at the time of choice the prospects of the two activities may have seemed very similar to both of them and it may have been a matter of almost random chance which determined the choice of career. In what follows the term 'fortune' will be used to describe the basic structural endowments of genes, property, education and social contacts, and the word 'luck' to describe the many chances in life which determine the actual outcome within these structures of basic endowments. One cannot, of course, draw any hard and fast line between these elements of fortune and elements of luck; they are both mixtures of recognisable laws of cause and effect and of strokes of pure chance; but the nature of society is such that it seems useful to think in terms of some such broad distinction.

Social scientists examine the general genetic, demographic, social and economic structure of society. They consider the characteristics of, and the factors affecting, various groups: income groups, property groups, IQ groups, social classes, age and sex groupings of the population, occupational classes, classes of educational attainment, and the like. A may be born into one set of groupings and B into another. When the souls of little A and little B were lining up in heaven to be sent forth on their sojourn in this wicked world, did they toss up as to which soul should occupy which niche in the social structure which they were joining? We cannot know. But the structured endowments which A and B receive in society by joining whatever group they do join we shall define as their good or bad fortune.

However, different people within the same niche in the structure of society may fare very differently in the course of their lives. It is the causes of these divergences in the fates of two persons within the same fortunate or unfortunate structural niche which are defined as factors of luck. This is not to assert that these factors are in any fundamental sense less subject to laws of cause and effect than are the factors of fortune. This category of luck certainly contains all those causes of inequality which are not explained by the structured influences of what has been defined as fortune; and there may well be disciplines other than present-day economics and sociology which would help to explain why two persons with the same structured fortune fare differently in the outcome.

The basic structural endowments of good or bad fortune are handed down from parents to child; but the child as he grows up moulds and modifies the basic endowments which he received as a child from his mother and father, before he amalgamates them with those of his wife and passes this package of *modified* and *mixed* endowments of fortune on to his own children. Let us start first with a consideration of the way in which an individual's initial endowments may be *modified* as he grows up, and turn later to the implications of the fact that he *mixes* these *modified* endowments with the already *modified* endowments which his wife received from her parents before the two of them hand on this modified mixture to the next generation.[1]

Let us then consider how a citizen's passage through life may affect the elements of basic structural fortune with which he was initially endowed. This is illustrated in Figure 20 in which we consider the way in which a particular citizen – let us call him Tom Jones – starting out as little Tommy receives his basic endowments from his home background, proceeds through life, and at length as poor old Tom or Thomas Jones Esquire or maybe even Sir Thomas Jones, GCB, himself contributes to a home background transmitting endowments to his children.

[1] This example is expressed in terms of a boy only because the English language does not possess a pronoun which covers both male and female. Solely for this reason, in what follows we shall analyse in terms of the male sex much that applies equally to the female sex.

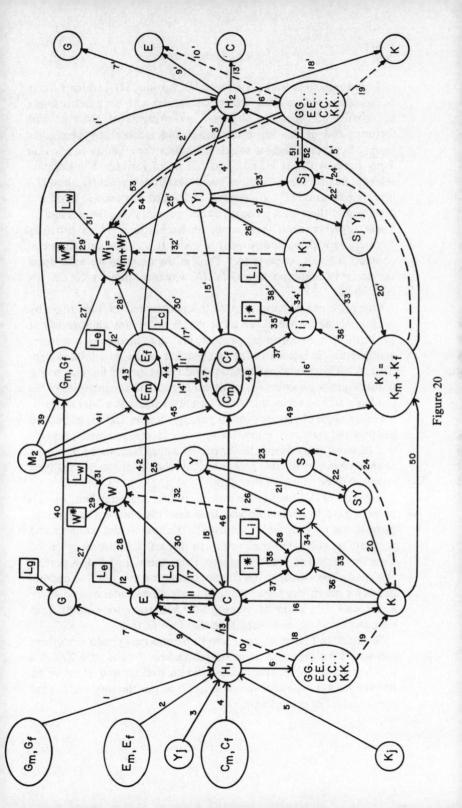

Figure 20

Tom Jones then starts in a home background (H_1) which is built by his father and mother. We are concerned with his parents solely as instruments affecting his basic endowments of good or bad fortune; and in this sense his father and mother are themselves simply bundles of factors which will affect their ability to provide Tom Jones with his initial endowments of fortune. The parents' relevant factors are the mother's and the father's genes (G_m, and G_f) (line 1), education (E_m, E_f) (line 2), and social contacts (C_m, and C_f) (line 4), and their joint income (Y_j) and property (K_j) (lines 3 and 5). These together constitute the home background which provides Tom Jones with an endowment of genes (G), education (E), social contacts (C) and property (K). Thus in the diagram we look upon the home background as a $GEYCK$ which produces a $GECK$ for each child.

One must not, however, regard this endowment of Tom Jones by his parents as a once-for-all affair which occurs instantaneously at his birth. It is a continuing process; and this introduces two inter-acting dynamic factors. In the first place, Tom Jones will be suscep-tible to different endowments at different stages of his life: to his parents' genes once-for-all on his conception, to the qualities of his mother's care as an infant, to his parents' friends at a later stage, to his inheritance of property on his parents' deaths, and so on. Second his parents' own education, income, social contacts and property will be developing during their years as home-builders and parents, so that what they have to give as well as what Tom Jones is ready to receive will be changing over time.

We shall at first neglect the influences affecting what Tom Jones's parents have to contribute and shall take the nature and develop-ment of his parents' genes, education, income, social contacts and property as given. We shall return to this set of problems when we close the cycle and come to regard Tom Jones himself as a parent. We shall then consider his development as a provider of endow-ments for his children. For the time being we consider him solely as a recipient of a given developing flow of basic endowments from his parents, which he himself then develops further.

To return to Figure 20, Tom Jones's parents may produce brothers and sisters for him, and these are represented by the little $GECK$'s which proceed from Tom Jones's home background H_1 (line 6). But the main purpose of the diagram is to put the individual Tom Jones under the microscope.

From his two parents Tom Jones receives his genetic endowment (G) (line 7). But while his genetic make-up is basically conditioned by that of his parents there is also an element of luck (L_g) (line 8). Two children of the same parents will not receive identical genetic endowments unless they are identical twins. Tom Jones can draw his genes only from those offered by his parents; but he may have good or bad luck in his draw from the parental stock.

Tom Jones will receive an education (E). In the absence of governmental intervention not only much of his early upbringing but also his formal education and training will be provided for him by his parents (line 9). However, the greater the number of Tom Jones's brothers and sisters, the less his parents may be able to afford out of their given time, income and property to invest in Tom Jones's individual education (line 10). In addition to his home background and formal education, much of what we have broadly defined as his education will be continued during his own career by his social contacts, that is to say, by the sort of friends and colleagues with whom he associates (line 11). But in all this there is a considerable admixture of luck (L_e) (line 12). To take only one example, his parents may make most carefully calculated decisions about the amount of money which they will invest in his education and about the educational institutions to which they will entrust him. But the outcome may be greatly affected in ways which it may be impossible to foresee by luck – as, for example, whether a particular teacher happens to fire young Tommy's imagination and interest in a particular subject or activity.

Tom Jones will inherit certain social contacts (C) from his parents (line 13), since the social environment of his home background will greatly affect his choice of friends and acquaintances. But as he grows up his social contacts will develop and will depend upon the way in which his own career develops. An important factor will be the social contacts which he makes at school or other educational institutions (line 14). Thereafter, the further development of his social contacts is likely to be affected by his material success in life. If he manages to earn a high income (Y) or to acquire much property (K), the fact that he is a man of riches will enable him to make contacts with people who will be useful to him in his career (lines 15 and 16). Finally, of course, there is an important element of luck (L_c) in the people he meets and the friends he makes (line 17).

From his parents Tom Jones may also receive property (K)

(line 18). But, once again, the greater the number of Tom Jones's competing brothers and sisters, the smaller – given an equal distribution of their property by the parents among their children – will be his own share of the family property (line 19). As time passes he may supplement this property from his own savings (SY) (line 20), his savings being simply his income (Y) multiplied by the proportion of his income which he saves (S) (lines 21 and 22). The proportion of his income which he decides to save will be affected by many considerations; but Figure 20 displays only two of the most important.

In the first place, the higher his income, the greater will be Tom Jones's ability to save and thus the higher his savings proportion (S) (line 23).

But, in the second place, the greater the property which he has already acquired (perhaps by inheritance), the smaller will be his need to save, since there will be less need to abstain from present consumption to acquire a property to support him in his old age or to give him security against adversity. This fact that the higher his property (K), the lower will be his savings proportion (S), is represented by the broken line 24.

It remains to consider the factors determining the level of Tom Jones's income as he passes through life. His income (Y) is simply the sum of his earnings or income from work (W) and of his income from property (iK) (lines 25 and 26).[2]

His earnings will be affected by many factors. First of all there is his capacity to earn which will be affected both by his genetic endowment and by his educational endowment (lines 27 and 28). But, given his ability, his actual earnings will depend upon the structure of wage rates that exist in the market for different kinds of ability (W^*) (line 29). Earnings, however, are not determined exclusively by a given market wage rate for a given ability. There is a further element of fortune in that good social contacts may enable a man to make a more rewarding choice of job (line 30); and there is also an element of luck (L_w) in determining whether Tom Jones will be successful in his choice of occupation or in the development of his particular job (line 31).[3]

---

[2] See Chapter XI (pages 169–71) for a discussion of some of the difficulties of drawing a clear dividing line between earnings and income from property.

[3] There are other important influences in the real world which are neglected in Figure 20 as a result of the assumption of free competition – influences such as trade

Tom Jones's earnings will depend in part upon the amount of effort which he chooses to put into the busness of earning a high income. This is influenced by many factors; but among these we may suppose that the higher is Tom Jones's income from property (iK), the lower – other things being equal – will be the effort which he puts into earning an income from work (line 32). Indeed if he has a sufficiently high income from property he may not bother to earn any additional income at all.

But does Figure 20 cover the undoubted fact that Tom Jones's own moral character and motivation will affect how hard he will work and what steps he will take to get on? Do not some people get on – and deserve to get on – because they try hard and others fail to make good – and deserve to fail – because they make little or no effort to help themselves? We are immediately faced by the riddle of free will. Do not a man's genetic and environmental endowments, together with some elements of pure luck, for which he can in no way be held responsible, determine his moral character and motivation as well as his ability? If so, it can all be comprehended in lines 27, 28, 30 and 31 of Figure 20. But it would then seem meaningless to assert that Tom Jones was in any way a free agent in deciding whether to deserve success or failure. If one does believe in some measure of free choice and personal responsibility for success or failure, there is something vital missing from the Figure. But the author of this volume has no contribution to offer to the solution of this philosophical enigma.

Let us turn now from Tom Jones's earned income to his income from property (iK). This is simply his property (K) multiplied by the average yield or rate of interest on it (i) (lines 33 and 34). The yield on property will be basically determined by the structure of the ruling market yields on various types of property (i^*) (line 35). But the actual yield obtained may well be affected by Tom Jones's investment opportunities. Thus the yield on property is likely to be higher for a man with much property to invest (line 36) and for a man with the right social contacts (line 37). A man with a large property can afford to take more risks in his investments, and the cost of advice from stockbrokers and of other investment services can be spread over a larger capital fund. For these reasons a large property

---

union or similar restrictions on entry into protected occupations or customary differentials in pay which interfere with market forces.

normally obtains a higher yield than a small property. Moreover, a wealthy man is more likely to have those social contacts which will enable him to be better informed about the chances of profitable investment. Finally, there will be an element of luck in Tom Jones's choice of investments for his property (L_i) (line 38).

Tom Jones grows up into mature manhood with a certain make-up of genes, income, property and social contacts, these elements of his make-up being, as we have seen, partly inherited from his original home background and partly made up by his own social and economic development. He is now ready to choose a wife and to become a father; and together these two bundles of genes, education, income, social contacts and property, having joined together in holy matrimony, are ready to make up a second-generation home background for the next generation of children.

Let us begin the analysis of Tom Jones's married life with the assumption that he has chosen, or been chosen by, a particular Mary Smith with her own particular bundle of genes, educaton, social contacts and property as they exist at the time of her marriage. We will discuss in the following chapter the very important question of what it was that brought Tom and Mary together. For the moment we are interested in the implications of their joint family life.

A family is more than a number of individuals. In the first half of Figure 20 we watched the development of Tom Jones as an individual bachelor. In the second half of the diagram we watch Tom and Mary Jones's family developing as a joint concern.

Mary Smith is represented as M_2, namely as a second-generation mother. For our purpose she is simply a bundle of factors relevant for the joint building of a second-generation home background (H_2) for the endowment of the second generation of children. She brings into the marriage her genes, education, social contacts and property, the nature of which depend upon what endowments she has received from her parents and the way in which she has developed them during her spinsterhood.

Thus Tom and Mary together provide a pool of mother's genes (G_m) and father's genes (G_f) for use by the family (lines 39 and 40). They provide mother's educaton (E_m) and father's education (E_f) to form part of the family background (lines 41 and 42). Their educations in any broad sense of the term continue during their married life; and this is partly due to the fact that they educate each other (lines 43 and 44). They provide the mother's and the father's social contacts for use by the family (C_m and C_f) (lines 45 and 46); and Tom's contacts enlarge Mary's contacts and *vice versa* (lines 47 and 48). They both bring some property into the family (K_m and K_f) (lines 49 and 50); and we assume that they form a close-knit family in which the two properties are for practical purposes merged into a single joint family property ($K_m + K_f = K_j$) with a corresponding joint family income from property ($i_j K_j$) derived from the yield on the joint family property (i_j). Similarly we assume also that Tom and Mary merge their individual earnings into a joint family income from work ($W_m + W_f = W_j$). Thus there is a joint family income (Y_j) from which joint family savings ($S_j Y_j$) are made.

The main relationships within this family are now similar to those in the first half of Figure 20. Tom and Mary may find many strokes of luck in their further education, their social contacts, their investments or their jobs, and the various elements in their family structure will feed back upon each other. The relevant lines in the second half of Figure 20 correspond exactly to the same relevant lines in the first half of the Figure.[4]

All that part of the second half of Figure 20 is a mere application to the joint family of the relationships considered at some length in the case of Tom Jones's bachelor life. But there is now an important additional consideration to be introduced.

At the far right of the Figure we have a new home background (H_2) made up of Tom's and Mary's genes, education, income, social contacts and property as these develop during their married life (lines 1^1, 2^1, 3^1, 4^1, 5^1); and these provide endowments of genes, education, social contacts and property as Tom's and Mary's little *GECK*'s are born and grow up. If we want now to consider the life-cycle of one of these in particular (for example, the life-cycle of Tom's and Mary's son Richard), we start from the large *GECK* at the far right of the diagram, which shows Richard Jones endowed with genes, education, social contacts and property from his home background (H_2) (lines 7^1, 9^1, 13^1 and 18^1), but competing for education and property (lines 10^1 and 19^1) with his brothers and sisters represented by the other little *GECK*'s proceeding from the

---

[4] In the Figure this is made clear by numbering the relevant lines on the right-hand half of the diagram with the same numbers as the corresponding lines on the left-hand half of the diagram. Thus line 1 on the left-hand is numbered 1^1 on the right-hand half; and similarly for the other numbers.

same home background (line 6^1). We have in fact cycled back to the extreme left-hand end of the Figure, but for generation 2 instead of generation 1.

But the size of Tom's and Mary's family will feed back into their own development as parents. The larger their family, the greater their financial responsibilities for feeding, clothing, housing, entertaining and educating their children. The greater these responsibilities, the more difficult will it be for them to save and accumulate property. The broken line 51 represents the fact the larger is the number of their children the more difficult will it be for Tom and Mary to accumulate property during their married life. It is probable that they will in fact accumulate a smaller property. But this is not absolutely certain since, while their ability to save will be less, their motivation to save may be greater, since the larger the family the more they must accumulate in order to be able to give each child an inheritance of any given absolute size. This increased motivation for saving is shown by the continuous line 52.

The size of their family will also affect their earnings. A large family may make it more difficult for Mary to go out to work and earn an income. On the other hand it will increase the need for income and may increase the parents' motivation to seek as high an income from work as they can manage to earn. The net result is uncertain; and this is indicated by the combination of the solid line 53 which represents the number of children as increasing the motivation to earn income with the broken line 54 which represents the reduction in the mother's opportunities to earn income.

Figure 20 is complicated enough; but even so it is a great simplification of reality. There are causal relationships which have been omitted from the Figure. Thus we have not allowed for the fact that a man's genetic and educational background may affect his ability and his effort in investing his property so as to obtain the highest possible rate of return on it; nor have we allowed for the fact that a man may during his career invest resources in his own further education and training, his ability to do so depending upon the level of his income and property. It would be easy to add the arrowed lines to the Figure to represent these further positive feedbacks; this has not been done simply in order to keep the picture clear.

Moreover there are certain other very important relationships which are perhaps implied in the Figure but which are not very clearly represented in it. Thus it fails to bring out the fact that the endowments which parents can give to their children may compete with each other. The more money a parent invests in a child's formal education (E), the less he may be able to leave to him in the form of other income-earning property (K). Moreover, parents who apply their minds to the direct care, education and amusement of their children at home may have less time and energy left for making money to leave to them.

Above all there is no representation of the factors which determine the number of children which a set of parents will produce. It may well be that the structured genetic, educational, social and economic characteristics of the parents do influence the size of their families, some types of family having on average a larger number of children than others. But there would certainly be important dispersions around these characteristic averages, the representation of which would need the introduction of yet another 'luck' factor. In Chapter XII we shall analyse some of the important *effects* of differential fertility between different types of family; but Figure 20 tells us nothing about the *causes* of differential fertility.

Finally, there is another very closely related demographic consideration. Figure 20 is based on the assumption of the permanent monogamous family in which Tom has children only by Mary and Mary has children only by Tom. This is still the basic pattern in our society, though the bonds of marriage are looser than they used to be. In a society in which human breeding pairs were frequently reshuffled the picture would be very different. In particular we would need to modify substantially what is said in Chapter X on the mating patterns of husband and wife.

A marked feature of the simple model presented in Figure 20 is the amount of positive feedback which it contains, that is to say of self-reinforcing influences which help to sustain the good fortune of the fortunate and the bad fortune of the unfortunate.

One example concerns job opportunities. A man who for any reason starts with a high income may be able to make appropriate social contacts which enable him to find exceptionally repaying jobs which will in turn help to raise his income still further (lines 15, 30, 25).

Another example concerns the accumulation of property. A man who for any reason of good fortune has a high income can save much and accumulate a large property (lines 20, 21, 22 and 23). But with a large property he has a high income from property (line 33) and thus a still higher income (line 26). Nor is that the end of the matter; with a high property he can probably get a high yield on his property, partly because a large property can be more cheaply and effectively managed than a small property (line 36) and partly because a man of wealth will be better able to make the sort of social contacts which will enable him to invest his property profitably (lines 16 and 37). Thus the yield on his property, as well as his property itself, will be raised simply because his initial fortune was good. We shall return to these important relationships in Chapter XI.

Positive feedback relationships of this kind may or may not be explosive in character. Let us take the job-opportunity example which we have just given of lines 30, 25, 15.

Suppose that pure luck (L_c) led to a chance improvement of 100 in social contacts (C) (line 17) which in turn caused earnings (W) to go up by $\frac{1}{2} \times 100$ (line 30) which caused total income (Y) to rise by the same amount (line 25). Suppose the increase in Y of $\frac{1}{2} \times 100$ caused C to go up by $\frac{3}{4}$ of $\frac{1}{2} \times 100$ (line 15). We would then have a secondary rise of $\frac{3}{4} \times \frac{1}{2} \times 100$ in C which would cause a secondary rise in W and so in Y of $\frac{1}{2} \times \frac{3}{4} \times \frac{1}{2} \times 100$ which would cause a tertiary rise in C of $\frac{3}{4} \times \frac{1}{2} \times \frac{3}{4} \times \frac{1}{2} \times 100$, and in W and Y of $\frac{1}{2} \times \frac{3}{4} \times \frac{1}{2} \times \frac{3}{4} \times \frac{1}{2} \times 100$, and so on. The ultimate rise in W and Y would be $\frac{1}{2} \times 100 \left(1 + \frac{3}{8} + \left(\frac{3}{8}\right)^2 + \left(\frac{3}{8}\right)^3 + \left(\frac{3}{8}\right)^4 + \ldots\right)$ which is equal to 75.

Suppose, however, that a rise in C of 100 caused W and Y to rise by $\frac{3}{2} \times 100$ instead of $\frac{1}{2} \times 100$ and that the rise in W and Y, as before caused C to go up by $\frac{3}{4}$ of the rise in W and Y, so that a rise of $\frac{3}{2} \times 100$ in Y caused C to go up by $\frac{3}{4} \times \frac{3}{2} \times 100$, which caused Y to go up by a further $\frac{3}{2} \times \frac{3}{4} \times \frac{3}{2} \times 100$ which caused C to go up by a further $\frac{3}{4} \times \frac{3}{2} \times \frac{3}{4} \times \frac{3}{2} \times 100$, and so on. Then the ultimate rise in Y would be $\frac{3}{2} \times 100 \left(1 + \frac{9}{8} + \left(\frac{9}{8}\right)^2 + \left(\frac{9}{8}\right)^3 + \left(\frac{9}{8}\right)^4 + \ldots\right)$. This series goes on rising indefinitely without limit since $\frac{9}{8}$ is greater than 1, $\left(\frac{9}{8}\right)^2$ is greater than $\frac{9}{8}$ and $\left(\frac{9}{8}\right)^3$ is greater than $\left(\frac{9}{8}\right)^2$, and so on. The series would be explosive. An initial chance improvement in social contacts would cause an explosion of earnings away from its initial level.

And conversely some worsening of fortune might either cause a limited downward spiral of income or, if the reactions were sufficiently great, it would cause an unlimited collapse of earnings towards zero.

In fact, in actual society upward or downward spirals which may start off in an explosive manner are likely sooner or later to come up against either a top ceiling or a bottom floor. This latter will be the certain effect of governmental policies which are designed to put a limit to excessive poverty but which we are neglecting in this chapter. It remains, however, true that the degree of inequality which will result from any chance variations of luck will be the greater, the more powerful are these forces of positive feedback.

On the other hand there are some negative feedback relationships; and the more powerful these negative feedbacks, the smaller will be the degree of ultimate inequalities.

While Figure 20 has many positive feedback loops, it contains through the broken lines 24 and 32 only two examples of negative feedbacks, of influence, that is to say, which damp down rather than multiply the results of initial good or bad fortune. Thus it is probable that the larger is a man's property, the smaller is his incentive to cut back his present consumption in order to save and accumulate; and this factor damps down the way in which large properties tend to lead to still larger properties (line 24). In a rather similar manner the existence of a high income from property reduces the need for income from work and may thus damp down the incentive to earn more (line 32); and this factor may reduce the positive, reinforcing effects which we have just examined, whereby high incomes lead to still higher incomes.

The assumption of *laissez-faire* has led to the omission from Figure 20 of some fundamental elements of negative feedback which may be at work in the real world through governmental interventions. Progressive taxation, the provision of free education and medicine, and the payment of social security benefits or other supplements to the incomes of those who are less well off, in so far as they are effective in redistributing income from the rich to the poor, are outstanding examples of such negative feedbacks. In such circumstances a rise in a man's gross income and wealth (before governmental adjustment) causes a less than proportionate increase in his net income and wealth (after governmental adjustment); and this diminishes the multiplier whereby initial good fortune feeds upon itself and magnifies the final outcome.

But there remain in society very strong elements of positive feedback which are illustrated in the Figure. Two results follow from this.

First, there is the obvious point that there are some apparently powerful built-in tendencies for the rich to sustain their riches and the poor their poverty which one would expect to help in explaining the persistent continuation of the large inequalities in income and wealth which we actually observe in society.

A second major result may be expected from the intertwining of the many positive feedback loops in Figure 20, namely that the various endowments passed from parent to child are likely to become highly correlated with each other. Thus, if Tom Jones is born with a set of useful genes which help him to earn a high income this will enable him to make useful social contacts and to accumulate a sizeable property. Thus as a father he is likely to be a bundle not only of useful genes, but also of a useful income, a useful property and useful social contacts. There will be a strong tendency in society for good or bad fortune to be handed on to the next generation in associated parcels of genes, income, property and social contacts.

CHAPTER X

ASSORTATIVE MATING AND SOCIAL MOBILITY

In the preceding chapter we simply assumed that a particular Tom Jones chose a particular Mary Smith for his wife, or that a particular Mary Smith chose a particular Tom Jones for her husband, without any discussion of the factors which influenced the choice of mating partners. But the degree to which the fortunate in society tend to marry the fortunate and the unfortunate to marry the unfortunate will have an important effect upon the transmission of inequalities from one generation to the next.

We will argue in this chapter that marriage is basically an equalising factor in the inheritance of endowments. At the same time, however, the selection of marriage partners may help to reinforce the correlation between the different elements of endowment, that is to say, it may help to cause good genes, good social contacts, good education and wealth in property to be combined together. Thus the final result of choice of marriage partners may well be to reinforce the tendency for those who are fortunate or unfortunate to be fortunate or unfortunate in all the basic elements of fortune simultaneously, but, at the same time, to cause the inheritance of such composite fortunes to be more equal than would otherwise be the case.

Let us first consider the possible effects of the choice of marriage partners in reinforcing the combination of the various elements of good or bad fortune. We argued at the end of the last chapter that there was a tendency for the basic components of good or of bad fortune – genes, property and social contacts – to become highly correlated with each other, simply because of the intertwining of the powerful positive feedback influences in the life of any one citizen. And in so far as there is any tendency for the fortunate to marry the fortunate and for the unfortunate to marry the unfortunate these influences which combine the elements of good or bad fortune are likely to be reinforced. Tom Jones marries Mary Smith. Tom Jones may be fortunately endowed with an educational and genetic make-up which turns him into an able, enterprising, perhaps ruthless, but anyhow successful businessman. Mary Smith may be fortunate in being the heiress to much property and endowed with the best social contacts. If in society there is a tendency for the fortunate to marry the fortunate and for the unfortunate to marry the unfortunate, whatever may be the primary cause of their good or bad fortune, then there will be a tendency for Tom Jones's useful genes and education to be joined with Mary Smith's useful property and social contacts. The various elements of basic endowments will become more highly correlated with each other.

In view of these strong forces which are at work in society, causing the basic components of good or bad fortune – genes, property and social contacts – to become highly correlated with each other, we shall start the analysis of the choice of mates by talking of the fortune of a man or woman as if there were some single index of the amount of genetic-property-social-contact 'fortune' which a man or a woman possessed at the time of his or her marriage, and show how marriage is an equalising factor in the inheritance of such a composite fortune.

While there is undoubtedly a tendency for the fortunate to marry the fortunate and for the unfortunate to marry the unfortunate, mating is not perfectly assortative. There will almost certainly be *some* difference between the degrees of fortune of Tom Jones and his mate, Mary Smith; and in view of this the fact that Tom Jones and Mary Smith must mingle their fortunes before they transmit endowments to the next generation will tend to limit the degree of inequalities in family backgrounds and endowments which would otherwise develop.

Let us imagine all the eligible bachelors drawn up in a strictly descending order of their fortunes and all the eligible spinsters similarly drawn up in a strictly descending order of their fortunes. We may say that there is perfect assortative mating if the most fortunate bachelor married the most fortunate spinster, the second most fortunate bachelor the second most fortunate spinster and so on down the two lists.

In this case there would be no averaging of fortunes as the generations succeeded each other. But consider, simply as an intellectual exercise, what might be called perfect anti-assortative mating. Suppose that through some organisational oversight one of the queues got lined up in the wrong direction so that the most fortunate bachelor married the most unfortunate spinster, the second most fortunate bachelor the second most unfortunate spinster, and so on down the bachelors' list and up the spinsters' list. The net result would be a tendency for the complete averaging of family fortunes in one generation, each family ending up with the same joint fortune.[1]

Completely random mating may be defined as the case in which each pair of bachelor and spinster was drawn at random from the two lists.

In fact mating is somewhere between the completely random and the perfectly assortative. A bachelor at a given position in the bachelor's pecking order will not inevitably marry the spinster at the corresponding position in the spinster's pecking order; but the choice is not purely random. The nearer any given bachelor and any given spinster are to the same position in their two pecking orders, the more likely they are to choose each other as mates.

But so long as mating is not perfectly assortative, there is some averaging and equalising tendency at work. If Tom's and Mary's fortunes do not correspond, then the joint family's fortune will be an average of whichever is the greater fortune and of whichever is the lesser fortune. This is an equalising tendency; and if this were the whole of the story, inequalities would progressively disappear as the generations succeeded each other. For as long as differences of fortune persisted there would be a force at work taking two different fortunes, joining them together and averaging them. This force is known as the regression towards the mean. Exceptionally large fortunes would tend to be averaged with lower fortunes, and exceptionally low fortunes with higher fortunes. Fortunes would regress towards the average of fortunes.

As long as mating is not perfectly assortative it will be probable that in any marriage one partner will be more fortunate than the other. The higher will marry below his (or her) own fortune and the lower will marry above his (or her) own fortune. Thus the higher a parent is initially above the average in the pecking order of fortune, the more likely is it that his (or her) offspring will on the average be endowed with a somewhat lower fortune. And conversely the lower the individual parent is below the average in the pecking order of

---

[1] On the assumption that the fortunes of the bachelors and of the spinsters were identically distributed.

fortune, the more likely that his (or her) offspring will be endowed with a somewhat better fortune. This phenomenon will be true of individual parents whether we consider the relationship between fathers and their children or the relationship between mothers and their children.

If this regression towards the mean were the whole of the story we would expect to find society continually moving towards a more and more equal distribution of endowments. But there is another set of forces at work tending all the time to reintroduce inequalities: forces which we may call the forces of dispersion around the average. These forces are expressed in all the elements of luck represented in Figure 20 – genetic luck (L_g), luck in education (L_e), luck in social contacts (L_c), luck in investments (L_i) and luck in one's work (L_w). We may illustrate this dispersion around the average by means of a much simplified genetic example.

Suppose that some genetic ability depended in a simple additive manner upon the quality of two possible allelic forms of one gene at a given locus on a particular chromosome. Let us call the two allelic forms a and b, form a giving a high ability and form b a low ability. Then a father with the pair $F_a F_b$ and a mother with the pair $M_a M_b$ would both have the average of this genetic ability. But of their children one quarter would be likely to inherit $F_a M_a$, one quarter $F_a M_b$, one quarter $F_b M_a$ and one quarter $F_b M_b$. In other words the probability would be that one quarter of their children would be above average, one half would be average, and one quarter would be below average in their genetic ability, even though both parents were of average ability and as a result produced children who *on average* themselves had average ability. This dispersion of their children about the average would restore some degree of inequality in the next generation.[2]

The random mating of average fathers would lead to a similar

----

[2] The genetic mechanism of dispersion can be much more complicated than that which is described in the text for at least three reasons. First, there may be more than two possible allelic forms of a gene occupying a particular locus on a particular chromosome. Secondly, a genetically inherited characteristic may depend upon the interaction of many genes at many different loci on different chromosomes, and not simply upon one particular gene. Thirdly, the interaction of allelic forms of a gene at a particular locus may not simply be additive; one allelic form may be dominant and the other recessive. The result of these three possible complications would be greatly to extend the range of possible dispersion about an average of any given genetically inherited characteristic.

distribution of their children. Suppose some average fathers $(F_a F_b)$ marry above them $(M_a M_a)$, producing half their offspring above the average $(F_a M_a, F_a M_a)$ and half at the average $(F_b M_a, F_b M_a)$. Suppose the same number of average fathers $(F_a F_b)$ marry below them $(M_b M_b)$, producing half their offspring at the average $(F_a M_b, F_a M_b)$ and half below the average $(F_b M_b, F_b M_b)$. In the combination of these two groups, one quarter of the children will be above, one half at, and one quarter below the average.

Indeed, if the allelic forms a and b were equally frequent in the population, perfectly random mating between all men and women would result in this same dispersion, since any child would have an equal chance of drawing any one of the following four possible combinations from the genetic pool: $F_a M_a, F_a M_b, F_b M_a, F_b M_b$.

But if mating were not perfectly random the dispersion would be more marked. Consider the extreme case of perfectly assortative mating. If men above the average $(F_a F_a)$ mated only with women above the average $(M_a M_a)$, all their children would be above the average; and similarly if men below the average mated only with women below the average, all their offspring would be below the average. But, as we have seen, if average men mated only with average women, only half their children would be average, the rest being either above or below the average. Thus with perfectly assortative mating the numbers at the average would be halved in each generation and the whole population would gradually be concentrated into two widely dispersed groups, one above and one below the average.

We have illustrated the forces of dispersion in society in terms of a very simple genetic example. But exactly similar influences are at work in the case of the other basic endowments. We have seen that if we take all the fathers in society with a given level of some genetic endowment, the genetic endowments of the children of these fathers will (i) regress towards the mean because of random mating (these fathers being on average likely to marry less well endowed spouses if we are considering a class of exceptionally highly endowed fathers, or better endowed spouses if we are considering a class of exceptionally poorly endowed fathers), but (ii) will be dispersed around some regressed average value both because of the random mating of their fathers (some marrying girls of exceptionally high and others marrying girls of exceptionally low ability) and (iii) also because of the luck in the genetic draw of the offspring from any particular pool of genes which their particular parents do offer to them.

But these points (i), (ii) and (iii) are all relevant in the case of the other endowments of fortune – namely, education, social contacts and property. We can take the whole class of fathers with any given level of endowments in any of these factors. Their random mating will cause a regression towards the mean in the endowments of their offspring. But the offspring's endowments will be dispersed about this new regressed mean, both because of the random mating of their fathers with wives of different levels of endowment and also because of the luck (L_e, L_c, L_w, L_i) of the offspring in what they are able to acquire from the endowments offered to them by their parents.

The ultimate inequality in the distribution of fortunes can thus be seen as depending upon the interaction of three forces. The less assortative is mating, the greater will be the regression towards the mean; and the greater the regression towards the mean, the greater the forces tending towards equality. But, whatever the degree of regression towards the mean, elements of pure luck, whether genetic, social or economic, will cause a dispersion about the average which might be expected for the children of any set of parents; and the greater the degree of dispersion around the average, the more markedly will inequalities tend to be restored and increased as the generations succeed each other. Finally, the more marked the positive feedbacks and the less marked the negative feedbacks which are discussed in Chapter IX in connection with Figure 20, the greater will be the ultimate inequalities to which these initial inequalities give rise.

It may be of interest to illustrate arithmetically the ultimate steady state degrees of inequality which will result from the interaction of the forces of the regression towards the mean and of the dispersion around the average. Case (a) and (b) of Table VII give a numerical example illustrating the interplay of these two forces. In both cases society tends to reproduce a stable pattern of inequality in the distribution of fortunes. Out of 120 fathers 10 have fortunes of 500, 20 fortunes of 400, 30 fortunes of 300, 20 fortunes of 200 and 10 fortunes of 100. In both cases each father is assumed to have one son and these 120 sons in aggregate have the same distribution of fortunes as do their fathers. But this is not because each son has the same fortune as his father; it is because the average regression towards the mean of the sons relatively to their fathers is offset by a dispersion about the average for each class of sons. But this same stable distribution of fortunes is brought about in case (a) by relatively little

Class of fortune	Number of fathers in class	Class of fortune					Average fortune of sons
		500	400	300	200	100	
500	10	6	3	1	0	0	450
400	20	3	11	6	0	0	385
300	30	1	6	16	6	1	300
200	20	0	0	6	11	3	215
100	10	0	0	1	3	6	150
		10	20	30	20	10	

Number of sons in class

(a)

Class of fortune	Number of fathers in class	Class of fortune					Average fortune of sons
		500	400	300	200	100	
500	10	4	3	2	1	0	400
400	20	3	8	7	1	1	355
300	30	2	7	12	7	2	300
200	20	1	1	7	8	3	245
100	10	0	1	2	3	4	200
		10	20	30	20	10	

Number of sons in class

(b)

Table VII

regression to the mean combined with relatively little dispersion about the average in each class, whereas in case (b) it is brought about by more marked regression towards the mean matched by a greater dispersion about each average.

Consider, for example, the second row of figures. In both cases 20 fathers with fortunes of 400 have 20 sons. In case (a) the average fortune of these sons falls to 385 and in case (b) it falls to 355. But in case (b) the dispersion of these sons over the various sizes of fortune (namely, $3 + 8 + 7 + 1 + 1$) is more evenly spread than in case (a) (namely, $3 + 11 + 6 + 0 + 0$). The same phenomenon is found for the other rows of cases (a) and (b). The greater regression to the mean in case (b) is offset by the wider dispersions of the fortunes of the sons issuing from each class of fathers. In both cases the same structure of inequality in society as a whole repeats itself from generation to generation.

We could conclude as a general principle that in order to reduce basic inequalities as the generations succeed each other it would be desirable (i) to promote random mating, (ii) to offset the impact of those pure strokes of luck in life which reintroduce inequalities by causing a dispersion of attainments about the average which one would otherwise expect and (iii) to mitigate the structural positive feedbacks and to accentuate the structural negative feedbacks in society which cause elements of good or bad fortune to react on each other.

So far we have been considering the degree of assortative mating in terms of a single composite 'fortune'. But as soon as we consider changes which might promote random mating it is necessary to consider the different elements of fortune separately. For it is very possible that while the degree of assortative mating may be reduced in respect of one element of fortune, it may by the same change be simultaneously increased in respect of some other element of fortune.

Consider the effect of social changes which introduce a greater degree of social mobility into society upon the ultimate distribution of the various components of fortune. Consider a society in which members of the fortunate classes consort only with and intermarry only with other members of the fortunate classes and in which members of the unfortunate classes consort only with and intermarry only with other members of the unfortunate classes. Suppose now that changes in social habits occur which break down these rigid social barriers. Members of different classes meet more frequently in clubs, sports and other social institutions. Above all, suppose that they meet as children and young adults more frequently in schools, universities and other places of education. What effect would one expect such a change to have ultimately on the distribution of endowments and so on the distribution of income and property?

Such changes would almost certainly make mating less assortative in terms of property and social contacts. The child of propertied parents with useful social contacts would be more likely than before to meet the child of propertyless parents with less useful social contacts.

But as far as ability to earn is concerned, whether this be due to genetic or to educational fortune, the change might lead to greater assortative mating. In particular the introduction of a system of higher education which was less structured according to social class would tend to bring boys and girls together according to their intellectual ability. This would be particularly true of a university system which ceased to be a finishing school for the sons of gentle-folk and started to provide an education for the able sons and daughters of all classes. Only the able children of gentlefolk would get to the university where, for the first time, they would meet the selected able children of the working class – and this just at the impressionable age when it has been known for young men and women to become fond of each other.

It would be tempting to conclude from this that such social changes might lead to a more equal distribution of property (as mating was less assortative according to property ownership) but a less equal distribution of earnings (as mating was more assortative according to those endowments which led to intellectual ability). But this overlooks the interconnections between the various endowments. High earnings lead to high incomes which enable large properties to be accumulated; and the great potential effects of this relationship will be discussed in the next chapter. It is possible, though not certain, that in the end the more unequal distribution of earning power leading to a more unequal chance of accumulating property would have so potent an effect in increasing inequalities in the ownership of properties that it would outweigh the equalising effects on property of less assortative mating according to property ownership. The easier rise of the meritocratic élite and descent of the aristocratic dud might in the end increase the concentration of property as well as of income at the upper end, unless, of course, offset by govern-mental measures for the redistribution of income and wealth.

All this is only one instance – probably one of the most important instances – of the argument in Chapter VIII that equality of oppor-tunity can be relied upon to produce greater equality of incomes and property only among those who have the same endowments. Where endowments differ, increased equality of opportunity may lead to greater inequalities in the outcome. Greater social mobility certainly leads to great equality of opportunity. The able man or woman from a less fortunate social class has a more equal opportunity with a member from a more fortunate class to obtain a good post. In so far as basic endowments are equal and inequalities have been maintained in society only through irrelevant social rigidities which imply inequalities of opportunity for people of basically equal endowments, greater social mobility will ultimately lead to greater equalities of income and property.

But if basic abilities differ, then in so far as greater social mobility enables greater ability to link itself more easily (and lesser ability to link itself less easily) with social and economic opportunities, and in so far as greater social mobility increases assortative mating on grounds of ability, there are important disequalising forces at work. Society may be faced with the possibility of the rise of a meritocracy which will ultimately increase social divisions, all the bright boys and girls from the less fortunate classes being drained off more promptly into the more fortunate classes and all the dullards from the more fortunate classes falling more rapidly into the less fortunate classes.

Whether greater social mobility and the greater equality of opportunity which it brings with it will ultimately reduce or increase inequalities in the distribution of incomes and property depends upon the degree to which people differ in their basic endowments of ability. It does not, of course, follow that an increase in social mobility should be resisted if it is expected to lead ultimately to greater inequalities. Equality of opportunity is desirable in and for itself; it is only just that people should have the same chances in life. Moreover, equality of opportunity has an important efficiency aspect; it enables people with a given ability to use that ability in the most repaying and productive jobs. All that is implied is that greater equality of opportunity may tend to lead to greater economic inequalities; and in so far as that is the case, it increases rather than decreases the need for other measures for the redistribution of incomes and properties.

CHAPTER XI

THE ACCUMULATION AND INHERITANCE OF PROPERTY

One of the most marked features of the distribution of incomes and property in most competitive economies is the much greater degree of inequality in the distribution of income from property than in that of earned income. In this chapter we shall examine briefly some of the special factors which affect the distribution of property and of income from property.

A preliminary question concerns the definition of the distinction between earned income and income from property. It is not always easy to make this distinction. For example, in the case of a self-employed person with a small workshop it is difficult to say how much of his income represents a payment for his labour and how much a return on the capital invested in his workshop.

The difficulty is even more marked in the case of capital invested in education and training. When funds are invested in someone's education, the resulting training is likely to increase the earning power of the person concerned. Is the resulting increase in his income to be defined as an increase in his earned income or as an increase in his income from property? For some purposes the definition as earned income would seem more natural, but for other purposes the increase in income can most appropriately be regarded as a yield on an expensive capital investment.

From a forward-looking point of view, people may consciously decide to invest in a certain degree and kind of education in order to improve the prospects of earning by the person who is being trained. From this point of view the amount invested in the education is most appropriately regarded as making up part of the income-yielding property of the person who has been trained. The amount of capital so invested may be a large sum, particularly in view of the fact that it should include not only the sums paid on the educational services provided to the pupil (teachers' salaries, cost of school buildings, books, equipment, etc.) but also any earnings foregone by the student during the process of education. The sum invested must represent the amount of real resources which the community could otherwise have used to increase consumption or investment in other lines of activity; and this includes not only the sums spent on school and university fees, etc., but also the wages which the student might have earned if, instead of staying at school or university, he had gone out to work to increase the community's real output.

But from a backward-looking point of view, once a man has received an education and training, the resulting skill becomes simply a factor – like his genetic make-up – affecting his earning capacity. He cannot divest himself of his property in his education any more easily than he can sell his genes. It has become part and parcel of himself; and it is just one of the factors determining his earning capacity.

It is, therefore, rather arbitrary which definition one adopts for a general exposition, provided that one remains aware of the implications of whatever definition one is using. In Figure 20 we have in fact treated increased earnings resulting from education as an increase in earned income (line 28). We have treated any resources which a man's parents have invested in his education (lines 9 and 10) quite separately from any income-yielding capital which he may have received from them (lines 18 and 19).

The inclusion of the amount of resources invested in a man's education as an element of property personally owned by him could in the modern world appreciably affect one's measure of the inequality in the personal ownership of property. Where the government provides free schooling to all citizens up to a certain level of education, there is an important factor at work reducing inequalities in the ownership of property, if such sums are included in personal properties. But even if we made allowances for this factor, the distribution of income from property would remain much less equal than the distribution of earned incomes.

We shall proceed on the basis of Figure 20 and conduct the analysis in terms of personal properties, excluding sums invested in education. In so far as we do this, we are in fact concerning ourselves solely with the marked inequalities in the distribution of property, narrowly defined in this way. However, we are at present concerned with a stylised *laissez-faire* competitive society in which there are no governmental expenditures on education. If education were in fact always privately financed, there would be no reason to expect that it would be an equalising factor. The rich could spend much more than the poor on the education of their children just as they could leave a greater amount of other property to their children than could the poor. There is no reason to believe in these circumstances that the ownership of property including sums invested in education would be more equally distributed than the ownership of property excluding such educational investments.

Let us start the analysis of the accumulation and inheritance of property by considering in isolation those influences which are likely to accentuate inequalities of ownership. In the last chapter we saw that if mating is at all random there will be some tendencies for the averaging and so the equalising of fortunes. Let us, therefore, suppose that the new biologists have made further advances in their arts and have eliminated sex as a method of reproduction, so that Tom Jones is reduced to producing offspring by a process of cloning. He decides to clone one son, who in turn decides to clone one son, and so on down the generations. Thus we have an immortal family with an unchanging genetic make-up and of an unchanging size, passing property down from generation to generation; and in our stylised *laissez-faire* economy there are as yet no death duties or other taxes to impede any process of accumulation.

In this context of a set of immortal families of unchanged genetic make-up, we will pick out and isolate those of the relationships illustrated in Figure 20 which are likely to lead to inequalities in the accumulation of properties. This is done in Figure 21, which abstracts from Figure 20 certain of the relationships which affect the accumulation of capital. For ease of reference the lines in Figure 21 are given the same numbers as the corresponding lines in Figure 20. We take the developments of the earning power of this immortal family as if, given the inborn genetic characteristics of the family, it depended solely upon the outside market forces which determined the wages offered to such persons (W*, lines 29 and 25). We wish to see how in this case the factors affecting the accumulation of capital will, as the generations succeed each other, determine the amount of property accumulated (lines 20, 21, 22, 23 and 24) and the income earned on this property (lines 33, 34, 35, 36, 37 and 16).

These relationships are of the same kind as those which we have explained in connection with Figure 20. In particular we are assuming that the proportion of income saved will be (i) higher, the higher the family's income (line 23) but (ii) lower, the higher the property already accumulated by the family (line 24). In the case of the yield on property we are assuming that the return will be (i) higher, the higher the size of the family property to be invested (line 36) and (ii) higher, the better the family's social contacts (line 37) and thus, indirectly, the higher the existing wealth of the family (line 16).

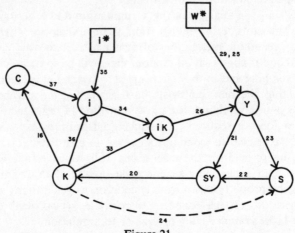

Figure 21

We proceed now to analyse the situation by the application of a simple form of the analysis developed in Chapter XIV of *The Growing Economy*. A family's income is $W + iK$. Let us suppose that its savings will be $S(W + iK) - \theta K$ where S and θ are constant. This expression is intended to illustrate the operation of the two factors which we are assuming to influence savings: (i) since S is constant, savings will be higher, the higher is the family's income $(W + iK)$; and (ii) since θ is constant, savings will be lower, the higher is the family's property (K).

The proportional rate of growth of the family's property is given by the ratio of its annual savings $\{S(W + iK) - \theta K\}$ to its existing stock of property, (K). Let us represent this rate of growth of its property by k, where

$$k = \frac{S(W + iK) - \theta K}{K} = iS - \theta + S(W/K)$$

Suppose that the family can obtain a constant yield on its property; that is to say, suppose that i, as well as S and θ, is constant. Its total savings are $SW + (iS - \theta)K$. We can regard SW as its savings due to its earnings and $(iS - \theta)K$ as its savings due to its ownership of property. We assume the latter element to be positive, i.e. $iS > \theta$.

We can then depict the rate of accumulation of the family's property in Figure 22(a) or (b). Measuring W/K along the horizontal axis and k up the vertical axis we can draw the straight line $k = iS - \theta + S(W/K)$ with i and S constant. We put the family history into a dynamic context by assuming that, as a result of technical progress and capital accumulation in the economy as a whole, its earnings (W) are rising continuously at a proportionate growth rate, w.

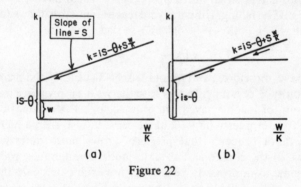

(a) (b)

Figure 22

Since $k = iS - \theta + S(W/K)$ and since i, S and θ are constant, k will be rising if W/K is rising. But W/K will be rising if the growth of W is greater than the growth of K, i.e. if $w > k$. It follows that k will be rising if $w > k$. Conversely, it can be seen that k will be falling if $w < k$.

There are thus two possibilities. In Figure 22(a) we consider the case where $w < iS - \theta$. Since $k = iS - \theta + S(W/K)$ we always have $k > iS - \theta$. In this case, therefore, $w < iS - \theta < k$ so that w is always less than k. But with the rate of growth of earnings (w) always less than the rate of growth of property (k), the ratio of earnings to property (W/K) will always be falling. The family will be continually moving to the left down the line of $k = iS - \theta + S(W/K)$ in Figure 22(a). Property will rise relatively to earnings without any limit.

In Figure 22(b) we examine the case where $w > iS - \theta$. In this case the ratio of earnings to property will reach a stable value at which both earnings and property will grow at the same rate. This can be seen in the following way. Suppose that the family possessed an exceedingly large property so that W/K was negligibly small. Then, since $k = iS - \theta + S(W/K)$, we would have k approximately equal to $iS - \theta$ which, *ex hypothesi*, is less than w. Property would be growing less rapidly than earnings, so that W/K would be growing. If, on the other hand, the family's existing property were very low, so that W/K were exceedingly high, then with $k = iS - \theta + S(W/K)$ we would have an exceedingly high rate of growth of property, k. At the extreme, if the family's property is zero and there are any positive savings at all, the growth rate of property is infinite. Thus with a very small initial property we would have $k > w$, and W/K would be falling. Ultimately we reach an intermediate situation in which $w = k = iS - \theta + S(W/K)$, so that

$$W/K = [w - (iS - \theta)]/S.$$

We have, therefore, two types of family. Type (a) is the property-explosion type of family. In this case the yield on property and the proportion of income saved are both so high that savings out of income from property $(iS - \theta)$ alone serve to give such a high rate of growth of property that property grows more quickly than earnings. In the consequential multi-millionaire families, property and income from property become so important that earnings are relatively quite insignificant. The probability of such property-explosion is reduced by the fact (line 24 of Figures 20 and 21) that as an excessive property is accumulated the incentive to save for further accumulation rather than to spend for current consumption is reduced. We have illustrated this influence by the factor θ. Nevertheless in some cases $iS - \theta$ may remain greater than w in spite of the existence of a positive θ.

The type (b) family may be called the property-stability type of family. In this case both the yield on capital and the proportion of income saved are moderate so that accumulation out of the income from capital alone $(iS - \theta)$ is not sufficient to give a rate of growth of property at a level equal to the rate of growth of earnings (w). In this case a certain proportion of savings must come out of earned income in order to maintain the rate of growth of property at a level equal to the rate of growth of earnings. If property is very high relatively to earnings, savings will be inadequate to bring the rate of growth of property up to the rate of growth of earnings; if property is very low relatively to earnings, savings will be more than sufficient to bring the rate of growth of property up to the rate of growth of earnings; there will result some intermediate ratio of property to earnings which will enable both to expand at the same rate.

Consider now two families of type (b), family 1 being a relatively rich family with relatively high earning capacity and family 2 a relatively poor family with relatively low earning capacity. Since, as we have seen, in stable equilibrium $W/K = [w - (iS - \theta)]/S$ or $K = WS/[w - (iS - \theta)]$ we have

$$\frac{i_1 K_1}{i_2 K_2} = \frac{i_1 W_1 S_1 [w_2 - (i_2 S_2 - \theta_2)]}{i_2 W_2 S_2 [w_1 - (i_1 S_1 - \theta_1)]}.$$

To take a numerical example, suppose that in a state of steady growth the rate of growth of earnings for both families were 3 per cent per annum ($w_1 = w_2 = 0.03$), though the earning capacity of family 1 remained all the time twice as high as that of family 2 $W_1/W_2 = 2$. Suppose that, apart from the θ-factor, the rich family saved 20 per cent and the poor family only 10 per cent of its income ($S_1 = 0.2$ and $S_2 = 0.1$), that the poor family's saving was not yet discouraged by the fact that it already owned much property ($\theta_2 = 0$), whereas the rich family's saving was reduced for this reason ($\theta_1 = 0.005$), and that the rich family could obtain a yield of 10 per cent per annum on its property while the poor family could invest only at 5 per cent per annum ($i_1 = 0.1$ and $i_2 = 0.05$). Then we would have

$$\frac{W_1}{W_2} = 2, \frac{K_1}{K_2} = 6.6, \text{ and } \frac{i_1 K_1}{i_2 K_2} = 13.3$$

While the rich family's earnings would be twice those of the poor family, its property would be more than six times as great and its income from property more than thirteen times as great.

In this chapter we have relied upon a much oversimplified model in order to isolate two factors which cause great inequalities in capital accumulation, namely the greater ability of the rich to save a high proportion of their income and to obtain a high yield on what property they do save. There can be little doubt that these two factors are important contributory causes of the phenomenon of the much greater inequalities in property and incomes from property than in earnings.

The model of capital accumulation which we have presented up to this point in this chapter is grossly oversimplified: (i) we have so far assumed that Tom Jones produces only one son. In the following chapter we will consider the important effect upon inequalities of property which may result from differences in the sizes of families; (ii) we have so far assumed that there are no death duties or other governmental fiscal arrangements which affect the ability of a family to accumulate property over the generations. We shall return to this issue in §4 of Chapter XIII; (iii) by the assumption that sex has been abolished as a method of reproduction, we ruled out of our analysis all the equalising influences of random mating which we discussed in Chapter X.

When we come to apply these equalising influences of random mating, there is an important distinction to be drawn between these equalising forces in so far as they affect the inheritance of genetic good fortune and in so far as they affect the inheritance of property. Until the new biologists have made the necessary advances in their art, it will remain impossible for Tom and Mary Jones to control the genes which they pass on to their children. They cannot decide that little Richard shall inherit all the good genes and little Jane all the bad genes; little Richard and little Jane must both take part in the same lucky dip. But Tom and Mary can decide that little Richard shall inherit all the family property while little Jane shall have none of it; and the laws and customs which regulate the inheritance of property can have a very important effect upon the ultimate degree of inequality in society.

One can illustrate this by means of the following artificial, but nevertheless instructive exercise. Imagine a society in which there is no capital accumulation but a constant stock of property which passes by inheritance from generation to generation. Suppose this property to be shared initially in equal parcels among a privileged 5 per cent of the families. Suppose each set of parents in the community produces the same number of children, equally divided in each family between boys and girls. Suppose every boy and girl survives and gets married and has in turn the same number of boys and girls as did their parents. If each family produces one son and one daughter, then the population will be constant. If each family produces two sons and two daughters, the population will grow, doubling in each generation.

We wish to watch the distribution of property as the generations succeed each other. Table VIII illustrates the way in which the combination of the degree of assortative mating according to property ownership, the growth rate of the population, and the laws and customs affecting the inheritance of property will combine to affect the outcome.

| | Percentage of Population Owning Property | | | |
| | Perfect Assortive Mating | | Completely Random Mating | |
Properties left to:	Stationary population	Growing population	Stationary population	Growing population
1 First son (*or* first daughter)	Percentage constant	Percentage falls (absolute number constant)	Percentage constant	Percentage falls (absolute number constant)
2 First child whether son or daughter	Percentage falls rapidly towards zero (concentration on one family)		Percentage falls slowly towards zero (concentration on one family)	
3 All sons (*or* all daughters)	Percentage constant		Percentage constant	
4 All children sons or daughters	Percentage constant		Percentage rises towards 100% (equality of ownership)	

Table VIII

In the first row of the Table we consider the case in which parents always leave their property to the eldest son. In this case the absolute number of property owners each owning an unchanged amount of property will remain unchanged, since each property owner leaves it all to one son, who leaves it all to one son, and so on *ad infinitum*. In a constant population the percentage of families owning property will, therefore, also remain constant. But in a growing population the constant number of property owners will come to represent a smaller and smaller proportion of the population, as all sons after the first son in each family join the growing ranks of those without property. The analysis would be exactly the same if all families always left all their property to the eldest daughter instead of the eldest son.

In the second row we consider as an instructive intellectual exercise what is probably an unusual set of laws and customs, namely that the whole property is left exclusively to the eldest child whether a boy or a girl. In this case, whether the population be stationary or growing, the ultimate outcome will be for the whole property of the community to be owned by one single individual. Two properties can in this case be joined together in holy matrimony, but once joined they can never be separated, since death does not part them. If an eldest daughter with a property marries an eldest son with a property, this becomes a single property which will be left to the eldest child of the marriage. If that child marries a property-less spouse, the enlarged property remains unchanged; but if he or she in turn marries a propertied spouse, then the already enlarged property is enlarged still further into a still bigger single property.

This process of concentration will continue indefinitely; but the speed with which it occurs will depend upon the degree of assortative mating. If there were perfect assortative mating among property holders, there would be a tendency for the number of property holders to be halved in each generation, since at every generation a male property and a female property would be merged into a single property. If mating were perfectly random, the process of property meeting property would be much slower. But the inexorable final result would be the complete concentration of all properties into a single ownership.[1]

---

[1] We have assumed that each family has one son and one daughter. If we modify this assumption and allow some families to produce only daughters, we can reach the same result (namely, a complete concentration of properties) with a more plausible type of primogeniture, namely that the whole family property is always left to the eldest son or, if there is no son, to the eldest daughter. Once again two properties may be joined together (when a propertied son marries a propertied daughter), but can never be separated, since the resulting enlarged property will always be left to a single heir or heiress. The process of concentration will, of course, be much slower, since propertied daughters will be much rarer than in the case examined in row 2 of Table VIII, but it will nevertheless be inexorable in its gradual operation.

Row 3 of the Table represents the case where only men own property but where, unlike row 1, the property is divided equally among all sons instead of being left only to the eldest son. In the case of the stationary population where each father has only one son, the effect in row 3 is identical with the effect in row 1. But where the population is growing there is a difference between rows 1 and 3. Where only eldest sons inherit, the absolute number of families owning property will remain the same. Where all sons inherit, and where propertied and propertyless families are growing at the same rate, the percentage of families owning property will remain unchanged at its original 5 per cent. Once again the analysis would be unchanged if it were the daughters and not the sons who inherited the whole of the family property.

Neither in row 1 nor in row 3 does the degree of assortative mating have any effect upon the result. Indeed, the degree of assortative mating is in these cases meaningless; since either all women or all men are propertyless, there is no meaning to be attached to the degree to which men and women select spouses with properties similar to their own.

In row 4, however, the absence of perfect assortative mating is crucial. We consider now the case where properties are split up equally among all children, whether they be sons or daughters. If there were perfect assortative mating, properties would remain in the ownership of a privileged 5 per cent of the population as in row 3. It makes no difference whether a property is left only to the sons in a family, or whether it is left half to the sons and half to the daughters, provided that these sons and daughters take as spouses the similarly endowed daughters and sons of similarly propertied families. Whether a whole property passes from a father to his sons who then marry propertyless wives or whether a half property passes to his sons who then marry wives who have received a similar half share of a similar property makes no difference to the property which they can then hand on to their children.

But if mating is not perfectly assortative, the difference between rows 3 and 4 is decisive. When properties are divided equally between sons and daughters and when the propertied sons may marry the daughters of propertyless parents and the propertied daughters may marry the sons of propertyless families, properties will be spread over a larger and larger number of the population. In the end there will result a complete equalisation of property ownership. If any properties of unequal size remained, sooner or later they would meet, marry and be averaged before being left to the next generation. Inequalities could thus be reduced; they could never be reintroduced. The smaller the degree of assortative mating, the quicker the process of equalisation.

In fact, of course, the process of equalisation depicted in the bottom right-hand box of Table VIII would not go unchecked. The situations depicted in Table VIII are based upon a number of very extreme abstractions from the conditions ruling in the real world with the express purpose of isolating for consideration one important set of factors. But the regression towards the mean in the case of the bottom right-hand box of Table VIII would, in fact, be offset by many factors causing a new dispersion of properties. First, some families would have more luck than others in investing their properties and thus adding to or subtracting from their value (L_i in Figure 20). Nor would each family in fact have exactly the same number of children, so that different properties would be continually resplit into different-sized fragments. Moreover, in Table VIII we have not allowed for the accumulation of new properties. When we do make allowance for capital accumulation, we must recognise that families would not accumulate additions to their inherited properties all at the same rate at the same time. Genetic luck, educational luck, luck in social contacts or luck in a job (L_g, L_e, L_c and L_w of Figure 20) would cause differences in earned incomes. If higher incomes lead to a higher proportion of income saved and if higher properties lead to a higher return on property (lines 23 and 36 of Figures 20 and 21), then on the basis of the earlier analysis in this chapter we may expect inequalities in accumulated properties to reappear. All that is maintained is that an equal distribution of properties among all the children of a family, combined with a minimum degree of assortative mating according to property ownership, will be a powerful factor tending to restrain the growth of inequalities in the ownership of property.

The difference between lines 3 and 4 of Table VIII also serves to illustrate a very important social phenomenon. Suppose that customs alter in such a way that parents who used to discriminate against their daughters by leaving all or most of their property to their sons start to divide their properties much more evenly between their sons and their daughters. The immediate result will be a much more equal distribution of property among individuals since the inequalities as between the sexes will be reduced. If one looks simply at the statistics of the distribution of wealth as between individual holders of property, inequalities will have fallen simply because the women as well as the men in any one property class now hold property.

This sexual equality is in itself a most important social change. But it does not in itself imply any direct diminution of interclass inequalities. Rich families may still remain as rich as before when husband and wife each own half the family property instead of the husband owning the whole of it. But, as the distinction between lines 3 and 4 of Table VIII make clear, if mating is not completely assortative, then the splitting up of properties between daughters as well as sons will ultimately help to reduce interclass inequalities as well as intersex inequalities. As long as sons only inherit property, random mating can have no effect in equalising family properties. But as soon as daughters as well as sons inherit, marriages mating rich men with poor women or mating rich women with poor men can help to promote interclass equality.

There is another dimension of inequality in the ownership of properties – namely, the intertemporal distribution between the young and the old at any one given date – which will be much affected by laws and customs relating to gifts and inheritances. Whether parents distribute their property among their children in part by gift during their own lives or whether they retain their properties intact until they die may be affected by governmental policies (for example, by differences in the rates of taxes on gifts and on inheritances at death) and by social conventions and customs. A change which led to an increased tendency for parents to pass on part of their properties by gift during their lives would reduce inequalities in the individual ownerships of properties by splitting a given property up between the old and the young instead of leaving the young without property. This increase in inequality of property ownership as between the young and the old, as in the case of the increase in equality of property ownership as between men and women, may well be desirable in and for itself. But whereas increased equality between men and women will, as we have seen, lead indirectly to increased equality as between the rich and poor classes in society, there is no reason to believe that increased equality between young and old will have any effect upon interclass distribution.

In so far as parents retain their properties until their deaths, the distribution of inherited property as between young and old will be determined by demographic factors. Thus, to take an extreme example, suppose that all parents married and had children at the age of twenty and lived until the age of eighty, by which time their children would be sixty years of age: in such a society there would be an extreme concentration of inherited property in the hands of the elderly between the ages of sixty and eighty, whereas no one below the age of sixty would have inherited any property. Early marriage and late death would concentrate the ownership of property among the elderly.

These particular demographic factors would affect the distribution of the ownership of property as between the old and the young, but not as between one class and another in society. However, there are other demographic factors which may have important effects on interclass distribution; and to these we shall turn in the next chapter.

CHAPTER XII

DIFFERENTIAL FERTILITY

Up to this point we have neglected the fact that fertility and mortality rates may differ as between the different classes in society. But differences in these fundamental demographic determinants, as between the fortunate and the unfortunate members of society, can have important implications for the distribution of income and property.

Suppose then that mortality rates were the same for all classes of society but that fertility rates were higher among the unfortunate than among the fortunate. This would result in two phenomena, both of which have important effects upon the distribution of incomes and properties.

First, the dependency ratio, i.e. the ratio of non-earning to earning members of the family, would be higher in the unfortunate than in the fortunate families.

Second, the rate of growth of population among the unfortunate would be higher than among the fortunate classes in society.

In order to discuss these matters in a clear and simple, if rather imprecise, manner,[1] we will talk of three age groups in society – young, middle aged and elderly – which for the sake of dramatic effect we will call children, parents and grandparents. Given the mortality rates in a population, the higher the fertility rates (i) the more rapidly will the population be growing, and (ii) the higher will be the proportion of children to parents and of parents to grandparents. This last effect upon the age distribution is easily explained by the fact that, if fertility was high in the past, then any given number of grandparents will have given birth in the past to a large number of present parents; and if present fertility rates are high, this number of present parents will have given birth to an exceptionally large number of present children.

---

[1] A more precise, formal and tedious discussion is to be found in Chapter X of *The Growing Economy*.

A population with high fertility will thus have a relatively small number of elderly grandparents but a relatively large number of young children. It is not clear, therefore, at once whether the dependency ratio will have gone up or down. In fact the increased burden of children is likely to outweigh the reduced burden of grandparents for a number of reasons. Population structures and maintenance costs are in fact such that child numbers are more important than the numbers of grandparents in determining dependency ratios; and the burden of child dependency relatively to that of elderly dependency is intensified by the fact that women of working age are more likely to be kept at home, and thus away from the possibility of supplementing the earned income of the family, by the need to look after small children than by the need to amuse Granny and Grandpa.

Differences in rates of mortality between one population and another can also affect both the dependency ratio and the rates of growth of different populations. But the effects of a reduction in mortality rates are more ambiguous, since they depend upon which mortality rates are reduced. Thus a fall in infant mortality rates is more or less equivalent in its demographic effects to a rise in fertility rates, since it makes little difference to the growth and structure of a population (though it may make all the difference in the world in terms of human joys and sorrows) whether more babies are born subject to unchanged infant mortality or whether the same number of babies are born subject to reduced infant mortality. At the other extreme a reduction in mortality rates among grandmothers who have passed the age of child-bearing will have no effect whatsoever upon the ultimate rate of growth of the population but will mean simply and solely a higher number of surviving grandmothers in any given population. It will increase the dependency ratio at the elderly end without affecting the rate of growth of the population.

Other possible effects can occur through a reduction of mortality rates among other age groups.[2] We shall not enter into these possibilities here but will confine our attention in this chapter to the case in which mortality rates are the same for the fortunate and for the unfortunate members of society, but in which fertility rates may differ. We do this for three reasons: first, because the effects of differential fertility are less ambiguous than those of differential

[2] See Chapter X of *The Growing Economy*.

mortality and provide therefore an easier exercise in economic-demographic analysis; secondly, because in a modern developed economy differences in mortality rates are in fact less than differences in fertility rates; and, thirdly, because when one considers policy measures one will wish to reduce mortality as much as possible for all classes (no one would advocate reducing the rate of growth of a population by taking steps to increase infant mortality) but one may seriously consider measures designed to effect fertility rates for economic reasons.

Let us then consider the effects on the distribution of incomes and properties of a state of affairs in which mortality rates are the same in all classes but in which fertility rates are higher in the unfortunate than in the fortunate families.

The first effect will be that the ratio of dependent to income-earning members of the family will be higher in the unfortunate than in the fortunate families. This has an obvious, direct effect in increasing inequalities in the real standard of living.[3] The fact that it is obvious means that it needs no more discussion, but this does not mean that it is unimportant.

The second effect will be that the unfortunate families will be growing more rapidly than the fortunate. The ultimate effects of this phenomenon on the distribution of incomes and properties are somewhat less obvious. In order to discuss them one must distinguish between the different component elements of good and bad fortune.

Parents who have five instead of two children can leave to each child only one fifth instead of one half of their own property. The larger the number of children, the more fragmented will be the ownership of property in the next generation. But parents who have five instead of two children can endow their children in each case with the same average genetic qualities. A genetically able parent can, as it were, leave all his ability to each child regardless of the number of his children, whereas he can leave only a *pro rata* proportion of his property to each child.

We can put the distinction this way. Suppose that the fertility of the fortunate were to rise and that of the unfortunate were to fall. As we have already pointed out, the fortunate parents would probably be able to accumulate somewhat smaller properties since

---

[3] Cf. Chapter IV, page 57 above.

they would have to support more children (line 51 in Figure 20) and, on the assumption that the custom was to leave property equally divided among all children in the family, these somewhat smaller properties would be split into a larger number of fragments (line 19 in Figure 20). Thus if parents have more children, each child can inherit a smaller share of what is probably a smaller total property. Conversely the less fortunate families having a smaller number of children to support might be able to accumulate somewhat larger properties, and in any case whatever properties they did accumulate would be less liable to be split into small fragments on the death of the parents. The effect of the differential fertility would undoubtedly be to mitigate inequalities in the ownership of property.

But there would be no such tendency to equalise genetic endowment. Having a large number of children in no way diminishes a parent's total genetic stock nor does it mean that this stock must be split into smaller fragments. An increase in the fertility of the fortunate relative to that of the unfortunate may raise the average quality of genetic endowments. But to equalise genetic endowment one would need to reduce the fertility both of the exceptionally fortunate and of the exceptionally unfortunate relative to the fertility of those with average fortune. No more geniuses and no more dullards, but only men and women of mediocre ability is the prescription for equalising genetic endowment, whereas many heirs for the rich and few heirs for the poor is the prescription for equalising property endowments.

Endowments in social contacts probably fall in this respect in between genetic endowments and property endowments. There are certain elements of social contact and atmosphere in the home which, like genetic endowments, can be enjoyed by all the children in the family, however few or many they may be. There are others which cost money (such as membership of a club or of an expensive school) and such outlays, like property inheritance, if spent on Richard are not available to be spent on Jane. There are other elements which are intermediate; to have four instead of two children to bring up may mean that each child gets somewhat less attention, but probably more than half as much attention, from his parents.

To summarise, we could expect a fall in the fertility of the most unfortunate to tend

(1) immediately to raise the average standard of living and to reduce

inequalities in the standard of living by reducing dependency ratios among the least fortunate,

(2) ultimately to raise the average of property holdings and to reduce inequalities in property holdings by reducing the fragmentation of small properties on each generational transmission,

(3) ultimately to raise the average of genetic endowments and to reduce the degree of inequality in the distribution of genetic endowments by reducing the numbers of the least well endowed, and

(4) ultimately to raise the average of social endowments and to reduce the degree of inequality in such endowments partly by reducing the number of the least well endowed and partly by reducing the fragmentation of the smaller endowments on each generational transmission.

The effects of a fall in the fertility of the least fortunate are thus consistently to raise the average, and to reduce the degree of inequality, in the various endowments. A change in the fertility of the most fortunate does not have quite such clear-cut results because of the differences in genetic and environmental inheritance which we have discussed in this chapter.

We may summarise by saying that a rise in the fertility of the most fortunate will tend

(1) immediately to lower the average standard of living and to reduce inequalities in the standard of living by increasing dependency ratios among the most fortunate,

(2) ultimately to lower average property holdings and to reduce inequalities in property holdings by increasing the fragmentation of large properties on each generational transmission,

(3) ultimately to raise the average of genetic endowments and to increase the degree of inequality in such endowments by increasing the numbers of the best endowed, and

(4) ultimately, (i) in so far as social endowments like property endowments must be fragmented among heirs, to lower the average of such endowments and to reduce inequalities in such endowments by increasing the fragmentation of the large endowments, but (ii) in so far as social endowments like genetic endowments need not be fragmented among heirs, to raise the average of such endowments and to increase the degree of inequality in such endowments by increasing the number of the best endowed.[4]

[4] In Chapter VII (pages 125–30 above) we drew a distinction between a Contraction of the Poor or of the Rich on the one hand and a Dilution of Poverty or of

Riches on the other hand. We have in fact a close analogy in the distinction between genetic inheritance and the inheritance of property. In so far as poor genetic endowment is concerned, a *reduction* in the number of children in a poorly endowed family implies simply a reduction in the number of persons with a given low endowment per head, i.e. a Contraction of the number of the Poorly Endowed. If, however, we are concerned with the fragmentation of properties, a *reduction* in the number of children in a family with little property will raise inherited property per head and we shall have a case of the Dilution of a Poor Endowment in Property.

In the case of those who are fortunately endowed, once again a *reduction* in the number of children will simply mean a Contraction of the number of the Well Endowed, in so far as we are concerned with genetic endowment. But an *increase* in the number of children who are to share an exceptionally large property will be needed in order to achieve any Dilution of a Rich Endowment in Property.

CHAPTER XIII

A CATALOGUE OF REDISTRIBUTIONAL
POLICIES

Up to this point we have discussed, first, what constitutes a desirable distribution of incomes and properties (Chapters IV to VI) and, second, what are the causes of the perpetuation of gross inequalities in society (Chapters VIII to XII). There remains for discussion the range of policies which might be adopted in order to bring the actual distribution of incomes and properties more closely into line with the desired distribution.

We do not, however, intend in this volume to tackle in any detail these problems of the choice of distributional policies. The reason is a simple one. Every policy which one might adopt in order to influence the distribution of incomes and properties will have other effects and, in particular, will affect the efficiency of the economic system. Consider, for example, the possible effects of a policy of taxes and subsidies devised in order to transfer present income directly from the rich to the poor. The possible effects of this re-distributional fiscal policy may be enumerated under eight heads:

(1) There will be the designed direct effect on the redistribution of income between the rich and the poor of the present generation.

(2) The redistributional fiscal policy may affect the total demand for goods and services, for example by changing incentives to save income rather than to spend it on consumption or by changing incentives to borrow funds to spend on investment in new capital equipment. If total demand is to be stabilised, these effects on total expenditures will have to be offset by counterbalancing inflationary or deflationary changes in general monetary or budgetary policies, whose effects must be taken into account in the final assessment.

(3) Even if the redistributional fiscal policy has no net effect upon the total demand for goods and services, it may affect the relation-ship between consumption and investment, causing, for example, a higher proportion of the national income to be spent on consump-

tion and a lower proportion to be saved and invested in capital equipment to the detriment of future generations. Thus the redistributional fiscal policy which was designed primarily to transfer incomes between the rich and the poor of the current generation may have indirect effects upon the distribution of income between the present and future generations.

(4) The redistributional fiscal policy may have effects upon incentives to work.

(5) It may have effects upon incentives to take risks.

(6) It may have effects upon the allocation of effort and of other resources as between different occupations or industries or regions.

(7) It may have effects upon fertility or mortality and so upon the size and composition of the future population.

(8) Finally – a point which is too often neglected in economic analysis – the application of the policy (for example, the assessment and collection of any new taxes involved) will impose administrative costs on the part both of the fiscal authorities and also of those who are subject to the fiscal intervention.

All these effects must be taken into account in the final assessment of the value of any particular economic policy, and many of these effects are concerned with economic efficiency rather than with the distribution of incomes and properties. For this reason it would involve intolerable repetition to discuss in detail the problems of redistributional economic policies in this volume and then on a subsequent occasion to discuss the efficiency aspects of the same catalogue of economic policies. Accordingly, on the plan outlined in the Preface to this volume, we shall confine ourselves at present to the presentation of a mere catalogue of policies which might be designed to have a significant effect upon the distribution of incomes and policies together with a very brief commentary upon them. In the next volume, namely *The Efficient Economy*, we intend to consider different forms of economic inefficiency and the various reasons which are likely to give rise to them, together with a succinct catalogue of the sort of policies which might be designed expressly to correct such economic inefficiencies. Finally in a closing volume, namely *The Mixed Economy*, we intend to discuss in more detail the balance of advantage and disadvantage in the adoption of different economic policies and institutions, taking into account the whole range of effects of those policies and institutions upon all the various economic objectives discussed in the preceding volumes.

Accordingly we close this volume with a catalogue of, and a brief commentary upon, the types of policy which might be adopted with the express purpose of affecting the distribution of incomes and properties. We do so under eight headings.

§1   *The Promotion of Competitive Conditions*

A first set of measures designed to equalise incomes is the removal of restrictive practices and other impediments to competitive conditions which prevent people from moving themselves and their resources from low-paid to high-paid occupations, industries, or regions. One great attraction of measures of this kind is that there is no conflict between the objectives of economic equality and of economic efficiency. When a restrictive practice which maintains an unduly high, monopolistic reward in a privileged and protected occupation is removed, the entry of new persons from lower-paid, unprivileged, unprotected occupations represents an increase in economic efficiency as well as an increase in economic equality.

In this category of measures to promote competitive conditions one may include measures (such as those discussed in Chapter XXIV of *The Controlled Economy*) which are designed to ensure that the general level of wage rates is not forced up by trade union action to a degree which causes either an explosive inflation or unnecessary unemployment. The inability of an unemployed man or woman to move into employment because the real wage rate for those in employment is maintained by monopolistic action at an unduly high level is only an extreme example of an interference with competitive conditions which causes both an economic inefficiency (the loss of output through unemployment) and an economic inequality (the difference between the unemployment benefit of the unemployed and the wage-earnings of the employed.)

Unfortunately there are three important reasons why one cannot rely solely upon the maintenance of competitive conditions to ensure simultaneously both economic efficiency and economic equality.

In the first place insistence upon competition between a large number of independent agents is incompatible with economic efficiency in those cases where, for technical reasons, efficiency demands that production be organised on so large a scale that there is not room in the market for a large number of independent competing units.

Second, the movement of resources from a low-paid to a high-paid occupation may be costly; for example, a worker and his family cannot move from a region in which wage rates are low to a region in which they are high without incurring considerable costs. In some cases these costs of movement might be great enough to maintain substantial differences in incomes as between different occupations, industries and regions, even though there were perfectly competitive conditions in each individual occupation, industry and region;[1] and in any case it is economically inefficient for the movement to take place if the real cost of movement is greater than the real increase in productivity of the factors which move.

Third, competitive conditions will tend to equalise incomes only between persons who are equally endowed with income-earning assets. But, as we have considered at length in Chapters IX to XII, individuals may differ greatly in their basic endowments of genes, education, social contacts and inherited property. Competitive conditions can ensure equality of opportunity for those who are equally well endowed; but this will, of course, result in inequalities of income as between those who are fortunate and those who are unfortunate in their basic endowments.

§2 *The Regulation of Particular Prices and Quantities*

The distribution of real income may be affected by measures which regulate the prices and/or ration the consumption of particular goods and services. For example, by instituting an equal ration of clothing for all consumers, rich and poor alike, the rich may be prevented from bidding up the price of clothing by their excessive demands against the interests of the poor. Or a control over the price which may be charged for a particular commodity or service may assist the consumers at the expense of the producers of that good or service; and if the consumers are poor and the producers are rich this will have an equalising effect upon the distribution of real incomes.

---

[1] The outstanding case in which the cost of movement is prohibitive is as between different periods of time. A worker of the hungry forties of the nineteenth century could not arrange at any cost for his soul to be sent back to heaven in order to be reborn in the better-paid fifties of the twentieth century. Such mobility can be achieved only by policies which reduce fertility at one point of time and increase it at another.

Action of this kind is liable to raise in an acute form a clash between the objectives of economic equality and of economic efficiency. Prices play a dual role: they can contribute to economic efficiency by inducing people to increase the supply and to economise in the use of things which are scarce and to turn to the substitute use of things which are plentiful; at the same time they will raise the incomes of those who are lucky enough to find themselves engaged in the production of scarce goods and services relatively to those who are unlucky enough to find themselves engaged in the production of plentiful goods and services. To hold down the price of the scarce goods and services in order to prevent this effect upon the distribution of real incomes is liable to remove the incentives to produce more of the scarce and less of the plentiful goods and to shift from the consumption of the scarce to the consumption of the plentiful goods.

Circumstances may, of course, exist in which there is no such clash between the objectives of economic efficiency and of economic equality. Thus in the case of a commodity which is inevitably produced under monopolistic conditions (because, for example, economies of large scale are so important that there is not room in the market for a large number of efficient competing concerns), it may be desirable on grounds of economic efficiency to impose a price control which removes the ability of the monopolist to make an excess profit by restricting output and thus raising his selling price above his costs of production. If the monopolist is rich and if the consumers of his product are poor, then the regulation of a maximum selling price for the product will increase both economic efficiency and economic equality.

But monopolists are not necessarily rich and consumers are not necessarily poor. If the monopolist were poor relatively to his consumers, then the price control would increase economic efficiency but would reduce economic equality. In fact situations are likely to be mixed. The monopoly profits of a large concern are likely to be distributed in dividends to many shareholders, some of whom are rich and some poor; the monopolistic dividends on the shares held in a pension fund may, for example, be supporting the income of a poor widow. At the same time among the many purchasers of the products of the monopolistic concern there are likely to be both poor individuals and rich individuals. The control of the price of the monopolistic concern will be in the interests of economic efficiency and it will improve economic equality in so far as the shareholders are richer than the customers; but it will worsen economic equality in so far as the customers are rich and the shareholders poor.

The organisation of an otherwise unnecessary monopolistic arrangement may help to improve the distibution of income. For example, measures which impose restrictions on the amount of produce which farmers may bring to market will help to maintain the selling price of farm products. This will improve the incomes of the farmers at the expense of the consumers of farm produce. But even though there may be many poor peasant farmers and a number of well-to-do consumers of food, by no means all farmers are poor and by no means all consumers of food are rich. The monopolistic intervention in the agricultural market will have subsidised some rich farmers at the expense of some poor consumers.

For these reasons one may start with a hunch that in general it is desirable to use the price mechanism in the interests of economic efficiency and to rely on more direct measures (and, in particular, on those of the kind discussed under § 8 below) to transfer purchasing power from the rich to the poor. But this cannot be regarded as an absolutely immutable principle. The progressive taxes on the rich and subsidies to the poor which are needed to make direct transfers of purchasing power from the rich to the poor may also introduce inefficiencies into the economic system through their adverse effects upon incentives to work, take risks and save. In general a given degree of redistribution may be achieved at a lower loss of efficiency through direct than through indirect transfers of purchasing power. But this is not necessarily invariably the case.

The amount of damage to efficiency caused by the regulation of particular prices will depend upon the extent to which the quantities of goods supplied and demanded respond to the distortion of prices. If the price distortions had no effect on quantities, there then would be no consequential misallocation of resources and thus no loss of economic efficiency. Suppose, therefore, that one could find two goods, X and Y, X being consumed exclusively by the rich and Y exclusively by the poor and the price elasticities of demand for X and for Y being both zero. To tax the price of X and to subsidise the price of Y would in this case simply transfer real purchasing power from the rich to the poor without the price change having any direct effect upon the use of resources. It would be equivalent to a lump-sum tax on the rich (equal to the quantity of X consumed by the rich multiplied by the rise in the price of X) combined with a lump-sum subsidy to the poor (equal to the quantity of Y consumed by the poor multiplied by the reduction in the price of Y). Alternatively suppose that one could find two goods X' and Y', X' being produced exclusively by rich men and Y' by poor men, and the price elasticities of supply of both X' and Y' being zero. Then a tax on X' and a subsidy to Y' would transfer real income from the rich producers of X' to the poor producers of Y' without any distortion in the levels of production. It is the difficulty of finding goods consumed (or produced) almost exclusively either by the rich or by the poor and for which the price elasticity of demand (or supply) is very low which gives rise to the hunch that it may be better to rely on the direct transfer of purchasing power than on the manipulation of relative prices as a means of improving the distribution of income.

§3   *The Public Provision of Social Goods*

An extreme form of the regulation of the prices and quantities of particular goods and services which we have discussed under §2 is the provision by the State to all citizens free of charge of certain services such as education and health. In this case we may regard the situation as one in which every citizen is given a quantitative ration of the good (e.g. so many years of education), the price being controlled at zero. Such a public provision of a free social service will clearly have an important equalising effect – indeed, such an equalising effect is often the basic reason for the arrangement – so long as the free social service is financed out of taxation which falls more heavily on the rich than on the poor· An equal ration for everyone financed by the taxation of the rich is clearly a major equalising institution.

But the question immediately arises whether this is the most efficient way of achieving the redistribution of real incomes. Why should one not apply to this extreme case the general conclusion of §2 against the use of such particular interventions? Why should it not be better to redistribute income directly from the rich to the poor and then let individuals buy their own educational and health services in free, private, competitive markets for schools and medicine?

There are three kinds of redistributional consideration which may be thought to justify a more direct intervention by the State in the provision of such social services.

First, outstandingly in the case of education and to a limited degree in the case of health, the question arises of the distribution of resources between one generation and the next. Should the State leave it to the free choice of parents whether, and if so to what extent, they should educate their children? The children cannot decide for themselves, and school learning which has been missed can only with difficulty, if at all, be repaired at an advanced age. If the principle is accepted that it is right that the State should concern itself with the redistribution of welfare between the rich and the poor, is it unreasonable that it should also concern itself with the distribution of welfare between parents and their children by ensuring that the parents invest a certain amount of their resources in their children's welfare through expenditure on their education? If this line of argument is accepted, then it is insufficient merely to transfer income from rich to poor parents; it becomes necessary also to ensure that some of that income is devoted to the children's education and health.

Second, the consideration raised in the previous paragraph would be met by some scheme for educational vouchers whereby parents were in effect given certain amounts of money which could be spent only on their children's education. The educational services could then be provided by private enterprise, subject to the provision that such services were of a given minimum educational standard. Parents would be free to choose the particular education for their children; and, if they so chose and were financially able to do so, they could spend private sums in addition to the State vouchers upon the further education of their children. But the redistributional argument for State intervention in the provision of educational services may be carried a step further. As we have argued in Chapter IX, a citizen's educational background and his social contacts are intimately interrelated. If all children go to the same school, whatever the social and economic status of their family backgrounds, there will be an important influence breaking down social barriers and reducing assortative mating. If it is desired to promote equality by equalising social and educational endowments, then there is an argument for encouraging State schools open to all classes at the expense of private schooling which may result in the concentration of the children of rich parents in one type of school which provides a more expensive and socially more select education than that provided at the schools attended by the children of poor parents. The extreme form of such policy is to require all children in a given district to go to the same State school. A less extreme form is to provide State schooling free of charge (i.e. with a 100 per cent subsidy) without giving any State financial support to private schooling.

Third, outstandingly in the case of health services and to a limited degree in the case of education, a desirable redistribution of resources will not be an egalitarian one but one which is based on needs. Not all children have the same educational needs. But, even more obviously, a healthy citizen does not need so large an income to spend on medical services as does a citizen who is ill. A simple distribution of income from the rich to the poor does not, therefore, adequately meet the situation. But if medical resources are to be distributed according to medical needs, one cannot leave the individual citizen to judge his or her own needs, partly because the individual citizen will not have the required technical knowledge and partly because with a free provision of any good the consumer will have no incentive to economise in his own use of that good. In the health service it will be the same set of persons – namely, the doctors – who must both judge the patient's needs and provide the medical service. The direct finance of the service by the State is the obvious straightforward administrative arrangement in this case.

There are at least two arguments concerning economic efficiency which may apply to State intervention in the provision of such social services as health and education.

First, there are important social benefits from a healthy and well-educated population which do not enter into the private calculus of cost and gain. In the case of infectious diseases, for example, the cure of citizen A will not merely be of direct benefit to citizen A; it will also indirectly protect citizens B, C, D and E from infection and from suffering from the disease. As far as education is concerned, communication and co-operation is much easier between literate and numerate persons than between illiterate and innumerate persons; and ease of communication and co-operation is essentially a social good. It is no use citizen A being able to write a message if citizen B cannot read it. Where social benefits exceed private benefits there is a well-established case for State promotion of the activity in question.

Second, the scale of efficient operations for a school or for a hospital may mean that there is room for only one such instituton in a given region or district. In this case the question arises, as in the case of other forms of productive industry, whether the desirable control of the resulting monopoly is best met by State socialisation of the activity in question.

There are thus many arguments both of a distributional and of an efficiency kind which must be assessed together in order to consider the best extent and form of State intervention in such social services as health and education. Nor do these distributional and efficiency aspects cover all the considerations which need to be taken into account. Particularly in the case of education, where freedom of thought and the need for experimentation in ideas are specialy desirable, there may be conflict between the objectives of equality of income, on the one hand, and of freedom and diversity of ideas, on the other hand.

Nor, of course, does the public provision of free health and educational services remove the possibility of conflict between the objectives of efficiency and equality within such services. The resources to be allocated to a State health service cannot be un-limited. How far should such limited resources be devoted to the possibly expensive prolongation of life and relief of severe suffering by old persons who are incurably ill and how far to the restoration of a full, healthy, productive life for young adults who are suffering from less painful but curable ills? The former category may have greater nccds from a distributional point of view, whereas investment in the cure of the latter category may have much more efficient effects in promoting production and the maintenance of real output per head in the community.

A similar possible conflict between the objectives of equality and efficiency may well occur in the design of educational services. Some children will have greater innate capacities than others. It is possible that in some conditions the return, measured in terms of extra productive ability, resulting from the education of able children will be much greater than the return to a similar amount of educational resources devoted to less able children. The efficient use of educa-tional resources is to apply them where the return in terms of future earnings is greatest. But this policy could imply adding extra educational endowment to those who start in any case with above-average genetic endowment. The objective of equality would require one to devote educational resources to the dullards in the hope that their extra educational endowment might help to offset their below-average genetic endowment.[2]

Nor, of course, is it necessary that the whole of the health or educational services should be treated in an exactly similar manner. In particular the first stages of education up to compulsory school-leaving age are likely (i) to be equalising (since every child receives such education) and (ii) to entail very considerable social benefits (since every child is receiving the minimum needs of literacy, numeracy and knowledge of the social culture to be able to communicate and co-operate with others).

But in the later stages of higher education the situation is more complicated. Higher education, unlike primary education, is not universal. Only a limited proportion of young men and women will be so educated. An expansion of such education over a greater proportion of the population will increase the number of skilled, highly trained persons and will reduce the number of unskilled, little-trained persons. It will for this reason tend to reduce inequalities of earnings by making the skilled more plentiful and the unskilled less plentiful relatively to the demand for them.[3] In so far as this influence is at work an expansion of higher education will increase equality. But it will not necessarily increase efficiency. If it is carried too far the pay of the higher trained will decline relatively to the pay of the untrained members of society to such an extent that the return at the margin on resources invested in the expansion of higher education will have fallen below the level of return which could have been earned on those resources if they had been invested in other forms of capital equipment.

[2] Such a possible conflict between the objectives of equality and efficiency in educational policy tends to reinforce the general conclusion of §2. The emphasis on efficiency in educational policy can properly be the more marked, the more effective are any direct measures for the subsequent direct transfer of income from the rich (i.e. those who have above-average educational and genetic endowments) to the poor (i.e. those who are below average in such endowments).

[3] In modern developed societies the supply of the skilled labour force which has received higher education is generally increasing relatively to the supply of those with little training. On the other hand technologies tend to become more sophisticated so that the demand for high skills is increasing relatively to the demand for unskilled workers. Whether there will result an absolute reduction or an absolute increase in the differentials between the pay of the skilled and that of the unskilled depends upon the relative speeds of the increases in the supply of, and in the demand for, skilled manpower.

But higher education is not only not universal; it is also highly selective. In so far as this involves adding extra educational endowment exclusively to those who are expressly selected because they are already endowed with a high innate ability, the process is a disequalising one, since it adds educational good fortune exclusively to those who are already blessed with genetic good fortune; and this disequalising effect will be particularly marked if equal opportunity for higher education increases assortative mating between those who are genetically well endowed (see Chapter X pages 166–8).

In addition to these possible disequalising effects of higher education, it is also true that the additional knowledge and skill acquired from higher education are likely to be of chief benefit directly to the student concerned who is thus equipped with income-earning professional and technical skills, whereas, as we have seen above, the primary education of a young child is likely to entail important social benefits for other members of society.

The case for the State provision of free education to all at the first stages is, therefore, much stronger both on distributional and efficiency grounds than in the case of the later stages of higher education for the selected few. In these later stages there is thus a case for a system which is less strictly subject to State control and in which a greater part of the finance is met privately by the select minority who will gain from the educational investment.[4]

§4   *The Redistribution of Private Property*
In so far as the public provision of social services which we have discussed in §3 is used as an instrument for the equalisation of incomes and wealth, it will operate through the equalisation of citizens' endowments of education and health. A similar type of effect might be achieved through measures aimed at equalising endowments of income-earning property. There are four possible ways in which inequalities in the inheritance of properties may be diminished.

First, if the number of children in the wealthy families is increased and in the less wealthy families decreased, large properties will be more fragmented and small properties will be less fragmented as

---

[4] State action might, of course, well be required in order to provide the necessary loans to students, who might have no more tangible security on which to raise finance than the hope that they will be able to earn high incomes in the future.

they pass by gift or inheritance from parents to children. We will note the result of such demographic developments under § 7 below.

Second, steps may be taken by the State through the heavy taxation of wealthy owners of property to diminish the size of the largest inherited properties. Such measures do nothing in themselves to redistribute private property. They equalise inherited properties by lopping off the top layers of large properties. If the accumulation of the community's capital as a whole is not to be diminished, the State must add to the socially owned State property as much as the privately owned property of the wealthiest citizens is cut down. We will, therefore, consider measures of this kind under § 5 when we come to examine the socialisation of property.

Third, in so far as measures are taken simultaneously both to reduce the ability and/or the incentive of the wealthy to save and to accumulate property and also to increase the ability and/or the incentive of the poor to save and to accumulate property, there will in the course of time be a redistribution of the ownership of property from the rich to the poor. Measures, such as those discussed in § 8 below, which are taken for the direct transfer of income and real purchasing power from the rich to the poor will have this indirect effect. They will decrease the ability of the rich and increase the ability of the poor to save and to accumulate property. This is an indirect longer-term distributional gain from such policies which must be added to the direct effects of such policies on the immediate redistribution of current consumption levels before the balance is struck between the distributional advantages and any efficiency disadvantages of such measures for the direct fiscal redistribution of incomes.

But it is possible to devise more direct measures to stimulate savings by small property owners relatively to savings by large property owners. Institutional arrangements may be introduced of a kind which make it easier for small savers to obtain a higher yield on their savings. Such arrangements might include profit-sharing schemes, investment trusts specially devised for spreading risks for small savings invested in risky but high-yielding assets, arrangements for the purchase by instalments of their houses by tenants of publicly owned dwellings. Finally, the return on small savings may be directly subsidised out of the proceeds of generally progressive taxation.

Fourth, heavy progressive duties on gifts and inheritances are generally a means for reducing the size of large private properties rather than a means for the redistribution of property from rich to poor owners. If the total sum of the community's capital is not to be reduced, the reduction in private ownership may require to be balanced by an increased social ownership of capital. But duties on gifts and inheritances can be devised in such a way as to give an incentive to a rich property owner to distribute his property by gift or by inheritance at his death in small amounts among a large number of otherwise relatively poor beneficiaries. In so far as this can be done, the result is a true redistribution of private property from wealthy to less wealthy owners.

The sort of arrangement which will have this result is a progressive tax on gifts or inheritances, where the rate of tax does not depend upon the wealth of the donor nor simply upon the size of the individual gift or the bequest, but upon the wealth of the recipient. The receipt of a gift or a bequest by an already wealthy man would be taxed at a high rate, whereas the receipt of a similar sum by a propertyless beneficiary would be subject to a low or zero rate of tax.[5] With this sort of arrangement a wealthy man could avoid all tax by leaving his property in small amounts to a number of persons who were not themselves at all wealthy. The incentive to redistribute property by gift or bequest would be at a maximum.

§5   *The Socialisation of Property*
Consider an economy endowed with a certain given amount of real property in the form of land, buildings, machines, stocks of goods, etc. One may contrast two extreme ways of ensuring an exact equality of the ownership of property and of the receipt of income from property. The first is to keep the whole of this property in private ownership but to distribute it in amounts of equal value between all the citizens in the community; and this is the extreme form of the redistribution of properties discussed in §4. The second is for the ultimate ownership of all property to pass into the hands of the State, which can then distribute the income from such property in the form of tax reductions or payments of income

---

[5] A variant of this scheme is an Accessions Duty where the rate of tax rises not according to the total wealth of the recipient but according to the total amount which he has already received up to date by way of gift or inheritance. Such a variant penalises wealth received by gift or inheritance but not wealth accumulated by the recipient from his own effort and savings.

supplements which raise the disposable incomes of every citizen by an equal amount to every citizen. In this case there is no inequality in the ownership of private property, simply because there is no private property; and the income from property is equally distributed in the form of an equal income supplement or Social Dividend paid to each citizen from the State's budget.[6]

It is important to distinguish between the ultimate beneficial ownership of property and the immediate management of property. The State can manage property (for example, the roads, State schools, State hospitals, or the capital equipment of nationalised industries) which it has acquired through the issue of debt to private owners, in which case it manages property the ultimate beneficial ownership of which (through the intermediary of the National Debt) remains in private hands. Indeed, the national debt owed by the State can well exceed the value of the nationalised capital which the State manages, because debt may well have been issued to finance expenditures in war time on goods and services other than lasting capital equipment. In this case the net value of the property owned by the State will be negative because its debts to the private sector exceed its nationalised real assets. On the other hand, the State could well own property without itself managing the property, if it had in the past accumulated budget surpluses which it had lent out to private enterprise or had invested in the ordinary shares of private companies.

For our present purpose we are not concerned with the question whether the State manages property or not. For example, whether or not monopolistic industries should be nationalised is a matter which is relevant to questions of economic efficiency rather than of economic distribution. In an analysis of the ultimate distribution of the income from property we are concerned with the ultimate net value of the property owned by the State and of the property owned

[6] Measures for the redistribution of private property of the kind discussed in §4 and measures for the socialisation of the ownership of property are not incompatible with each other; nor, of course, need such measures be taken to the extreme of eliminating literally all inequalities in the receipt of income from property. There may well be some policies (such as an Accession Tax on the receipt of gifts and inheritances) which cause some redistribution of private properties combined with some policies (such as a levy on private wealth used to redeem National Debt) which result in some increase in the social ownership of property. The two sets of policies may be such as to cause some reduction, but not the complete disappearance, of inequalities in properties and in incomes from property.

by private owners. Let K represent the value of the total real property in the community; let D represent the value of the national debt; and let K_s represent the amount of real property managed by the State. Then $K - K_s + D$ is the net value of property in private hands and $K_s - D$ is the net value of property owned by the State. If the State had accumulated out of past budget surpluses enough not only to redeem the whole of the National Debt (D) but also to invest in what might be called a National Asset (A) in the form of net loans to private enterprise in addition to its holding of nationalised property K_s, then the net value of private property would be $K - K_s - A$ and the net value of State property would be $K_s + A$.

Given K and K_s we are interested at present in the case for reducing D or increasing A (i.e. in transferring an amount of net property from the ultimate ownership of private persons to ownership by the State) as a means of reducing inequalities arising from the unequal ownership of private property. In this connection two questions arise: first, what are the advantages and disadvantages of equality achieved through a redistribution of private property (of the kind discussed in §4) as compared with equality achieved by a transfer of property to State ownership? and, second, what are the relative difficulties involved in achieving a redistribution of private property or a transfer of such property to State ownership?

We can examine the essential features of the first question by undertaking the following mental exercise. Suppose the State to have acquired a certain amount of private property from rich property owners through, for example, a highly progressive capital levy. It could dispose of this private property in either of two ways: first, it could hand back this property to private owners but redistribute it in equal shares among all citizens; or, secondly it could retain this property in State ownership.

To choose the second of these two alternatives is to choose a transfer of property to State ownership rather than a redistribution of private property as a means of equalising incomes from property. Such a transfer would endow the State with an additional income from property and would reduce private incomes from property by a similar gross amount. If the interest on the property would have been subject to an income tax if it had been returned to private ownership, then the net loss to private incomes and the net gain to the State's current budget would be the gross interest on the transferred property less the tax which would have been payable on it in private ownership. But in any case there would be a net gain to the State's budget; and this would enable the State, without any reduction in its other current expenditures, to reduce all round rates of taxation on other private incomes to an extent which matched the State's net gain in income from State-owned property. Individuals' net incomes would be unchanged; what they lost in net income from the transferred property, they would recover from the reduction of other taxes; but they would now own less property.

This change would bring with it both gain and loss. The gain would consist in the improvement in economic incentives due to the reduction in rates of taxation. But the reduction in the private ownership of property would itself have its disadvantages. A man with £1,000 of net income after tax and £10,000 of property is better off than a man with £1,000 of tax-free income but without any property. Property gives security and independence. Moreover, for the organisation of a free society without excessive governmental regulation, private property and private enterprise is an essential feature.

There is thus a balance of advantage and disadvantage: the more property is transferred to State ownership, (i) the more readily can incentives be improved by the reduction of rates of taxation, but (ii) at the same time the smaller is the amount of security, independence and freedom obtainable from the private ownership of property. Somewhere there is an optimal situation, since the greater is the amount of State property, the less can be gained under (i) from a still further reduction of rates of tax but the more severe will be the loss under (ii) from a still further diminution of private property.

The transfer of property from private to State ownership involves some form of levy or tax, just as the redistribution of private property discussed under §4 implies some governmental fiscal or other intervention. Any final assessment of the relative desirability of such a transfer must take into account any disincentive effects of the levy or taxation imposed for the purpose of making the transfer. Since the whole purpose of the operation is to transfer the ownership of property, it is no objection to the transfer operation that the tax or levy raised to acquire property for the State may itself be paid out of savings and capital rather than out of consumption. Indeed, it would be positively desirable to find a form of levy which was paid out of private capital resources. Charges such as a once-for-all capital levy or a recurrent tax on private wealth or on transfers of property by way of gift or inheritance are perhaps more likely than taxes on income or consumption to be paid out of capital. For this reason they might be the most appropriate ways of raising revenue which is going to be devoted by the State not to current public expenditures but to the redemption of the National Debt or, if that were completely eliminated, to the building up of a National Asset. But such charges would undoubtedly have other effects on incentives to work, to take risks and to save in the future. This is not the occasion to consider in detail these efficiency effects; but they would need to be assessed before any final decision was reached about the desirable degree of State ownership.

§ 6   *Measures for the Control of Savings*

The arguments for and against the State ownership of property which we have examined in §5 were concerned solely with the *interclass* distribution of income and property; that is to say, they were concerned with the possibility of distributing more equally the indirect enjoyment of the income earned on the community's capital resources by the transfer of such property from rich property owners to the State. The State would be in a position to use the net budget revenue obtained from the interest on the transferred property to reduce taxes or to pay out income supplements in ways which would make more equal the distribution of current incomes. We turn now to the problem of the *intergenerational* distribution of welfare, namely, the transfer of consumption as between the present and future generations. The solution of this problem may also affect the desired amount of State ownership of property.

As we have already seen in Chapter VI, the distribution of welfare as between the present and future generations depends upon the proportion of the national income which is saved rather than devoted to current consumption. A reduction in current consumption which enables more resources to be devoted to the building up of real capital assets or to the conservation of exhaustible resources will enable more to be produced in the future for consumption by future generations. If it is desired to transfer more resources from present to future generations, then the State must do something to stimulate current savings; if, on the other hand, it is desired to transfer resources from future generations to the present generation, the State must do something to reduce current savings.

There are two different types of reason why the government may wish to influence the level of total national savings in order to redistribute income between the present and future generations.

In the first place the government may wish, by a political decision, to over-ride the market valuations put upon the welfare of future generations. The body of citizens in their joint governmental role may be more farsighted than in their separate individual roles as private savers.

In the second place, tax measures (of the kind implied by the policies discussed in §§3, 4, 5 and 8 of this chapter) may involve a distortion of the private citizens' calculus of the balance of gain and loss to present and future generations which results from their savings. State intervention would be necessary to correct this distortion if it were desired to adjust savings to the levels which would rule if private judgements were not distorted.

Let us start by examining this second case. Progressive rates of tax, imposed in the interests of interclass redistribution, are likely to reduce the post-tax yield on savings below the market rate of interest, i.e. below the marginal product of capital. Suppose that there is a 50 per cent tax on income and that the market rate of interest is 10 per cent per annum. Then a citizen with a pre-tax income of £200 will have £100 which he can spend on consumption or save. If he saves the £100 he will earn in future interest £10 per annum gross but only £5 per annum net after tax. He will obtain 5 per cent on his savings although the market return on capital is 10 per cent. If the tax were not on income but on expenditure on consumption, this distortion would be avoided. The citizen would now have the choice of spending £100 (after tax) on consumption or of saving and investing £200 (free of tax). If he chose to save, he would obtain £20 per annum gross on his savings which would enable him to spend £10 per annum (after tax) on consumption. By giving up £100 worth of consumption, he obtains £10 worth of consumption per annum in the future, a yield equal to the full market rate of interest of 10 per cent.

But even in this case there would probably be other taxes which would reduce the net yield on savings below the market yield. Taxation of wealth or of capital transfers by way of gift or inheritance mean that the citizen who saves resources does not gain for himself or for his heirs the whole of the productive return on the capital which he has accumulated.

The measures taken to improve interclass distribution are thus likely themselves to introduce distortions into the private calculus of the return on savings of a kind which reduce the apparent return on savings to the private saver below the real return to the community.

The removal in part or whole of such a distortion will raise the return on private savings. This may cause a rise or a fall in private savings according as private savers regard future consumption levels as being good or bad substitutes for present consumption levels.[7] But whichever result the removal of the distortion may have, it will bring the distribution of consumption standards as between the present and future consumers more nearly into line with the intergenerational valuations set by individual citizens.

As one means for the removal of this distortion, the State may, as we have seen, shift from a progressive tax on all incomes to a progressive tax on consumption expenditures (i.e. to a progressive tax on income less investment financed out of savings or plus consumption financed out of dissavings). Such a shift will have a double effect.[8] In the first place the exemption of savings from tax, if it had no effect on the level of private consumption, would cause an increase in private savings at the expense of tax revenue. If the rate of tax and the level of government expenditure remained unchanged, this would cause an equivalent fall in the budget surplus. The effect so far would be to substitute private savings for public savings. If, however, the consequential rise in the net rate of return on private savings up to the market rate of interest induced a rise (or a fall) in the proportion of disposable income which was spent and thus a fall (or a rise) in the real level of private consumption, these would be an increase (or decrease) in private savings over and above the reduction in public savings.

But the government might wish to take further measures to influence the proportion of the national income which was saved, either because it was not possible to remove entirely the distortions caused by taxation (e.g. by death duties) from the private calculus of gain and loss as between the generations or else because the government wished to over-ride such private intergenerational valuations. The government might wish to raise or to lower the savings proportion. We will confine our analysis to the case in which the

[7, 8] See Note to Chapter XIII (pages 215–19 below).

government wishes to raise the savings proportion in order to transfer resources from the present to future generations; and the reader is left to consider the application of the analysis to the opposite case in which the State wishes to reduce total savings.

The State could increase total savings by raising rates of taxation of a kind which would reduce the current consumption of private citizens and by devoting the increased revenue to public savings and thus to the accumulation of State-owned property.

This argument for the accumulation of State-owned property must be clearly distinguished from that discussed in § 5, which was concerned solely with the transfer of *existing* property from private to State ownership in the interests of *interclass* redistribution. The case which we are now discussing concerns the accumulation of *additional* property in the interests of *intergenerational* redistribution. A noticeable feature of the difference is that the argument in § 5 is in support of a budget surplus financed by taxes which are paid out of private capital, whereas the present argument is in favour of a budget surplus which is financed by taxes which are paid out of current consumption.[9]

There are in effect two broad philosophies which may be applied both to the interclass problem of § 5 and to the intergenerational problem of § 6. If one attempts to bring about a redistribution of private property under § 5 (e.g. by an Accessions Duty on gifts and inheritances) and to remove distortions from private savings under § 6 (e.g. by shifting from the taxation of income to the taxation of expenditure), then one is adopting essentially what may be called 'liberal' solutions. One is encouraging the privately desired accumulation of private property and a more equal distribution of private property. If one attempts under § 5 to transfer private property to the State (e.g. by a budget surplus financed by taxes paid out of

---

[9] The sizes of the budget surplus and of the amount of State-owned capital which are desirable in order to achieve an optimal level of total savings have been analysed in more precise terms on certain simplified conditions in Chapter XXIII and the Note to Chapter XXIII of *The Growing Economy*. In conditions of steady growth the State will come to own a certain growing stock of property, part of the income from which it will at every stage be using to finance the consumption of the current generation (otherwise there would be no increase in the welfare of the present generation at the expense of past generations) and part of which it will be using to accumulate still further capital in the interests of still later generations (otherwise there would be no increase in the welfare of future generations at the expense of the present generation).

private property) and under §6 to adjust the level of State savings
(e.g. by adjusting the level of a budget surplus financed by taxes paid
out of private consumption), then one is adopting essentially
'socialist' solutions. One is attempting to solve both interclass and
intergenerational redistribution by measures which affect the
amount of property owned by the State relatively to the amount in
private ownership.

§7   *Measures for the Control of Population Growth*

The intergenerational distribution of welfare will be affected not
only by the proportion of current income which is saved and thus
used to aid the future population but also by the current rates of
fertility which will affect the size of the future population which is
to enjoy the fruits of whatever capital is accumulated for its use. An
increase in fertility leading to an increase in the future population
will have a double 'distributional' aspect. In the first place, an
increase in the future population may well reduce output per head
and so the standard of living of the future population. Even if we
neglect altogether the additional members of the future generation,
the increased fertility may thus affect intergenerational distribution
by affecting standards of consumption of future generations relatively to the standards of consumption of the present generation.
But, in the second place, we may not wish to neglect the welfare of
the additional members of the future generation who, in the absence
of the increase in fertility, would never have been born. We have in
this case also to consider the 'distribution' of welfare between the
born and the unborn. (Cf. Chapter V above.)

Just as in §6 of this chapter (page 207 above) we found two broad
reasons why the government might wish to influence the amount of
current income which was being saved, so there are two similar
broad reasons why the government might wish – if it knew how – to
influence fertility rates and so the size of the future population.

In the first place, the government might put more or less weight
on the evaluation of the welfare of additional members of the
population than the individual citizens did on the welfare of additional numbers in their own private families. The government might
wish to stimulate growth if it considered that individual parents
were underestimating the desirability of a larger national family and
to restrict growth in the opposite case.

In the second place, there may be taxes and subsidies or other factors in the economic system which distort the individual's calculus as between the costs and benefits of additional members of the family.

Just as in the case of the proportion of income saved in §6 (pages 207–8), such distortions are in fact likely to be introduced by fiscal measures which are expressly designed to reduce interclass inequalities. One reason for being relatively rich is having no children to support; and one reason for being relatively poor is having a large family to support. Redistribution from rich to poor is bound, if it is to be effective, to contain a large element of subsidisation to large families – free health and education, family allowances, allowances for children under the income tax, and so on – at the expense of bachelors, spinsters and parents with small families. Such redistributional subsidies will make the large family seem much less expensive to the parents concerned than it is in fact to society as a whole.

Let us suppose then that the government would like, if it could, to intervene in a manner which would reduce the general level of fertility. But at the same time, for the reasons which we have discussed in Chapter XII, it may want on both distributional and efficiency grounds to encourage fertility among the fortunate relatively to fertility among the unfortunate, since this will (i) promote interclass equality by increasing the number of children in rich families relatively to those in poor families among whom the family incomes and properties have to be shared and (ii) promote a higher average output per head by improving the average level of ability in the population.

This second reason for promoting a differential rate of fertility among the fortunate becomes the stronger, the greater is the degree of social mobility and of equality of opportunity in society. For the easier it is for the innately able to rise in society and for the dullards to decline in society, the more probable will it be that those who are genetically well endowed will be found among the prosperous members of society and that those who are genetically less well endowed will be found among the less prosperous members of society; and this concentration of innate ability at the upper end will be even more marked if high social mobility leads (as we suggested in Chapter X that it might well do) to a high degree of assortative mating according to innate ability. The more probable it thus becomes that high innate ability is concentrated among the prosperous members of society, the more effective will differential fertility rates be in affecting the average level of ability in society.

Is it possible for the government to intervene in such a way as (i) to subsidise large families in the interests of direct equalisation of incomes per head but (ii) to reduce the average size of families and (iii) to raise the size of fortunate families relatively to that of unfortunate families?

One possible set of measures is to take steps to make access to knowledge and means of birth control equally available to all citizens. At present the fortunate often have easier access to methods for the control of their fertility than do the unfortunate. This is so for two broad sets of reasons: first, knowledge of new methods of control is more readily available in the social, intellectual and educational atmosphere of the fortunate classes; and, second, the rich can more readily afford the medical and other expenses of contraception and abortion.

Measures designed to enable everyone to avoid having more children than they want can take many forms: sterilisation and abortion on demand, the development of family planning advice and services in maternity hopsitals, the supply of free family planning advice and free supplies of contraceptives in a national health service, the development of domiciliary family planning services whereby the service is taken to the citizens rather than requiring the citizen to come to the services clinic, the inculcation in school education of the need and the means to ensure that sexual intercourse should never occur without contraception unless a child is planned, and governmental promotion of research into contraceptive methods.

In a free liberal democratic society, in the absence of Platonic police-state measures, it is difficult to devise further measures to achieve the desired combination of results. Simply to deter large families, especially among unfortunate parents, by fiscal measures such as taxes on the number of children produced, runs directly counter to the need to subsidise such families in the interests of the children who would otherwise be condemned to poverty.

One conceivable set of fiscal policies might be to offer a lump-sum subsidy to any potential parent who would agree to be sterilised and at the same time to tax rich bachelors more heavily than rich parents with large families.[10] The lump-sum subsidy on sterilisation might be an important incentive to the relatively poor parent, but could be more than counterbalanced by the tax advantages to married couples with large families in the higher ranges of the progressive scales of taxes on incomes or expenditures.

§8 *The Direct Redistribution of Personal Incomes*

The final item in our catalogue of redistributive measures is the straightforward policy of taxing the rich and subsidising the poor. This can be achieved by a system of progressive taxation on current incomes or on current levels of expenditures on consumption in the case of the rich, combined with a system of subsidies to supplement the incomes or the current levels of expenditure on consumption of the poor. This is the most direct form of interclass redistribution.

Such a direct redistributional fiscal policy will have a large range of economic effects which we have already enumerated under eight headings (pages 189–90 above). We will confine ourselves now to a very brief development of one or two salient points.

We have already noted the fact that if standards of living are assessed (as they should be) according to the level of income or of consumption per head in the family concerned, then such a redistributive system is bound to involve some element of subsidisation of large families at the expense of those who are unmarried or who have only a small number of children. It will also involve an element of what we have called (page 109 above) intertemporal redistribution. In so far as citizens do not save sufficient during their working years to avoid being worse off during the years of their old age and retirement, a straight redistribution from the relatively rich to the relatively poor will involve an element of taxation of those of working age to finance the elderly as well as dependent children.

The straightforward redistribution of purchasing power from the rich to the poor, carried out in the interests of interclass redistribu-

---

[10] One method of doing this is by means of a progressive scale of tax on income (or on consumption expenditure) which proceeds to aggregate the total incomes (or consumption expenditures) of the members of a family, to divide this aggregate sum by the number of members of the family, and to allot the resulting average income (or expenditure) separately to each member of the family for the purpose of taxation under the progressive scale of tax. The larger the number of children, the smaller the average income (or expenditure) imputed to each member of the family and the lower, therefore, the rate of tax which that member pays under a progressive tax system. A similar, but somewhat less extreme, form of this principle would be to count minor children not as whole persons, but as half persons, in computing the above-average income (or expenditure) per head in the family.

tion, is thus likely to intensify some of the other problems of redistribution discussed in this chapter. It may, as we have seen in §7,
intensify the population problem through the implied subsidisation
of large families. It may also intensify the problem of the control of
savings, discussed in §6, by reducing a citizen's incentive to save for
his old age if he knows that his standard of living in his old age will
be supported by public subsidy or for his heirs if he knows that they
will not gain so significantly from his abstinence.

The fiscal measures necessary to finance the direct redistribution
of purchasing power may have important effects upon economic
efficiency. A direct redistributive fiscal system must announce to the
individual that the more he increases his real purchasing power by
raising his own earnings or the income from his own private
property, the higher the rate of tax which he will pay. This will affect
his incentive to increase his pre-tax income by earning more, by
taking more risks and by accumulating more property. Such changes
in incentives may have important effects upon the efficiency of the
economic system, that is to say, upon the total income available for
distribution between the members of the community. The taxation
which is imposed for the direct redistribution of purchasing power
from rich to poor may take many forms, such as a progressive
income tax, a progressive tax on consumption expenditures, a
progressive wealth tax and various forms of progressive death
duties. These different taxes may differ in their effects on incentives
to work, risk and save; and they may thus differ in important ways
upon economic efficiency. But this aspect of the subject must be
held over until there has been an analysis of the problems of *The
Efficient Economy.*

Any complete policy for the redistribution of income and wealth
would probably comprise elements of all the eight types of policy
which we have catalogued in this chapter. What form the precise
combination should take will depend upon many factors.

First, it will depend above all upon the attitude taken to the basic
questions posed in Chapters I to VI of this volume. What does one
mean by a desirable distribution of income and property? And how
much weight does one give to this distributional objective relatively
to other social objectives, such as economic efficiency, economic
freedom, and so on?

Secondly, it will depend upon the analysis of the causes of inequalities. In Chapter IX we distinguished between structural elements of good or bad 'fortune' in endowments of genes, education, social contacts and property on the one hand, and random strokes of 'luck' on the other hand. The relative weight which one would put upon policies designed to equalise the socially structured endowments of fortune (such as those discussed under §§3 and 4 of our catalogue) as compared with policies designed directly to transfer purchasing power from people who happen to be rich to those who happen to be poor at any given point of time (such as those measures mentioned in § 8 of our catalogue) should clearly depend upon the degree to which it is important indirectly to correct for structured 'fortune' or directly to offset the strokes of random 'luck'.

Finally, one must take into account in the selection of the complete package of policies their efficiency effects through the effects which the various measures will have upon economic incentives of various kinds.

This general assessment of policy packages is at the heart of the problems of political economy. It is a desperately difficult task. One very attractive way of dealing with a difficult task is to put it off till tomorrow. Accordingly we will postpone any further discussion of this problem until we come to write, if we ever do, the final volume in this series on *The Mixed Economy*.

Note to Chapter XIII

THE EFFECT OF AN INCOME TAX AND AN EXPENDITURE TAX
ON SAVINGS

Consider an economy in which a representative citizen has an income at factor cost of Y, i.e. a receipt of earnings and income from property of Y before payment of tax. Table IX shows his distribution of this income between consumption, savings, and tax payment under an income tax and an expenditure tax. It is assumed that the same rate of tax, t, is applied to the representative citizen's income or to the market value of his expenditure on consumption and that in both cases he decides to save the same proportion, s, of his disposable income.

With the income tax the citizen has to pay tY in tax. His disposable income is $(1 - t)Y$ and of this he saves a proportion s, so that his savings are $s(1 - t)Y$ and his consumption $(1 - s)(1 - t)Y$, both these sums being equal to the factor cost of the goods used up in private consumption or in privately financed investment.

With the expenditure tax our citizen has a disposable income of Y out of which he saves sY. He spends the remainder $(1 - s)Y$ on consumption at market prices, but of this the government takes $t(1 - s)Y$ in revenue, leaving $(1 - t)(1 - s)Y$ to be spent on consumption goods at their factor cost.

	Income Tax	Expenditure Tax	
	I	II	II − I
Tax revenue	tY	$t(1 - s)Y$	$-tsY$
Consumption	$(1 - s)(1 - t)Y$	$(1 - t)(1 - s)Y$	0
Private savings	$s(1 - t)Y$	sY	$+tsY$
Total	$1Y$	$1Y$	0

Table IX

It is to be observed that with t and s the same in both cases, the factor cost value of private consumption will be the same in both cases. But with the expenditure tax there will be a shift of tsY from government revenue to private savings at factor cost; tsY is the loss of revenue to the government through the exemption of private savings from tax, this additional amount being available for the private finance of investment.

Thus a shift from an income tax to an expenditure tax (i.e. a tax on income which exempts private savings) will lead to an increase in private savings in the absence of any change in the proportion of private disposable incomes which are saved. It will thus enable the same amount of total savings to be achieved with a smaller public savings (i.e. a smaller budget surplus and an increased amount of private savings).

But the shift from an income tax to an expenditure tax will also raise the net return on an individual's savings. Suppose that the market rate of interest is i. Assume the factor cost of a unit of consumption goods and of a unit of capital goods both to be £1. Then with the income tax, an individual who purchases 1 less unit of consumption goods will be able with his savings of £1 to purchase 1 more unit of capital goods. On this capital of £1 he will receive a future gross income of £i per annum with a post-tax net value of £$(1 - t)i$, which will enable him to purchase $(1 - t)i$ more consumption goods per annum, a net return of $(1 - t)i$ on his savings of 1 unit of consumption.

With the expenditure tax, if he purchases 1 less unit of consumption goods he will save the market price of the consumption goods which is equal to £$1/(1 - t)$, since the expenditure of this sum after consumption tax at t leaves £1 with which to purchase one unit of consumption goods at factor cost. On his savings of £$1/(1 - t)$ he obtains £$i/(1 - t)$ per annum, which, if he spends it on consumption, will be taxed at t, leaving £i per annum worth of consumption goods at factor cost to add to his annual consumption. Thus by giving up 1 unit of consumption goods he can add i units to his future consumption level, a rate of return of i.

Will this rise in the rate of return from $(1 - t)i$ to i induce the citizen concerned to increase or to decrease the factor cost value of his consumption from the level of which it was running under the income tax? Will it, in other words, cause him to decrease or increase s, the proportion of his disposable income which he will save? As is well known, there are two conflicting influences. There is an income effect which will tend to reduce his savings; the higher yield will make him better off in the future in any case, so that he could increase his current consumption as well as his future consumption if he saved somewhat less. On the other hand there is a substitution effect which will tend to increase his savings; any sacrifice of today's consumption will now give a bigger return in terms of tomorrow's consumption.

If we confined ourselves to a two-period model, the interplay of these tendencies can be illustrated by Figure 23 (which corresponds to Figure 18 on page 202 of *The Growing Economy*).

We measure this year's consumption $\hat{C}_1$ up the vertical axis and next year's consumption $\hat{C}_2$ along the horizontal axis. The curves I and I′ are indifference curves showing the combinations of $\hat{C}_1$ and $\hat{C}_2$ between which the citizen is indifferent. He starts with the possibility of consuming OF this year if he mortgages the whole of this year's and next year's income and leaves nothing for consumption next year. With a rate of interest i, for every unit of consumption which he gives up this year he can consume $1 + i$ units next year, either because he borrows less or because he saves more at the rate of interest i. His budget constraint line is, therefore, given by the line FG which starts at F and falls with a slope such that $OG/OF = 1 + i$. If the rate of interest goes up from i to i', the line FG swings round to FG' where $OG'/OF = 1 + i'$. Our citizen will have decided to save more (or less) according as Q' is lower (or higher) vertically

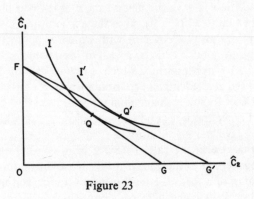

Figure 23

	Income tax	Expenditure tax	
	I	II	II − I
Tax revenue	tY	$t(1 - s - \Delta s)Y$	$-t(s + \Delta s)Y$
Consumption	$(1 - s)(1 - t)Y$	$(1 - t)(1 - s - \Delta s)Y$	$-(1 - t)\Delta s Y$
Private savings	$s(1 - t)Y$	$(s + \Delta s)Y$	$(1 - t)\Delta s Y$
			$+t(s + \Delta s)Y$
Total	$1Y$	$1Y$	0

Table X

than Q. Clearly he is likely to save less (or more) according to whether there is a low (or high) substitutability between consumption at different times in his preference function. On page 206 of *The Growing Economy* we gave reasons to believe that this substitutability might well be low for very low and for very high standards of living, but might be much higher at intermediate standards.

Since the shift from an income tax to an expenditure tax will raise the net rate of return on an individual's savings, it may cause a change in the proportion of his disposable incomes which an individual saves. Let us suppose that it changes the proportion of disposable income saved from s to $s + \Delta s$. Then we can rewrite

Table IX as in Table X. In this case private consumption at factor cost would be reduced by $(1 - t)\Delta s Y$ as a result of a decision to increase the proportion of disposable income which is saved by Δs. This would result in an increase of private savings of $(1 - t)\Delta s Y + t(s + \Delta s)Y$ and a decrease in tax revenue and so in public savings of $t(s + \Delta s)Y$.

A MATHEMATICAL MODEL OF THE DYNAMICS OF SOCIAL WELFARE IN A SECOND-BEST ECONOMY

I

We are concerned with the question whether a given small change in today's policy decisions may be expected to cause an improvement or a deterioration in social welfare, given that the effects of the policy change will occur over an uncertain future. For this purpose we must regard the policy-makers as looking ahead and having an idea of the controls (rates of tax, etc.) which they will set at each future point of time and at each given state of the environment at that point of time. In earlier examples[2] we have illustrated environmental influences by the question whether the weather will be wet or fine. Thus the authorities will have it in mind to set next year's taxes at one level if it is fine next year and at another level if it is wet next year.

We must then have in mind a branching pattern of time-cum-environmental points, illustrated in Figure 24. Thus starting now at the beginning of year I at point 1, one may find oneself at the beginning of year II either at environmental point 2 or at environmental point 3 (e.g. according as to whether it has been wet or fine during year I.) If one starts at the beginning of next year at point 2 one may find oneself at the beginning of year III either at point 4 or at point 5; and so on. We will call a typical environmental-cum-

---

[1] This Appendix contains a development of the model given in Chapter XVI of *The Controlled Economy*. In particular (i) the demographic aspects of the model have been greatly extended, (ii) allowance has been made for the existence in the production system of exhaustible resources and of a fixed factor like land, (iii) the range of possible divergences between marginal social costs and values has been extended and (iv) alternatives to pure utilitarianism have been considered for the social welfare function.

[2] See Chapters X, XI and XII of *The Controlled Economy*.

time point q. We will mean by point $\overline{q-1}$ the point from which q must have proceeded, and by $\overline{q+1}$ the points which may follow point q. Thus if, on Figure 24, q stood for point 6, then $\overline{q-1}$ must stand for point 3 and $\overline{q+1}$ for points 12 and 13. We will call v the number of time-cum-environmental points which are being considered in the policy-makers' control plan.

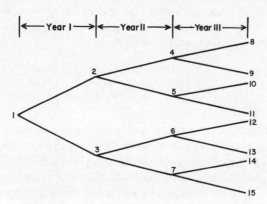

Figure 24 Time-cum-Environmental Points.

In this uncertain dynamic setting we wish to construct a welfare function which depends in some way upon the evaluation of the policy-makers of the possible future patterns of individual utilities. For this purpose we must first define the categories of all future individuals. This we can do by specifying both the type of individual and also the time-cum-environmental point of his birth. Down each column of Table XI we consider the individuals of all types who

		Points of birth			
		$1 \ldots$	$j \ldots$	$q \ldots$	v
Types of individuals	1	$(11) \ldots$	$(1j) \ldots$	$(1q) \ldots$	$(1v)$
	$\vdots$	$\vdots$			
	h	$(h1) \ldots$	$(hj) \ldots$	$(hq) \ldots$	(hv)
	$\vdots$	$\vdots$			
	m	$(m1) \ldots$	$(mj) \ldots$	$(mq) \ldots$	(mv)

Table XI

are born at a given point of time and environment; along each row we consider the individuals of any one type who are born at various points of time and environment. Thus an individual of the kind (hj) is an individual of type h born at point j. The division of individuals into the types 1 to m must take account of all relevant differences other than point of birth, i.e. differences such as sex, genetic endowments, social and economic class, etc. There will thus be mv kinds of individuals specified both by their types and by the point of their birth. Let $mv = s$ and let us use r to specify one particular kind of individual in the series $1 \ldots r \ldots s$. We will write N_r for the number of individuals of kind r with $N = \sum_r N_r.$[3]

We write

$$\hat{U}_r = \sum_q \varepsilon_q \lambda_{rq} \hat{U}_{rq} \qquad \ldots\ldots\ldots\ldots\ldots\ldots(A.1)$$

to represent the total life-time utility of an individual of kind r which is expected today (i.e. at point 1). $\hat{U}_{rq}$ is the utility which he can expect to enjoy at point q if he is alive at point q. But this depends upon two probabilities: first, the probability (expressed by ε_q) that the economy starting from point 1 will in fact move through point q; and, second, the probability (expressed by λ_{rq}) that an individual of kind r will be alive at point q if the economy does in fact pass through point q. Suppose $r = (hj)$, i.e. referred to an individual of kind h born at point j; and suppose, for purposes of illustration, that j was point 6 on Figure 24. Then λ_{rq} would necessarily be zero for all points other than 6, 12 and 13, since an individual born at point 6 could not pass through any of those other points. We would have $\lambda_{r6} = 1$, $1 \geqslant \lambda_{r12} \geqslant 0$ and $1 \geqslant \lambda_{r13} \geqslant 0$ since by definition the

[3] N will be much greater than the actual total of future mankind over the whole control-plan period. The economy will in fact move only over one environmental path; but N includes all potential persons over all possible environmental paths. This may involve counting one actual person as a large number of potential persons. Consider points 4, 5, 6 and 7 on Figure 24. It may be that a particular individual of type h would be born at the beginning of year III whatever the environment at year III. In this case this particular individual of type h born at the beginning of year III counts as four individuals of kinds $(h4)$, $(h5)$, $(h6)$ and $(h7)$ respectively. We treat him as different persons with different probabilities of existence according to the different probabilities of reaching points 4, 5, 6 or 7 from point 1. This treatment is necessary because environment may affect births so that an individual baby of type h which would be born at point 5 may not exist at all if the economy does not in fact pass through point 5.

individual will exist at point 6 but the chances of his living till point 12 or point 13 will depend upon his expectation of life in these different environmental circumstances.

Let us write

$$\hat{U}_{rq} = (1 - \rho_{rq}) \, \hat{U}_{rqe} + \rho_{rq}\hat{U}_{rqu} \quad \ldots\ldots\ldots\ldots(A.2)$$

where ρ_{rq} is the probability of an individual of kind r if he exists at point q finding himself involuntarily unemployed at point q. $\hat{U}_{rqe}$ is the utility he can expect at point q if he exists in employment at point q and $\hat{U}_{rqu}$ is the utility he can expect at point q if he exists in enforced unemployment at point q. In what follows for convenience of notation we will write $k = rq$ or, since $r = (hj)$, $k = (hj)q$. In other words k refers to the experience at point q of a individual of type h who is born at point j.

Differentiating (A.1) and using (A.2) we have

$$d\hat{U}_r = \sum_q \varepsilon_q \lambda_k \left\{ \hat{U}_k \frac{d\lambda_k}{\lambda_k} - (\hat{U}_{ke} - \hat{U}_{ku}) \, d\rho_k \right.$$

$$\left. + (1 - \rho_k)d\hat{U}_{ke} + \rho_k d\hat{U}_{ku} \right\} \ldots\ldots\ldots\ldots\ldots\ldots\ldots\ldots\ldots\ldots\ldots(A.3)$$

Write

$$\hat{U}_{ke} = \hat{U}_{ke}\{\hat{C}_{xke}, \, \hat{C}_{yke}, 1 - \hat{L}_k, C_{xq}, C_{yq}, \overline{X}_q, \overline{Y}_q, G_{xq}, G_{yq}\}\ldots(A.4)$$

We assume that there are only two goods, X and Y. $\hat{C}_{xke}$ is the amount of X consumed by an employed individual of type r at point q; and similarly for $\hat{C}_{yke}$. $\hat{L}_k$ is the proportion of his time which an employed individual of kind r spends at work instead of at leisure at point q. $C_{xq}, C_{yq}, \overline{X}_q, \overline{Y}_q$ are the total amounts of X and Y consumed (C_{xq}, C_{yq}) or produced ($\overline{X}_q, \overline{Y}_q$) at point q. They are included in the arguments of $\hat{U}_{ke}$ in case the total consumption or production activities of others have some external effects on the welfare of the individual concerned. G_{xq} and G_{yq} are the total amounts of the goods X and Y consumed by the government, i.e. represent the effect of public goods on the individual's welfare.

We next differentiate (A.4) and obtain

$$d\hat{U}_{ke} = \mu_{ke}d\hat{H}_{ke}\ldots\ldots\ldots\ldots\ldots\ldots\ldots(A.5)$$

where

$$\begin{aligned}
d\hat{H}_{ke} = {} & P_{xke}d\hat{C}_{xke} + P_{yke}d\hat{C}_{yke} - P_{lk}d\hat{L}_k \\
& + P_{cxke}dC_{xq} + P_{cyke}dC_{yq} \\
& + P_{\bar{x}ke}d\overline{X}_q + P_{\bar{y}ke}d\overline{Y}_q \\
& + P_{gxke}dG_{xq} + P_{gyke}dG_{yq} \ldots\ldots\ldots\ldots\ldots\ldots(A.6)
\end{aligned}$$

The term μ_{ke} represents the marginal utility of money at point q to an employed individual of kind r; $d\hat{H}_{ke}$ represents the increase in his real consumption, the different elements in his real consumption being valued at their current money values. Thus P_{xke}, P_{yke} and P_{lk} represents the amounts of money which the employed individual of kind r at point q would be willing to give up for an additional unit of X, Y or leisure to consume.[4] $P_{\bar{x}ke}$ and $P_{\bar{y}ke}$ represent the prices which he would be willing to pay to receive any external benefit (or, if negative, to avoid any external cost) from a marginal change in the total community's consumption or production of X or Y. P_{gxke} and P_{gyke} represent the additional taxes he would be prepared to contribute to obtain one more unit of public good G_x or G_y.

We will write

$$P_{lk} = W_q\theta_k(1 - \delta_{lk}) \ldots\ldots\ldots\ldots\ldots\ldots(A.7)$$

where W_q is the ruling market wage for a given amount of 'effective work' done, θ_k is the amount of 'effective work' per unit of time which an individual of kind r can produce at point q, and $W_q\theta_k(1 - \delta_{lk})$ is the additional amount of money which the individual will add to his income by working for one more unit of time. The term θ_k is a crude way of capturing the fact that an hour's work has different values according to the *quality* of the work done; we simply assume that some people are more capable than others in producing a larger *quantity* of some homogeneous 'effective work' per unit of

---

[4] These may well be the ruling market prices of these goods, but are not necessarily so. For example, if the individual had a monopsonistic influence in the market for X, then P_{xke} would represent not the price he paid for X but the marginal payment for X (see J. E. Meade, *Trade and Welfare*, pages 16–17).

time. The term δ_{lk} measures the marginal divergence between the wage rate paid to a man per hour of work $(W_q \theta_k)$ and the addition to his wage income due to doing one more unit of work (P_{lk}). The most obvious reason for such a divergence would be any marginal rate of income tax on his earnings.

We can have similar terms for an unemployed individual of kind r at point q, namely,

$$d\hat{U}_{ku} = \mu_{ku} d\hat{H}_{ku} \dots \dots \dots (A.8)$$

but in this case there is no term corresponding to the term $P_{lk} d\hat{L}_k$ in (A.6), since it is a definition of unemployment that the amount of work done is constrained to be zero.

Substituting in (A.3) from (A.5), (A.6), (A.7) and (A.8) we obtain

$$d\hat{U}_r = \sum_q \varepsilon_q \lambda_k$$

$$\begin{bmatrix} \hat{U}_k \dfrac{d\lambda_k}{\lambda_k} - (\hat{U}_{ke} - \hat{U}_{ku})\, d\rho_k \\[2mm] + (\mu_{ke} - \mu_q)(1 - \rho_k)\, d\hat{H}_{ke} + (\mu_{ku} - \mu_q)\, \rho_k d\hat{H}_{ku} \\[2mm] + \mu_q(1 - \rho_k)\, \delta_{lk} \hat{W}_k \dfrac{d\hat{L}_k}{\hat{L}_k} \\[2mm] + \mu_q(\Delta_{1k} + \Delta_{2k} + \Delta_{3k}) \\[2mm] + \mu_q(1 - \rho_k) \left(d\hat{C}_{ke} - \hat{W}_k \dfrac{d\hat{L}_k}{\hat{L}_k} \right) \\[2mm] + \mu_q \rho_k\, d\hat{C}_{ku} \end{bmatrix} \dots (A.9)$$

In equation (A.9):

(i) μ_q represents a weighted average of the marginal utilities of money to all consumers of all kinds at point q. Algebraically it is immaterial what weighting we choose; but economically the choice of the weights will define a situation of no change in the distribution of real consumption at point q;[5]

(ii) $d\hat{C}_{ke} = P_{xq} d\hat{C}_{xke} + P_{yq} d\hat{C}_{yke}$, which represents the change in the consumption standard of an employed man of kind r at point q, the components of his consumption being valued at the current

[5] For a discussion of this point and of the various sets of weights which might be chosen, see *The Controlled Economy*, pages 260–2.

average prices at which they are sold to all consumers; and similarly for $d\hat{C}_{ku}$;

(iii) $\hat{W}_k = W_q\theta_k\hat{L}_k$ or the wages paid to an employed man of kind r at point q;

(iv) $\Delta_{1k} =$

$$(1 - \rho_k)(P_{xke} - P_{xq})\, d\hat{C}_{xke} + \rho_k(P_{xku} - P_{xq})\, d\hat{C}_{xku}$$
$$+ (1 - \rho_k)(P_{yke} - P_{yq})d\hat{C}_{yke} + \rho_k(P_{yku} - P_{yq})d\hat{C}_{yku};$$

(v) $\Delta_{2k} =$

$$\{(1 - \rho_k)P_{cxke} + \rho_k P_{cxku}\}\, dC_{xq} + \{(1 - \rho_k)P_{cyke}$$
$$+ \rho_k P_{cyku}\}\, dC_{xq}$$
$$+ \{(1 - \rho_k)P_{\bar{x}ke} + \rho_k P_{\bar{x}ku}\}d\bar{X}_q + \{(1 - \rho_k)P_{\bar{y}ke}$$
$$+ \rho_k P_{\bar{y}ku}\}\, d\bar{Y}_q;$$

(vi) $\Delta_{3k} =$

$$\{(1 - \rho_k)P_{gxke} + \rho_k P_{gxku}\}\, dG_{xq}$$
$$+ \{(1 - \rho_k)P_{gyke} + \rho_k P_{gyku}\}\, dG_{yq}; \text{ and}$$

(vii) P_{xq} represents the average price to private consumers of X at point q, and similarly for P_{yq}.

II

Equation (A.9) expresses the effect of various changes on the present expectation at point 1 of the life-span utility to be enjoyed by an individual of kind r (i.e. of type h to be born at point j). We turn now to the weight which the policy-makers would put at point 1 on any such changes in such expected life-span utilities of various kinds of individuals. In general we will suppose that the policy-makers have a social welfare function of the kind

$$Z = Z(\hat{U}_1 \ldots \hat{U}_r \ldots \hat{U}_s, N_1 \ldots N_r \ldots N_s) \quad \ldots\ldots\ldots(A.10)$$

That is to say, we suppose that in assessing any plan for the future they are concerned with the expected utility per head of the various kinds of individual and also with the numbers of individuals of each kind.

If the policy-makers were pure utilitarians, then the social welfare function would take the form

$$Z = \sum N_r\hat{U}_r \quad \ldots\ldots\ldots\ldots\ldots\ldots\ldots\ldots(A.11)$$

This function has constant returns to scale both in the N's and the $\hat{U}$'s. That is to say, if every N increased by 10 per cent, then Z would increase by 10 per cent; alternatively if every $\hat{U}$ increased by 10 per cent, then Z would increase by 10 per cent. It is important to bear in mind that while a pure utilitarian must use a social welfare function in which both forms of constant returns to scale occur, it is not necessary that they should go together.

Consider for example the function

$$Z = \sum_r \hat{U}_r^2 N_r$$

If all the N's increase in the ratio dN/N, then $dZ/Z = dN/N$. But if all the $\hat{U}$'s increase in the ratio $d\hat{U}/\hat{U}$ then $dZ/Z = 2(d\hat{U}/\hat{U})$. Such a function puts more weight on an increase in the total of utility if it is brought about by a given rise in utility per head than if it is brought about by a corresponding increase in the number of heads. Nevertheless at the same time this social welfare function considers the existence of two identical societies, in each of which there is the same number of people with the same utilities per head, as twice as valuable as the existence of only one of these societies, though it would consider as still more valuable a doubling of utility per head for every citizen in one of these societies.

Or consider a function of the kind

$$Z = \sum_r \hat{U}_r^{\alpha_r} N_r$$

where the exponents α_r may differ for the different kinds of individual. For example one could have a low exponent α for a class of wealthy individuals and a high exponent α for a class of poor individuals. In this case a rise in total utility which was caused by a rise in the utility of the rich would be counted as less valuable than an equal rise in total utility which was caused by a rise in the utility of the poor. In other words, policy-makers would count as more valuable a given rise in total utility which was associated with a more equal distribution of utilities than the same rise in total utility which was associated with a less equal distribution of utilities.

As far as the scale of total population is concerned we will consider only two extreme types of social welfare function. In the first case, which we will denote simply by Z, we will assume that there are constant returns to scale of population and we will have

$$Z = Z(\hat{U}_1 \ldots \hat{U}_r \ldots \hat{U}_s, N_1 \ldots N_r \ldots N_s)$$

with $Z = \sum_r \dfrac{\partial Z}{\partial N_r} N_r$ ....(A.12)

In the second case which we will denote by Z^*, we will have the same valuation of the $\hat{U}$'s but with no weight at all put upon the scale of the total population, so that

$$Z^* = Z/N \quad \ldots\ldots\ldots\ldots\ldots\ldots\ldots(A.13)$$

In (A.12) and (A.13), policy-makers have similar concerns about the pattern of distribution of the $\hat{U}$'s; but in (A.13) they judge the value of a society merely by its pattern of distribution of welfares per head as between different kinds of citizens and not at all by the absolute scale of these populations of different kinds of citizen. In (A.12) they make the same kind of judgements about the pattern of distribution of utilities per head, but regard a 10 per cent increase in the absolute scale of each and every population as marking a 10 per cent improvement in total social welfare.

Consider then the function in (A.12). We have by differentiation

$$dZ = \sum_r N_r \frac{\partial Z}{N_r \partial \hat{U}_r} d\hat{U}_r + \sum_r \frac{\partial Z}{\hat{U}_r \partial N_r} \hat{U}_r dN_r$$

If the policy-makers were pure utilitarians (as in equation (A.11) we would have $\partial Z/N_r \partial \hat{U}_r = 1$ and $\partial Z/\hat{U}_r \partial N_r = 1$. Write $\partial Z/N_r \partial \hat{U}_r = (\bar{\mu}/\mu)_r$ and $\partial Z/\hat{U}_r \partial N_r = (\bar{\hat{U}}/\hat{U})_r$ where $(\bar{\mu}/\mu)_r$ is the modification to the marginal utilities and $(\bar{\hat{U}}/\hat{U})_r$ the modification to the total utility of an individual of kind r which the policy-makers make because of their interest in the pattern of distribution of utilities among various kinds of individual. We may call $\bar{\mu}_r$ and $\bar{\hat{U}}_r$ the pattern-modified distributional weights of marginal and total utilities. We have then

$$dZ = \sum_r N_r (\bar{\mu}/\mu)_r d\hat{U}_r + \sum_r (\bar{\hat{U}}/\hat{U})_r \hat{U}_r dN_r \quad \ldots\ldots(A.14)$$

From (A.1) we obtain

$$\sum_r (\bar{\hat{U}}/\hat{U})_r \hat{U}_r dN_r = \sum_r (\bar{\hat{U}}/\hat{U})_r \sum_q \varepsilon_q \lambda_{rq} \hat{U}_{rq} dN_r$$

so that we can express (A.14) as

$$dZ = \sum_r N_r (\bar{\mu}/\mu)_r d\hat{U}_r + \sum_r \sum_q \varepsilon_q \lambda_k (\bar{U}/\hat{U})_r \hat{U}_k \, dN_r \quad \text{....(A.15)}$$

From (A.13) we have by differentiation

$$dZ^* = (1/N)(dZ - Z^* dN) \quad \text{.................(A.16)}$$

But since $\partial Z/\hat{U}_r \partial N_r = (\bar{U}/\hat{U})_r$ we have from the second equation in (A.12) $Z = \sum_r \bar{U}_r N_r$ and from (A.13) $Z^* = \sum_r \bar{U}_r (N_r/N)$ which is the weighted average of the pattern-modified $\hat{U}$'s. Write this average $\sum_r \bar{U}_r (N_r/N)$ as $\bar{U}$. Then from (A.16) we have

$$dZ^* = (1/N)(dZ - \bar{U} \, dN) \quad \text{.................(A.17)}$$

III

Equation (A.9) gave us the formula for a change in the expected value of the life-cycle utility of an individual of kind r. Equations (A.15) and (A.17) tell us how the policy-makers might incorporate these changes in their social welfare function. Substituting from (A.9) into (A.15) we obtain

$$dZ = \sum_r \sum_q \varepsilon_q N_r \lambda_k$$

$$\begin{bmatrix} (\bar{U}/\hat{U})_r \, \hat{U}_k \, (dN_r/N_r) + (\bar{\mu}/\mu)_r \, \hat{U}_k (d\lambda_k/\lambda_k) \\ \quad - (\bar{\mu}/\mu)_r (\hat{U}_{ke} - \hat{U}_{ku}) \, d\rho_k \\ + (\bar{\mu}_{ke} - \bar{\mu}_q)(1 - \rho_k) \, d\hat{H}_{ke} + (\bar{\mu}_{ku} - \bar{\mu}_q) \, d\hat{H}_{ku} \\ + \bar{\mu}_q (1 - \rho_k) \, \hat{W}_k \, (d\hat{L}_k/\hat{L}_k) \\ + \bar{\mu}_q (\Delta_{1k} + \Delta_{2k} + \Delta_{3k}) \\ + \bar{\mu}_q (1 - \rho_k)(d\hat{C}_{ke} - \hat{W}_k \, [d\hat{L}_k/\hat{L}_k]) \\ + \bar{\mu}_q \rho_k d\hat{C}_{ku} \end{bmatrix} \quad \text{...(A.18)}$$

In equation (A.18) $\bar{\mu}_{rqe} = (\bar{\mu}/\mu)_r \, \mu_{rqe}$ and $\bar{\mu}_{rqu} = (\bar{\mu}/\mu)_r \, \mu_{rqu}$, since the pattern-modification $(\bar{\mu}/\mu)_r$ is applied to the marginal utilities of an individual of kind r through his life-cycle. Since μ_q is merely a weighted average of the various μ_{rqe}'s and μ_{rqu}'s, by multiplying all the relevant μ_{rq}'s by $(\bar{\mu}/\mu)_r$, we replace the weighted average of the $\bar{\mu}_{rq}$'s (namely μ_q) with the weighted average of the $\bar{\mu}_{rq}$'s (namely $\bar{\mu}_q$).

IV

We next turn to the structure of the total level of the economy's production, income and consumption at point q.

We have first

$$L_{xq} + L_{yq} = \sum_r N_r \lambda_k (1 - \rho_k)\, \theta_k \hat{L}_k \quad \ldots\ldots\ldots\ldots (A.19)$$

which states that the demand for labour to produce X and Y at point q (L_{xq} and L_{yq} respectively) is equal to the supply which is the sum over all kinds of individuals of the number of hours worked by an individual of kind r (i.e. $\hat{L}_k$) multiplied by the work-effectiveness of that kind of labour (i.e. θ_k) multiplied by the number of that kind of workers who are in employment (i.e. $[1 - \rho_k]\, \lambda_k N_r$).

We have next the two production functions

$$\bar{X}_q = \bar{X}_q(L_{xq},\, X_{xq},\, Y_{xq},\, E_{xq},\, F_{xq})$$
$$\bar{Y}_q = \bar{Y}_q(L_{yq},\, X_{yq},\, Y_{yq},\, E_{yq},\, F_{yq}) \quad \ldots\ldots\ldots\ldots\ldots (A.20)$$

which state that the output of either industry at the point q is a function of the inputs at that point of labour, of instruments of production, of an exhaustible resource and of a fixed factor. We assume there to be one exhaustible resource (E), such as oil, which can be used at any point q to produce X or Y until it has been exhausted and one fixed factor (F), such as land, which is constant in amount and indestructible and which also can be used at any point q to produce X or Y. Thus $\bar{X}_q$ is the output of X at point q. L_{xq} is the input of labour into the production of X at point q. X_{xq} and Y_{xq} are the inputs of X and Y respectively as instruments of production into the production of X at point q. E_{xq} and F_{xq} are similarly the inputs of E and F into the production of X at point q. And similarly for $\bar{Y}_q$.

We have two equations expressing the equality of demand and supply for each product at any point q, namely,

$$\sum_r N_r \lambda_k \{(1 - \rho_k) \, \hat{C}_{xke} + \rho_k \hat{C}_{xku}\} = \overline{X}_q - G_{xq} - X_{x\overline{q+1}} - X_{y\overline{q+1}}$$

$$\sum_r N_r \lambda_k \{(1 - \rho_k) \, \hat{C}_{yke} + \rho_k \hat{C}_{yku}\} = \overline{Y}_q - G_{yq} - Y_{x\overline{q+1}} - Y_{y\overline{q+1}}$$

$$\dots\dots\dots(A.21)$$

The left-hand sides of these equations express the total personal consumption of X and Y respectively at point q by all employed and unemployed persons of all types. The right-hand sides express the supplies available for consumption. In the case of X this is the total output ($\overline{X}_q$), less the amount bought by the government (G_{xq}), less those amounts put aside for use in industry X or industry Y in the next period of production ($X_{x\overline{q+1}}, X_{y\overline{q+1}}$). And similarly for the supply of Y.[6]

We can derive ten marginal-product terms from (A.20) and introduce divergences between the prices paid for productive inputs and the values of their marginal products. Thus we write for the industry producing X:

$$\left.\begin{aligned}
(1 + \delta_{lxq}) \, W_q &= P_{xq} \frac{\partial \overline{X}_q}{\partial L_{xq}} \\[6pt]
(1 + \delta_{xxq}) \, P_{x\overline{q-1}}(1 + i_{\overline{q-1}}) &= P_{xq} \frac{\partial \overline{X}_q}{\partial X_{xq}} \\[6pt]
(1 + \delta_{yxq}) \, P_{y\overline{q-1}}(1 + i_{\overline{q-1}}) &= P_{xq} \frac{\partial \overline{X}_q}{\partial Y_{xq}} \\[6pt]
(1 + \delta_{exq}) \, P_{eq} &= P_{xq} \frac{\partial \overline{X}_q}{\partial E_{xq}} \\[6pt]
(1 + \delta_{fxq}) \, R_q &= P_{xq} \frac{\partial \overline{X}_q}{\partial F_{xq}}
\end{aligned}\right\} \dots\dots\dots(A.22)$$

---

[6] The above model and its notation differ from that used in *The Growing Economy* and *The Controlled Economy*. In the previous volumes we assumed that inputs were applied in an industry at the beginning of a period t and produced an output at the end of period t, this output being available for use at the beginning of the next period $t + 1$. Thus, as in equation (10.9) on page 255 of *The Controlled Economy*,

$$\overline{X}_t = C_{x\overline{t+1}} + G_{x\overline{t+1}} + X_{x\overline{t+1}} + X_{y\overline{t+1}}$$

We now assume that production and consumption take place instantaneously at point t, but that the inputs of X and Y necessary for production at point $t + 1$ must be saved out of production at point t. Thus

$$\overline{X}_t = C_{xt} + G_{xt} + X_{x\overline{t+1}} + X_{y\overline{t+1}}$$

with similar expressions for the industry producing Y. In the first expression in (A.22) the value of the marginal product of L_{xq} is given on the R.H.S. Since W_q is the wage rate paid for L_{xq}, δ_{lxq} is the proportionate divergence between the wage rate and the value of the marginal product of L_{xq}. In the second expression in (A.22) the RHS expresses the value of the marginal product in the X-industry of X used as an input in the X-industry. But the X so used at point q must have been purchased at point $\overline{q-1}$ at the price $P_{x\overline{q-1}}$, which will have accumulated at the rate of interest ruling at point $\overline{q-1}$ (namely, $i_{\overline{q-1}}$) to a cost of $P_{x\overline{q-1}}(1 + i_{\overline{q-1}})$ at point q. δ_{xxq} thus represents the proportionate divergence between the cost of X_{xq} and the value of its marginal product. The third expression in (A.22) gives a similar expression for the marginal product of a unit of Y used at point q to produce a unit of X. In the fourth expression in (A.22) the RHS represents the value of the addition to the output of X due to using up one more unit of the exhaustible resource, E, in the production of X at point q; if P_{eq} is the market price of E at point q, δ_{exq} represents the proportionate divergence between the price of E and the value of its marginal product in the X-industry at point q. In the fifth expression in (A.22) the RHS expresses the value of the marginal product of the fixed factor, F, in the production of X at point q, R_q measures the market rent for a unit of F at point q and δ_{fxq} then measures the proportionate divergence between this rent and the value of the marginal product of F in the X-industry at point q.

We now differentiate (A.19), (A.20) and (A.21); and we add the results. We assume full employment of the fixed factor, F, so that $dF_{xq} + dF_{yq} = 0$. Making use of this relationship and substituting from (A.22) for the partial derivatives which represent the marginal products of the various inputs in the two industries, we obtain:

The difference of substance is that we now assume labour to be applied at the end rather than at the beginning of each short discrete production period. In a continuous process the distinction would become insignificant. We make this change because, when we incorporate the productive process into the utility and social welfare functions, it is convenient to be able to assume that the individual's choice between consumption and leisure at any one time can be compared with the technological opportunity cost at the margin between leisure and additional consumption goods at that same point of time.

$$\sum_r N_r \lambda_k \{(1 - \rho_k)(d\hat{C}_{ke} - \hat{W}_k[d\hat{L}_k/\hat{L}_k]) + \rho_k d\hat{C}_{ku}\}$$

$$= \sum N_r \lambda_k \left\{ \begin{array}{l} (\hat{C}_{ke} - \hat{C}_{ku} - \hat{W}_k)\,d\rho_k \\[2mm] +[(1 - \rho_k)(\hat{W}_k - \hat{C}_{ke}) - \rho_k \hat{C}_{ku}]\left[\dfrac{dN_r}{N_r} + \dfrac{d\lambda_k}{\lambda_k}\right] \end{array} \right\}$$

$$+ (1 + i_{\overline{q-1}})\,dI_{\overline{q-1}} - dI_q$$

$$+ \Delta_{4q} + W_q(\delta_{lxq}\,dL_{xq} + \delta_{lxq}\,dL_{yq})$$

$$- dG_q + P_{eq}\{(1 + \delta_{exq})\,dE_{xq} + (1 + \delta_{eyq})\,dE_{yq}\}$$

$$+ R_q(\delta_{fxq} - \delta_{fyq})\,F\,d(F_{xq}/F) \quad\ldots\ldots\ldots\ldots\ldots\text{(A.23)}$$

where

(i) $\hat{C}_{ke} = P_{xq}\hat{C}_{xke} + P_{yq}\hat{C}_{yke}$ and $d\hat{C}_{ke} = P_{xq}\,d\hat{C}_{xke} + P_{yq}\,d\hat{C}_{yke}$, and similarly for $\hat{C}_{ku}$ and $d\hat{C}_{ku}$;

(ii) $dI_q = P_{xq}(dX_{x\overline{q+1}} + dX_{y\overline{q+1}}) + P_{yq}(dY_{x\overline{q+1}} + dY_{y\overline{q+1}})$;

(iii) $\Delta_{4q} = (1 + i_{\overline{q-1}})\left\{ \begin{array}{l} P_{x\overline{q-1}}(\delta_{xxq}\,dX_{xq} + \delta_{xyq}\,dX_{yq}) \\[1mm] + P_{y\overline{q-1}}(\delta_{yxq}\,dY_{xq} + \delta_{yyq}\,dY_{yq}) \end{array} \right\}$;

(iv) $dG_q = P_{xq}\,dG_{xq} + P_{yq}\,dG_{yq}$; and

(v) $F = F_{xq} + F_{yq}$ and represents the constant amount of the fixed factor.

Let us write $V_{xq} = P_{xq}(\partial \overline{X}_q/\partial L_{xq})$ for the value of the marginal product of L_{xq} and similarly for V_{yq}. Let V_q represent the weighted average of these two marginal products so that $V_q = (L_{xq}/L_q)\,V_{xq} + (L_{yq}/L_q)\,V_{yq}$ where $L_q = L_{xq} + L_{yq}$. Using (A.22) we obtain

$$(V_q - W_q) = W_q([L_{xq}/L_q]\delta_{lxq} + [L_{yq}/L_q]\,\delta_{lyq}) \quad\ldots\ldots\text{(A.24)}$$

V

If we multiply (A.23) by $\varepsilon_q \bar{\mu}_q$ and sum the result over q, we obtain an expression for the last two terms on the RHS of (A.18). If we substitute this expression into (A.18), making use of (A.24), we obtain the equation (A.25) on page 234. In this equation, by analogy with $\hat{W}_{rq}$, $\hat{V}_{rq} = V_q \theta_{rq} \hat{L}_{rq}$ and

$$dZ = \sum_r \sum_q \varepsilon_q N_r \lambda_{rq}$$

$$
\begin{aligned}
&\left[(\bar{U}/\hat{U})_r \, \hat{U}_{rq}(dN_r/N_r) + (\bar{\mu}/\mu)_r \, \hat{U}_{rq}(d\lambda_{rq}/\lambda_{rq}) \right. \\
&\quad - (\bar{\mu}/\mu)_r (\hat{U}_{rqe} - \hat{U}_{rqu}) \, d\rho_{rq} &\text{(i)} \\
&\quad + (\bar{\mu}_{rqe} - \bar{\mu}_q)(1 - \rho_{rq}) \, d\hat{H}_{rqe} + (\bar{\mu}_{rqu} - \bar{\mu}_q) \, \rho_{rq} \, d\hat{H}_{rqu} &\text{(ii)} \\
&\quad + \bar{\mu}_q \{ (1 - \rho_{rq})(\hat{V}_{rq} - \hat{C}_{rqe}) - \rho_{rq}\hat{C}_{rqu} \} \{ (dN_r/N_r) \\
&\quad + (d\lambda_{rq}/\lambda_{rq}) \} &\text{(iii)} \\
&\quad + \bar{\mu}_q (\hat{C}_{rqe} - \hat{V}_{rq} - \hat{C}_{rqu}) \, d\rho_{rq} &\text{(iv)} \\
&\quad + \bar{\mu}_q (1 - \rho_{rq}) \, \hat{W}_{rq}(\delta_{lrq} + [L_{xq}/L_q] \, \delta_{lxq} \\
&\quad + [L_{yq}/L_q]\delta_{lyq}) \, (d\hat{L}_{rq}/\hat{L}_{rq}) &\text{(v)} \\
&\left. \quad + \bar{\mu}_q (\Delta_{1rq} + \Delta_{2rq} + \Delta_{3rq}) \right] &\text{(vi)}
\end{aligned}
$$

$$+ \sum_q \varepsilon_q \bar{\mu}_q$$

$$
\begin{aligned}
&\left[(1 + i_{\overline{q-1}}) \, dI_{\overline{q-1}} - dI_q \right. &\text{(vii)} \\
&\quad + \Delta_{4q} + (V_{xq} - V_{yq}) \, L_q \, d(L_{xq}/L_q) &\text{(viii)} \\
&\quad - dG_q &\text{(ix)} \\
&\quad + P_{eq}\{ (1 + \delta_{exq}) \, dE_{xq} + (1 + \delta_{eyq}) \, dE_{yq} \} &\text{(x)} \\
&\left. \quad + R_q(\delta_{fxq} - \delta_{fyq}) \, F \, d(F_{xq}/F) \right] &\text{(xi)}
\end{aligned}
$$

$$\ldots\ldots\ldots(A.25)$$

represents the average value of the marginal product of an employed citizen of kind r at point q, given the number of hours which he works, $\hat{L}_{rq}$ and the effectiveness of his work, θ_{rq}.

Using (A.17) we can obtain dZ^* by two modifications of (A.25): first, by subtracting $\sum_r \bar{U} \, dN_r$ from the RHS of (A.25); and second, by dividing the resulting expression by N, so that

$$dZ^* = (1/\sum_r N_r)\{dZ - \sum_r \bar{U} \, dN_r\} \quad \ldots\ldots\ldots(A.26)$$

Equation (A.25) and its modified form (A.26) give us the final formulae for dZ and dZ^*.

We may briefly enumerate the meaning of the various items on the RHS of (A.25).

Item (i) represents the effect on Z of the structural changes to an individual's utility of being born rather than unborn, of having a longer life, or of being employed instead of unemployed. (Cf. Components I and II in Chapter XVI of *The Controlled Economy*.)

Item (ii) represents the effect of the redistribution of consumption at various points of time and environment (Cf. Component IV in Chapter XVI of *The Controlled Economy*.)

Item (iii) represents the excess (or deficiency) at various stages of life of additional individuals' marginal products over their consumption (allowing for the probability of unemployment); and it measures, therefore, the net contribution (or the net claim) made to existing members of society through the activities of additional members, whether the addition to the population is due to more births or to longer life-expectancy. (Cf. Component I in Chapter XVI of *The Controlled Economy*.)

Item (iv) represents the contribution (or drain) which an increase of unemployment makes on other members of the community. The unemployed's consumption goes down by the difference between his consumption in employment and his consumption in unemployment, but his contribution to the community's output also goes down. The result for the rest of the community depends upon the balance between these two changes. (Cf. Component II in Chapter XVI of *The Controlled Economy*.)

Item (v) allows for the effect of a change in hours worked.

Item (vi) covers inefficiencies due to any differences in the market prices which are charged to various consumers (Δ_{1rq}), external economies and diseconomies (Δ_{2rq}), and the value of public goods

(Δ_{3rq}). (For Δ_{2rq} and Δ_{3rq}, cf. Component VI in Chapter XVI of *The Controlled Economy*.)

Item (vii) is concerned with the optimal time pattern of savings and investment. Thus an increase in the amount saved for investment at point q (i.e. dI_q) will reduce the amount of goods available for consumption at q by a similar quantity and will thus in itself reduce welfare by $\bar{\mu}_q \, dI_q$. But at q there will be an increased output available for consumption due to any increase in the amount saved for investment at point $\overline{q-1}$ and this increased output (apart from any inefficiencies which will be caught in the term Δ_{4q}) will be worth $(1 + i_{\overline{q-1}}) \, dI_{\overline{q-1}}$ at point q. The changed pattern of savings-investment will thus have increased welfare at q by the net amount $\bar{\mu}_q\{(1 + i_{\overline{q+1}}) \, dI_{\overline{q-1}} - dI_q\}$.

An alternative way of expressing this relationship is as follows. Suppose that point $\overline{q-1}$ were point 2 on Figure 24. The point q would then be represented by point 4 or point 5; dI_2 will, therefore, appear in item (vii) with the negative value of $\varepsilon_2 \bar{\mu}_2 \, dI_2$ at point 2 and the positive value of $(\varepsilon_4 \bar{\mu}_4 + \varepsilon_5 \bar{\mu}_5)(1 + i_2)$ at points 4 and 5. Its net contribution to social welfare will therefore be $\{(\varepsilon_4 \bar{\mu}_4 + \varepsilon_5 \bar{\mu}_5)(1 + i_2) - \varepsilon_2 \bar{\mu}_2\} \, dI_2$, which is positive or negative according as

$$ i_2 \gtrless \frac{\varepsilon_2 \bar{\mu}_2 - (\varepsilon_4 \bar{\mu}_4 + \varepsilon_5 \bar{\mu}_5)}{\varepsilon_4 \bar{\mu}_4 + \varepsilon_5 \bar{\mu}_5} \quad\text{...............(A.27)} $$

i.e. according as the money rate of interest is greater or less than the expected rate of decline of the marginal utility of money purchasing power. (Cf. Component III in Chapter XVI of *The Controlled Economy*.)

In item (viii) the term $\bar{\mu}_q \Delta_{4q}$ covers any increase in welfare due to a reduction in inefficiencies in the use of the instruments of production (X and Y) used to produce outputs of goods ($\overline{X}$ and $\overline{Y}$) at point q. For example, $(1 + i_{\overline{q-1}}) \, P_{x\overline{q-1}} \, dX_{yq}$ represents the cost (as valued at point q) of an additional amount of X saved at point $\overline{q-1}$ for use at point q in the production of Y; and δ_{xyq} represents the excess of the value at point q of the consequential increase in Y over this cost. The term thus covers a multitude of sins. Two examples must suffice. (i) Suppose that all the δ-terms in Δ_{4q} were positive and equal. We would have $\Delta_{4q} = \delta(1 + i_{\overline{q-1}}) \, dI_{\overline{q-1}}$. The value at point q of the products of goods saved for investment at point $\overline{q-1}$ would exceed the cost with accumulated interest by a divergence δ.

The social yield on capital would exceed the private yield on capital and an increase in investment at the expense of consumption would *pro-tanto* be socially desirable. (ii) In so far as $\delta_{xxq} > \delta_{xyq}$ then a shift of X as an instrument of production from Y-production to X-production at point q would be socially desirable.

As far as labour is concerned we have already accounted for all changes in the total amount of work done in items (iii), (iv) and (v). In item (viii) we catch the possibility of improvement through a change in the proportion of labour going to one industry rather than the other; if $V_{xq} > V_{yq}$ an increase in L_{xq}/L_q, the proportion of labour devoted to the production of X – which implies, of course, an equal reduction in L_{yq}/L_q – will raise the value of total output. (Cf. Component VII in Chapter XVI of *The Controlled Economy*.)

Item (ix): if we take item (ix) together with Δ_{3rq} from item (vi) we obtain

$$\sum \varepsilon_q \bar{\mu}_q \left\{ \begin{array}{l} \left[\sum_r N_r \lambda_{rq} \overline{(1 - \rho_{rq}} P_{gxqe} + \rho_{rq} P_{gxrqu}) - P_{xq} \right] dG_{xq} \\ + \left[\sum_r N_r \lambda_{rq} \overline{(1 - \rho_{rq}} P_{gyqe} + \rho_{rq} P_{gyrqu}) - P_{yq} \right] dG_{yq} \end{array} \right\}$$

These terms measure the changes in public goods multiplied by the excess of the sum of their marginal values to all consumers over their average market price as private goods, i.e. over their opportunity costs. (Cf. Component VI in Chapter XVI of *The Controlled Economy*.)

Item (x): since there is only a finite amount of E, if more E is used at one point of time, so much less can be used at another. Consider the desirability of planning to postpone the use of a small amount of E – namely, dE – from one point of time to the next point of time, for example from point 2 to points 4 or 5 in Figure 24. We would have

$$dE = - (dE_{x2} + dE_{y2}) = (dE_{x4} + dE_{y4}) = (dE_{x5} + dE_{y5})$$

Then the total contribution of this change to social welfare would be

$$- \varepsilon_2 \bar{\mu}_2 P_{e2} \{ (1 + \delta_{ex2}) \, dE_{x2} + (1 + \varepsilon_{ey2}) \, dE_{y2} \}$$
$$+ \varepsilon_4 \bar{\mu}_4 P_{e4} \{ (1 + \delta_{ex4}) \, dE_{x4} + (1 + \delta_{ey4}) \, dE_{y4} \}$$
$$+ \varepsilon_5 \bar{\mu}_5 P_{e5} \{ (1 + \delta_{ex5}) \, dE_{x5} + (1 + \delta_{ey5}) \, dE_{y5} \}$$

If we neglect the δ-terms, this gives

$$\{\varepsilon_4\bar{\mu}_4 P_{e4} + \varepsilon_5\bar{\mu}_5 P_{e5} - \varepsilon_2\bar{\mu}_2 P_{e2}\}\, \mathrm{d}E$$

which is positive or negative according as

$$P_{e2} \gtrless \frac{\varepsilon_4\bar{\mu}_4 P_{e4} + \varepsilon_5\bar{\mu}_5 P_{e5}}{\varepsilon_2\bar{\mu}_2} \quad\ldots\ldots\ldots\ldots\ldots(A.28)$$

Suppose that in terms of (A.27) we had the optimal distribution of savings – investment between the generations, so that $\varepsilon_2\bar{\mu}_2 = (\varepsilon_4\bar{\mu}_4 + \varepsilon_5\bar{\mu}_5)(1 + i_2)$, then the postponement of $\mathrm{d}E$ by one period of time would make a positive or negative contribution to social welfare according as

$$P_{e2} \gtrless \frac{\varepsilon_4\bar{\mu}_4 P_{e4} + \varepsilon_5\bar{\mu}_5 P_{e5}}{(1 + i_2)(\varepsilon_4\bar{\mu}_4 + \varepsilon_5\bar{\mu}_5)} \quad\ldots\ldots\ldots\ldots(A.29)$$

If we were dealing with a certain future (e.g. $\varepsilon_4 = 1$ and $\varepsilon_5 = 0$), then this would become $P_{e2} \gtrless P_{e4}/(1 + i_2)$. In other words, if the future were certain, if in terms of (A.27) the optimal amount of capital accumulation were taking place, if there were no divergences between the price of E and the value of its product at each point in time in each use (i.e. the δ_e's = 0), and if there were no divergence between the market rate of interest and the social rate of return on investment (i.e. the δ's in $\varDelta_{4q} = 0$), then the use of E should be so distributed over time that its market price rose at a rate equal to the rate of interest. If the future were uncertain but the other conditions were all fulfilled, then its planned distribution over future time-environment paths should be such that the weighted average of its expected price (the weights being the relevant $\varepsilon\bar{\mu}$'s) rose at a rate equal to the market rate of interest.

Item (xi) presents no problem. It states simply that the use of the fixed factor should at each time-environment point be shifted from one use to another, if the divergence between the value of its marginal product and its market rent were greater in the latter than in the former use.

VI

We can make various simplifications of (A.25) in order to isolate for consideration particular features of the model.

Let us consider the following simplified stationary economy.

(i) There is full employment, so that $\rho_{rq} = 0$.

(ii) There are no demographic changes so that $d\lambda = 0$.

(iii) There is no saving or investment, so that $dI = 0$.

(iv) We are in a stationary economy in which we need to consider the position at only one point of time, so that $q = \varepsilon_q = 1$.

(v) The amount of hours worked by each individual member of the population is constant, so that $d\hat{L}_{rq} = 0$.

(vi) There are no public goods and no marginal inefficiencies, except divergences between the values of the marginal product of labour in the two industries X and Y, so that $\Delta_{1rq} = \Delta_{2rq} = \Delta_{3rq} = \Delta_{4q} = 0$.

(vii) There are only two classes in the population, so that $r = a, b$.

(viii) As a result of (ii), (v) and (vi) the only arguments in the individual utility functions are the levels of consumption of X and Y, so that $d\hat{H}$ becomes $d\hat{C}$.

(ix) We neglect both the exhaustible resource and the fixed factor, so that the dE's and dF's are zero.

In this case (A.25) can be rewritten into the form

$$dZ = (\bar{\mu}_a - \mu) N_a d\hat{C}_a + (\bar{\mu}_b - \mu) N_b d\hat{C}_b$$
$$+ \{\bar{U}_a + \bar{\mu}(\hat{V}_a - \hat{C}_a)\} dN_a$$
$$+ \{\bar{U}_b + \bar{\mu}(\hat{V}_b - \hat{C}_b)\} dN_b$$
$$+ \bar{\mu}(V_x - V_y) L d(L_x/L) \dots\dots\dots\dots\dots\dots(A.30)$$

where the terms in dN_a and dN_b show what would be the effects in the stationary economy if the populations were constant at somewhat different levels, all other conditions remaining unchanged.

In (A.30) we could write

$$(\bar{\mu}_a - \bar{\mu}) N_a d\hat{C}_a + (\bar{\mu}_b - \bar{\mu}) N_b d\hat{C}_b$$
$$= (\bar{\mu}_a - \bar{\mu}_b) C d(C_a/C) \dots\dots\dots\dots\dots\dots(A.31)$$

where for the existing numbers in the two groups, namely N_a and N_b, C is the total amount of money spent on consumption goods by the members of both groups, and $d(C_a/C)$ is the change in the proportion of consumption goods *valued at constant unchanged prices* going to class a; i.e. it is the change in the proportion of the quantity of real consumption which goes to group a. Equation (A.31) is a valid expression if $\bar{\mu}$ is a weighted average of $\bar{\mu}_a$ and $\bar{\mu}_b$ where the weights are the original expenditures on consumption by group a and group b respectively.[7]

VII

A second set of simplifying assumptions may be made in order to bring out some of the underlying dynamic considerations of a demographic character. For this purpose we modify (A.25) in the following respects.

(i) There is full employment, so that $\rho_{rq} = 0$.

(ii) There are no marginal inefficiencies or external economies or diseconomies so that $\Delta_{1rq} = \Delta_{2rq} = \Delta_{4q} = 0$, $V_{xq} = V_{yq}$ and $\delta_{exq} = \delta_{eyq} = \delta_{fxq} = \delta_{fyq} = 0$.

(iii) The numbers of hours worked by each individual is constant so that $d\hat{L}_{rq} = 0$.

(iv) There is no governmental expenditure on goods so that $\Delta_{3rq} = dG_q = 0$.

With these simplifications we can rewrite (A.25)

$$dZ = \sum_r \sum_q \varepsilon_q N_r \lambda_{rq}$$

$$
\begin{bmatrix}
(\bar{\mu}_{rq} - \bar{\mu}_q)\, d\, \hat{C}_{rq} & \text{(i)} \\
+ (\bar{U}/\hat{U})_r \, \hat{U}_{rq}\,(dN_r/N_r) + (\bar{\mu}/\mu)_r \, \hat{U}_{rq}\,(d\lambda_{rq}/\lambda_{rq}) & \text{(ii)} \\
+ \bar{\mu}_q(\hat{V}_{rq} - \hat{C}_{rq})(dN_r/N_r + d\lambda_{rq}/\lambda_{rq}) & \text{(iii)}
\end{bmatrix}
$$

---

[7] Write C_a and C_b for the original levels of total consumption of groups a and b respectively, so that

$$\bar{\mu} = \frac{C_a}{C_a + C_b}\bar{\mu}_a + \frac{C_b}{C_a + C_b}\bar{\mu}_b$$

Then

$$(\bar{\mu}_a - \bar{\mu})dC_a + (\bar{\mu}_b - \bar{\mu})dC_b$$

$$= (\bar{\mu}_a - \bar{\mu}_b)\frac{C_b dC_a - C_a dC_b}{C_a + C_b}$$

$$= (\bar{\mu}_a - \bar{\mu}_b)(C_a + C_b)\frac{(C_a + C_b)dC_a - C_a(dC_a + dC_b)}{(C_a + C_b)^2}$$

$$+ \sum_q \varepsilon_q \bar{\mu}_q$$

$$\left[\begin{array}{l} (1 + i_{\overline{q-1}})\, dI_{\overline{q-1}} - dI_q \\ + P_{eq}(dE_{xq} + dE_{yq}) \end{array} \right] \qquad \begin{array}{l} \text{(iv)} \\ \text{(v)} \end{array}$$

$$\ldots\ldots\ldots(\text{A.32})$$

Apart from the distributional term in (i), the investment term in (iv) and the exhaustible resource term in (v) we are left only with variations in the demographic factors, N_r (i.e. the number of persons of type h born at point j) and λ_{rq} (i.e. the expectation that a person of type g born at point j will live till point q, if the economy does in fact pass through point q). Changes in the λ_{rq}'s thus represent directly the changes in mortality rates. The N_r's depend, however, upon fertility rates which are not directly shown in (A.32).

We can express the factors determining N_r as follows:

$$N_{(hj)} = \sum_c \sum_f \lambda_{(cf)j} N_{(cf)} \beta_{(cf)(hj)} \ldots\ldots\ldots\ldots\ldots(\text{A.33})$$

where $\beta_{(cf)(hj)}$ is the chance of an individual of type c who is born at point f producing a child of type h at point j.

If one knew the past demographic history up to point 1 and knew all the future λ's and β's, one could in principle trace out the future course of the numbers of individuals of every kind who would exist at every future point of time and environment. We know $N_{(cf)}$ for all types c up to point 1 (i.e. up to the point $f = 1$) from the past demographic history. From this we can deduce the $N_{(c, f+1)}$'s for all types from the basic demographic formula (A.33) if we know the λ's and the β's for all the points $\overline{f + 1}$. We shall then know the total demographic history up to all the points $\overline{f + 1}$, from which we can proceed by a similar process to all the points at the next time period. And so on indefinitely. In these calculations the λ's represent the mortality parameters and the β's the fertility parameters.[8]

---

[8] In considering $\beta_{(cf)(hj)}$ one would have to allow for the genetic and social make-up of both of the parents. Thus when a man and a woman have a child that child would have to be allotted as one half to the man and one half to the woman. The chance of a father of type c having a half share in a child of type h would depend as much upon his wife's as upon his own genetic and social make-up and would thus be affected by the degree of assortative mating (See Chapter X.)

If there were only one type of person and only one environmental path we could rewrite the basic demographic relationship as

$$N_j = \sum_f \lambda_{fj} N_f \beta_{fj} \quad\text{.........................(A.34)}$$

The number of births at time j is the sum of births to all parents born at all earlier dates f; and this depends on the number of births at each f, the proportion of those potential parents who survive till j and their fertility at point j. Given the earlier demographic history and the future values of the λ's and β's, the future course of the population can be forecast.[9] In principle it follows that if one knows the small changes in the demographic parameters, λ and β, one can forecast the resulting changes in the number of births, N, at each point of time.

[9] For a simple exposition of some of these relationships see Chapter X and the Note to Chapter X of *The Growing Economy*.

INDEX

243

smoothing consumption 93–5, 107
social contacts 144–5, 148–53, 155–6, 158, 160, 166, 180, 186–7, 196
social costs and benefits 14, 15, 197
social goods: choice of 16–18; public provision of 195–200
social mobility 167–8, 211
social services 84, 195–200
social welfare: changes in 86, 104–5; changes in total future 81; defined as sum of individual welfares 40, 44ff, 66, 69; effects of redistribution 82; utilitarian criterion of 61–2, 64, 66; *see also* utility; welfare
social welfare dynamics, model of 220–42
socialisation of property 202–6: taxation for 205–6
Stationary Economy IX, X, 13n, 30n, 35n, 41n, 136n, 138n
sterilisation 212
stocks, idle 88–9, 106
stocks, terminal 103, 105
streams, consumption 94–5, 110–11
streams, income 110–11
structure of economic activities 14
subsidies 17, 19, 33–4, 38, 189–90, 194–5, 210–14
subsidies on sterilisation 212–13
super-egalitarian criterion 49–50
sympathy 61–3, 65, 67

tastes and needs, individuals': different 53ff, 57, 61; same 44ff
taxation 33–4, 37–8, 89, 98, 107, 109, 194–5, 201; for socialisation of property 205–6; on consumption 208–10, 213n, 215ff; on gifts and inheritances 201–2, 207; *see also* income tax
temperamental factors 20–3
terminal stocks 103, 105
tests for welfare levels 26–9
Theory of Economic Externalities X
Theory of International Policy X
Theory of Justice X
time: cost of movement in 192n; distribution over Ch. VI *passim,* 109, 213;

welfare changes in 80–4
time and space, distance in 59–60
Trade and Welfare 224
trade unions 136, 139–40, 191
training, *see* education

ultimism and selfishness 98–101
unemployment 16, 139, 191, 223, 225, 235
Unequal Shares XI
units of consumption 57
utilitarian criterion of social welfare 61–2, 64, 66
utilities: coefficient of variation of 122, 124–5· life-span 226; maximising total 53ff, 74–5, 98–101, 118
utility: average proportionate divergence of 121–2, 124–5; Gini coefficient for distribution of 122–5; hill of 26; proportionate loss of 118–21, 124–5, 131–4; *see also* social welfare; welfare
utility functions, individuals': different 53ff, 61; same 44ff

voluntary charitable clubs 65, 65n, 66n
vouchers, educational 196

waste of consumption, proportionate 118–21, 124–5, 131–5
weights: distributional 46ff, 58–60, 86; pattern-modified distributional 47–8, 53, 62, 70–1, 73n, 228–30
welfare: changes in 23, 80–4, 118–21; criteria for 26–9, 39, 83; intergenerational distribution of 206ff; interpersonal comparisons of Ch. II *passim;* levels of 25–9; methods of increasing 45ff; per head 69–71, 73ff, 119, 220–42 *passim;* tests for levels of 26–9; total 69–71, 73ff, 119–22, 220–42 *passim; see also* social welfare; utility
Well Endowed, Contraction of the Number of the 188n
workers and landlords 32–43, 136–40